COMPUTERS OUR LIFELINE

8

Based on NEP

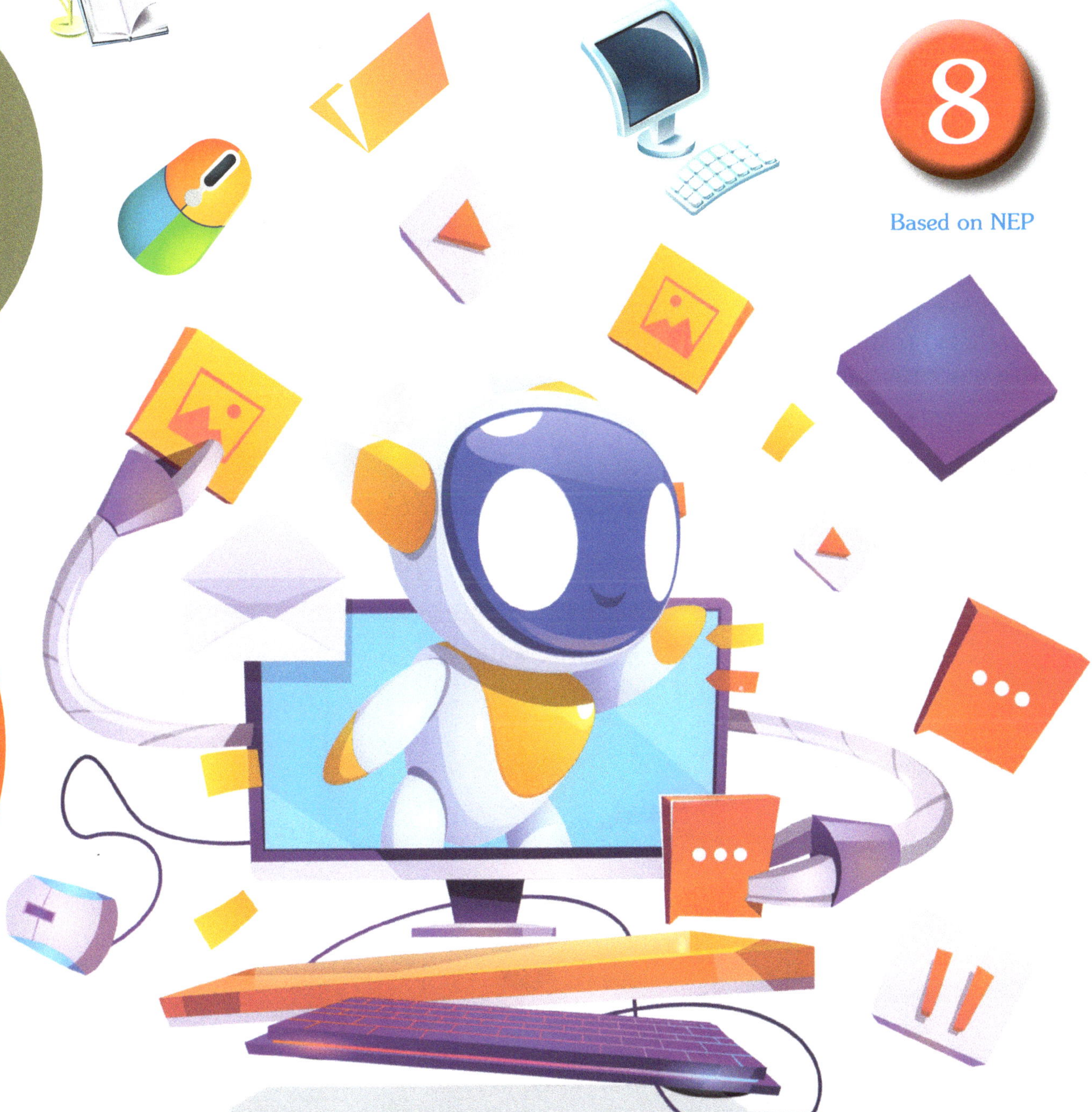

MANOJ PUBLICATIONS

COMPUTERS
Our Lifeline - 8

Publishers:
MANOJ PUBLICATIONS
761, Main Road, Burari, Delhi-110084 (INDIA)
Mobile : 09999476076, 09868112194, 08178823569, 08178854810
Email : info@manojpublications.com

For online shopping visit our website :
Website : www.sawanonlinebookstore.com

ISBN : 978-81-310-1646-6

Concept:
Puneet Gupta
M.B.A. (William & Mary, U.S.A.)

Edited by:
Davinder Singh Minhas
Rohan Kumar

PREFACE

This is the Age of Computers. In every nook and corner of the globe, computers have made their presence felt, be it school, office, post office, bank, shop, mall, hotel, restaurant, airport, railway station, Metro station and so on. Needless to say, they have become our lifeline as we can't do anything without them. In order to keep pace with the modern world, it is important to familiarise our children with computer applications right from the start. They ought to be taught the uses of computer in a lucid, interesting and enjoyable style: from basic to intermediate to advanced level.

Keeping in view the requirements of students, all the books in the series—Computers : Our Lifeline—have been designed to meet the purpose of acquiring a sound in-depth knowledge on computers with their uses. The contents of the books are based entirely on recently approved NEP (National Educational Policy).

The chapters in all the books contain a fairly good amount of illustrations which make the text very easy to understand. There are many computer books flooding the market. Our books are the books with a difference in order that they are well equipped with exhaustive exercises which test a student's mental horizon by making him take Formative Assessment as well as Summative Assessment. The knowledge of the latest software with their applications and types of computer language have been made available. Nay, students have been introduced to coding, the process of designing computer apps. The main goal of books in the series is to make a student computerate, *i.e.* computer literate.

We sincerely hope that all the books in this series will prove fruitful both to students and teachers. We shall be highly pleased to receive constructive suggestions in order to make the series more qualitative in the forthcoming editions.

– Author

CONTENTS

Artificial Intelligence

In this chapter, we will learn:

⇒ Meaning of Artificial Intelligence
⇒ Goals of Artificial Intelligence
⇒ Types of Artificial Intelligence
⇒ Examples of Artificial Intelligence in our Daily Life
⇒ Advantages of Artificial Intelligence
⇒ Disadvantages of Artificial Intelligence
⇒ Major Areas of Applications of Artificial Intelligence

MEANING OF ARTIFICIAL INTELLIGENCE

The term 'Artificial Intelligence' is composed of two words, *i.e.* Artificial and Intelligence. The word 'Artificial' means non-natural, *i.e.* anything that is man-made and the word 'Intelligence' refers to the ability to understand, think and learn. So, combining both, we can define artificial intelligence as below:

- An intelligent entity created by humans.
- Capable of performing tasks intelligently without being explicitly instructed.
- Capable of thinking and acting rationally and humanly.

We can understand the term 'Artificial Intelligence' through the given definition –

AI is a branch of computer science concerned with the study and creation of computer systems that exhibits some form of intelligence: system that learns new concepts and tasks, system that can reason and draw useful conclusion about the world around us, system that can understand a natural language or perceive and comprehend a visual scene, and system that performs other types of feats that require human types of intelligence.

– Patterson

Can You Explain What Human Intelligence Is?

Human Intelligence is mental quality that consists of the abilities to learn from experience, adapt to new situations, understand and handle abstract concepts and use knowledge to manipulate one's environment.

GOALS OF ARTIFICIAL INTELLIGENCE

The basic goal of AI is to enable computers and machines to perform intellectual tasks such as problem-solving, decision-making perception and understanding human communication.

The general problem of stimulating or creating intelligence is broken down into sub-problems. These problems include special abilities that users expect an intelligent system to exhibit. We must emphasize planning and learning that is relevant and applicable to the given situation.

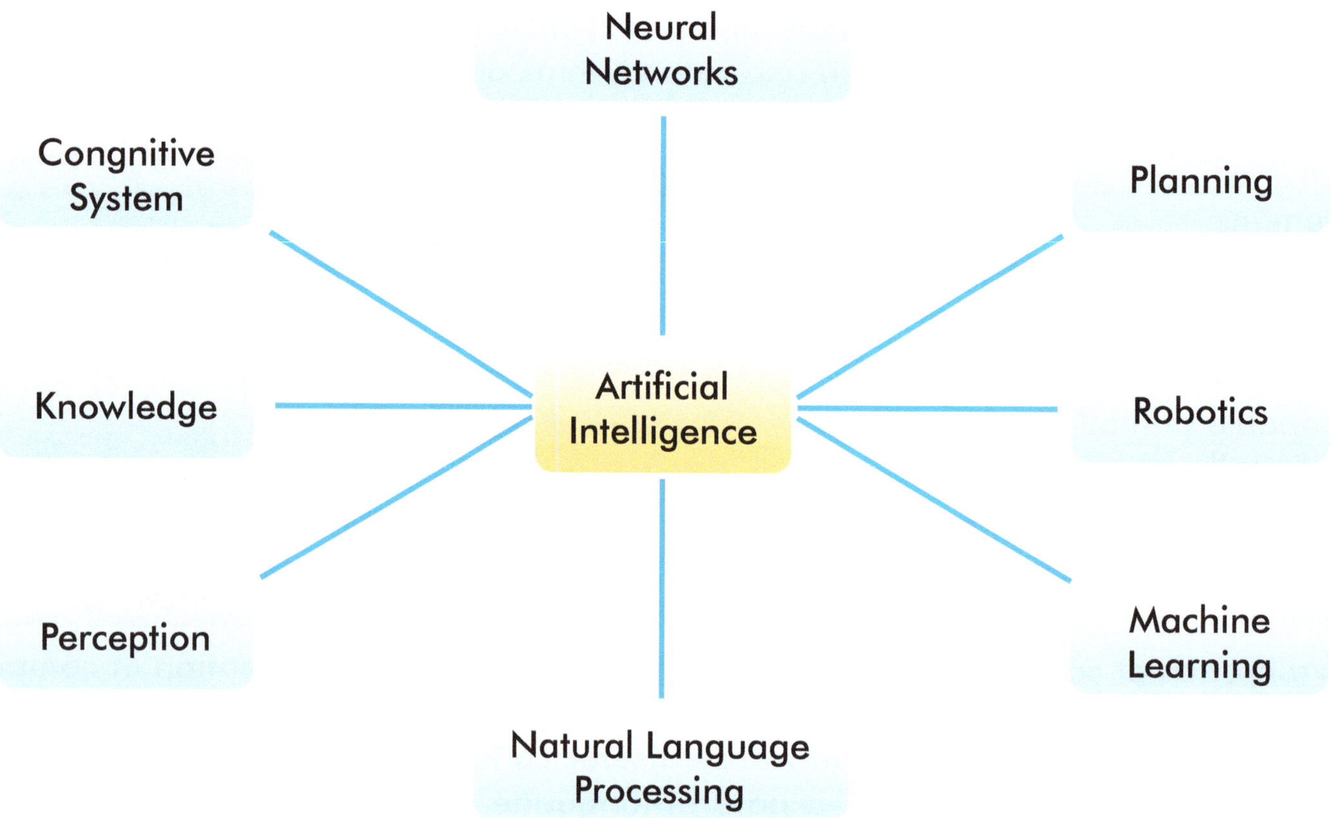

Creating expert systems: The computers and the machines that are mentioned here should have the ability to display intelligent behaviour, learn, demonstrate, explain and provide users with best of advice.

TYPES OF ARTIFICIAL INTELLIGENCE (AI)

Different artificial intelligence entities are built for different purposes, and that's how they vary. AI can be classified as Type 1 and Type 2 based on functionalities.

Narrow Artificial Intelligence (Narrow AI)

Narrow Artificial Intelligence is said to be narrow when the machine can perform a specific (single) task extremely well, even better than humans. It is also called as weak AI. Programmed to perform a single task, it lacks self-awareness, consciousness to perform Intelligence tasks. An example would be a poker game wherein a machine beats a human because all rules and moves are fed into the machine.

Artificial General Intelligence (AGI)

Artificial General Intelligence reaches the general state when it can perform any intellectual task with the same accuracy level as a human would. It means the machines can actually think and perform tasks on their own just like human beings. They are self-aware and conscious to take decisions. We are still a long way from building an AGI system.

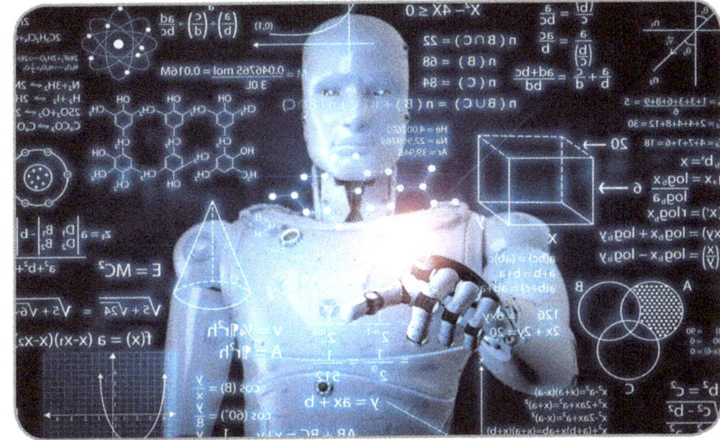

Strong Artificial Intelligence (Strong AI)

AI is strong when it can beat humans in many tasks. However, this type of AI is only theoretical at this point. It's the type of AI that writers have fictionalized in Sci-fi movies such as The Terminator and i-ROBOT.

Examples of Artificial Intelligence in our daily life:

- **Smart Cars and Drones:** Talking about AI, there is no better and more prominent display of this technology than what smart car and drone manufacturers are doing with it. Just a few years back, using a fully automatic car was a dream; however, now companies like Tesla and Google have made so much progress that we already have a fleet of semi-automatic cars on the road.
- Companies like Amazon and Walmart are heavily investing in drone delivery programs and it will become a reality far sooner than you expect. If you think that's far-fetched, do note that militaries all over the world have already been using successful drone programs.
- **Digital Assistants:** Apple's Siri, Google's assistant, Amazon's Alexa and Microsoft's Cortana are digital assistants that help users perform various tasks, from checking their schedules and searching for something on the web, to sending commands to another app. AI is an important part of how these apps work because they learn from every single user's interaction. This allows them to better recognize speech patterns and serve users' results that are tailored to their preferences.

Apple's Siri

Google's Assistant

Amazon's Alexa

- **Robots:** A robot is a machine designed to execute one or more tasks automatically with speed and precision. There are as many different types of robots as there are different tasks for them to perform.

- **Roomba J7 model vacuum:** It uses AI to scan the size of a living area, looks for objects that might be in the way and remembers the best route for cleaning the carpet.

- **Smartphones :** Smartphones have become the most indispensable tech products that we own today and we use them almost all the time. Well, if you are using a smartphone, you are interacting with AI whether you know it or not.

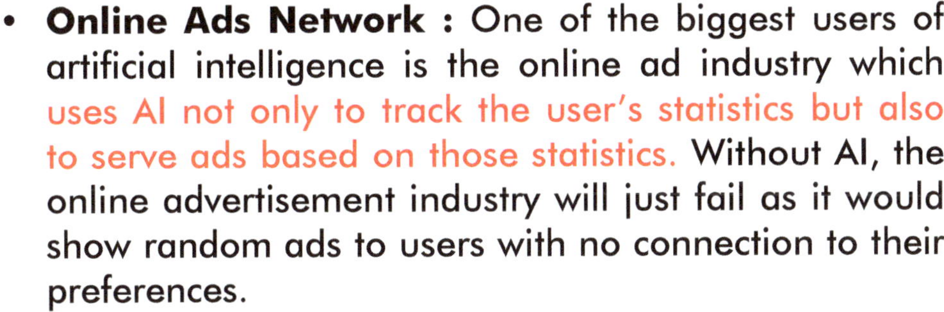

- **Online Ads Network :** One of the biggest users of artificial intelligence is the online ad industry which uses AI not only to track the user's statistics but also to serve ads based on those statistics. Without AI, the online advertisement industry will just fail as it would show random ads to users with no connection to their preferences.

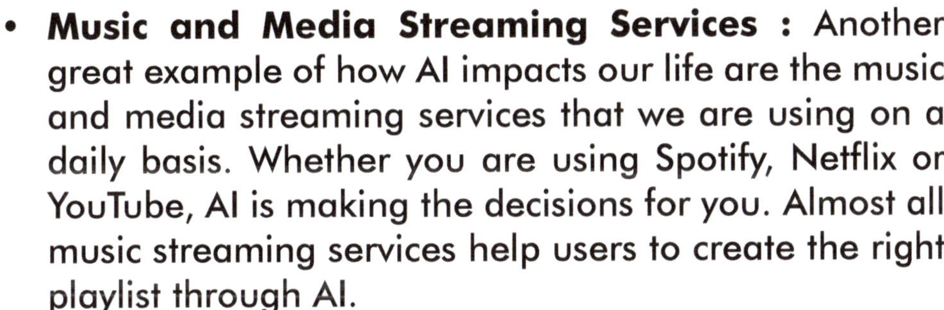

- **Music and Media Streaming Services :** Another great example of how AI impacts our life are the music and media streaming services that we are using on a daily basis. Whether you are using Spotify, Netflix or YouTube, AI is making the decisions for you. Almost all music streaming services help users to create the right playlist through AI.

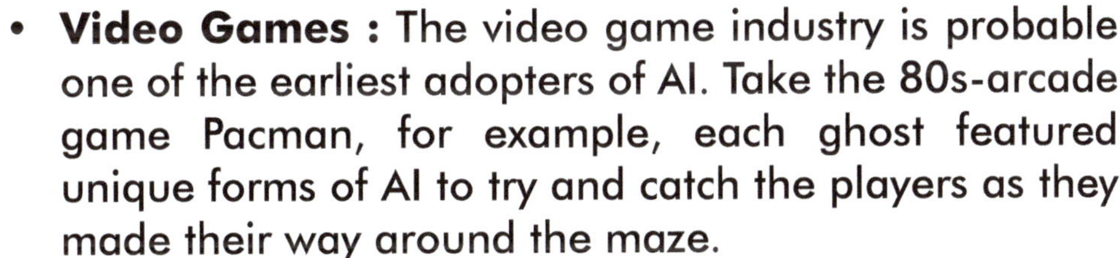

- **Video Games :** The video game industry is probable one of the earliest adopters of AI. Take the 80s-arcade game Pacman, for example, each ghost featured unique forms of AI to try and catch the players as they made their way around the maze.

Hence, we can say that the advantages of Artificial intelligence applications are enormous and can revolutionize any professional sector. Let us see some of them.

ADVANTAGES OF ARTIFICIAL INTELLIGENCE

Reduction in Human Error:

As decisions are taken on previously gathered information and certain algorithms, without the interference of humans, errors are reduced and the chance of reaching accuracy with a greater degree of precision is a possibility.

Faster Decisions

Using Artificial intelligence, decisions can be taken very fast. For example, we all have played chess game in Windows. It is nearly impossible to beat CPU in hard mode because of the AI behind that game.

Can Work Continuously

Unlike humans, a machine does not get tired even if it has to work for consecutive hours. This is a major benefit of AI (Artificial intelligence) over the humans, who need rest and time to be efficient.

Taking Risks on Behalf of Humans

In various situations, a robot can be used instead of humans to avoid the risks. Robots can be programmed to explore space because their metal bodies can adapt to external changes in different situations but the human body cannot. In military forces, robots can be programmed to defuse a bomb.

No Emotion

The complete absence of emotions makes machines to think logically and take a right decision whereas human emotions are associated with different moods that can affect human efficiency. Complete absence of emotions allows machines to take correct decisions.

Daily Applications

In today's era, AI is used in many applications, like Apple's Siri, Window's Cortana, Google's Assistant. Using these types of applications we can communicate with the device using our voice which makes our work easy.

New Inventions

Artificial intelligence is powering many inventions in almost every domain which will help humans to solve the majority of complex problems. Recently, doctors can predict breast cancer in the woman at earlier stages using advanced Artificial intelligence based technologies.

As every bright side has a darker version in it, Artificial Intelligence also has some disadvantages. Let's see some of them.

DISADVANTAGES OF ARTIFICIAL INTELLIGENCE

High Cost of Creation

Creation of Artificial Intelligence requires huge costs as machines containing it are very complex. Hardware and software need to get updated with time to meet the latest requirements. Machines need repairing and maintenance which is costly and often time-consuming.

Unemployment

The increasing number of AI machines is leading to unemployment and job security issues. As machines are replacing human resources, the rate at which people are losing their jobs will increase.

Can't Think Out of Box

Robots can only do the work that they are programmed to do. They cannot act on anything different outside of whatever algorithm or programming is stored in their internal circuits. When it comes to a creative mind, nothing can beat a human mind.

Highly Dependent on Machine

In today's generation, most of the people are highly dependent on applications like Siri. With so much assistance from machines, humans may not use their thinking abilities and this will gradually decrease their mental capacities.

Making Humans Lazy

Artificial Intelligence is making humans lazy with its applications automating the majority of the work. Humans tend to get addicted to these inventions which can cause a problem to future generations.

MAJOR AREAS OF APPLICATIONS OF ARTIFICIAL INTELLIGENCE

We can say that the most important application of artificial intelligence is to be able to design human-like intelligence system. Major tech companies are still working on it for a while but it is still not achieved accurately. It might take some time to achieve that goal. Apart from that, many important areas of applications of artificial intelligence can be found and we can classify them as follows:

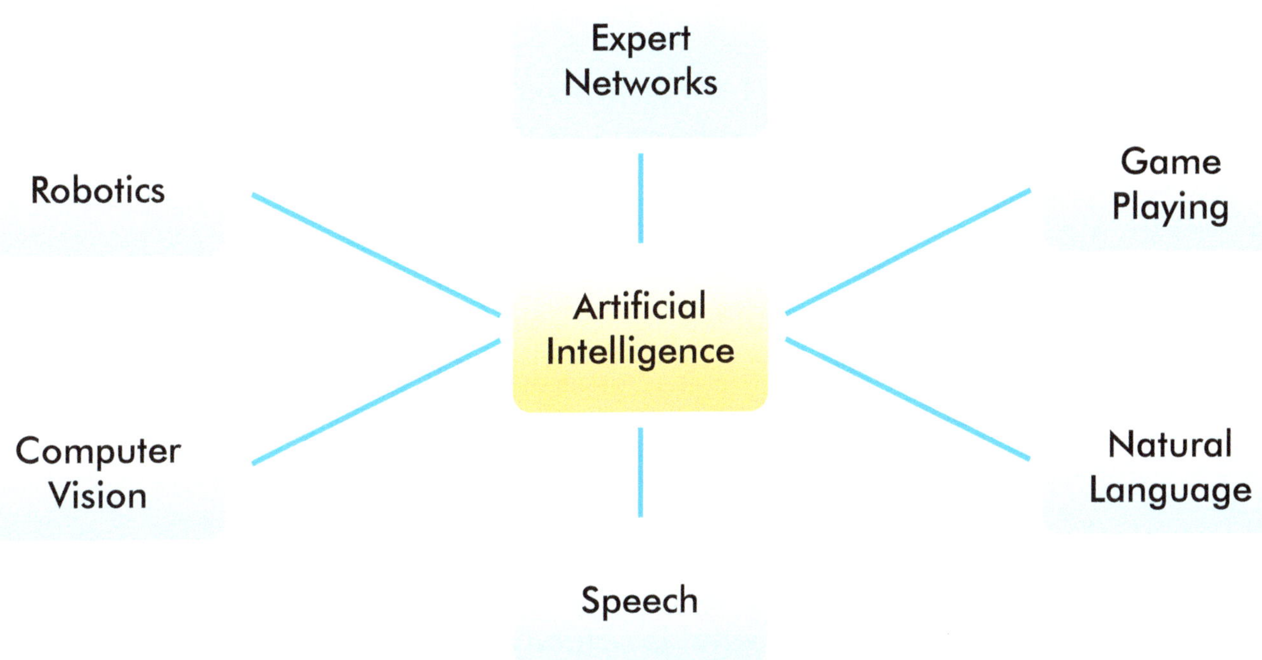

Expert System

The expert systems are one of the important applications of artificial intelligence. The expert systems are basically some computer applications that store the experience and knowledge of human experts based on some particular domain.

Game Playing

In the beginning of the twenty-first century, game playing was not that much enjoyable or interesting as graphics quality was not good and the artificial intelligence used at that time was also not well developed. If we see nowadays, we can play the high-end games online which are more realistic in nature. The concept of artificial intelligence is implemented in modern games and we even don't feel that we are playing with a machine; it is so real.

Natural Language Processing

We know that a machine doesn't recognize the languages like English, Hindi, Spanish, etc. that we speak. It only understands machine language, *i.e.* the language based on the binary and hexadecimal number system. But the problem is that human beings can't understand that language. So, to recognize and understand our natural languages by a machine, the concept of natural language processing comes up.

Natural language Processing mainly consists of two components:

Natural Language Understanding: It means how a machine can understand our languages, how our speech gets transformed into machine-understandable form, etc. A complex processing algorithm is required to achieve this because a natural language can be very ambiguous.

Natural Language Generation: It is the reverse process of Natural Language Understanding. The machine converts its language into human understandable natural languages.

Speech Recognition

Speech recognition is one of the most commonly used applications of artificial intelligence. Basically, it refers to the ability of the machine that understands the words we say. When a machine receives our voice, it first records, analyses and then finally translates the sounds into some predefined words to recognize them.

Computer Vision

Computer vision is the ability to obtain a high-level of the digital images and videos by machines. The primary goal of computer vision is to recognize and interpret images. It means what is present in a scene or what is actually going on.

Robotics

Robotics is a branch derived from the Mechanical, Electronics and Computer Science Engineering. It is the study of designing, constructing, operating some intelligence that can make our tasks easy. A robot can do repetitive work without getting bored.

Some Popular Social Robots in the World

Sophia

Created by Hanson Robotics, Sofia is a humanoid-like robot that is capable of holding a conversation. This robot has appeared in several high-profile interviews and appearances, including a spot on the Jimmy Fallon show. Sofia is unusual as she has been given official citizenship of Saudi Arabia and also the United Nations title of 'Innovation Champion'.

REEM

REEM is a full-size humanoid service robot, created by PAL Robotics. This robot can act as a receptionist, provide entertainment for guests, make presentations and give speeches in different languages and help with a variety of chores.

ASIMO

ASIMO is a humanoid robot created by Honda in 2000. Since then, it has been continually developed and has become one of the world's most advanced social robots with the ability to walk, run and even use the stairs.

Pepper

Introduced in 2014 and manufactured by SoftBank Robotics, Pepper is the world's first robot that is capable of recognizing human emotions. Pepper is social and capable of having conversations with people, giving them directions and even dancing with them.

Gita Robot

Carrying your own bags is such a chore. With Gita Robot, worry no more. It is a robot created by Piaggio. This compact robot is designed to follow you around while you're out and about in town or on the way to work.

LET'S HAVE A LOOK

- Artificial Intelligence (AI) is an area of computer science that emphasizes the creation of intelligent machines that work and react like humans.
- The word 'Artificial' means non-natural, *i.e.* anything that is man-made and the word 'Intelligence' means the ability to understand, think and learn.
- Human intelligence is defined as the general mental ability in humans for reasoning, problem- solving and learning.
- Narrow artificial intelligence or weak AI does only a specific type of task, for example, Poker game.
- Robotics is a branch derived from the Mechanical, Electronics and Computer Science Engineering.

BRAIN TEASER

1. Multiple Choice Questions:

Tick (✓) the correct answer:w

a. Artifical intelligence is an intelligent entity created by

i. Animals ☐ ii. Computers ☐ iii. Humans ☐

b. Which type of artificial intelligence is known as weak AI?

i. Strong AI ☐ ii. Narrow AI ☐ iii. General AI ☐

c. Apple's Siri is used as-

i. Drone ☐

ii. Digital assistance ☐

iii. Video game ☐

d. ASIMO is a humanoid robot created by __________ in __________.

i. Softbank Robitics in 2014 ☐

ii. Honda in 2014 ☐

iii. Honda in 2000 ☐

2. Fill in the blanks:

a. General Artificial Intelligence are __________ and __________ to take decisions.

b. One of the biggest users of artificial intelligence is the __________ ad industry.

c. In __________ forces, robots can be programmed to defuse a bomb.

d. Complete absence of __________ allows machines to take a right decision.

e. The most important application of artificial intelligence is to be able to design ______________________.

f. Computer vision is the primary vision to __________ and __________ images.

3. Write 'T' for True and 'F' for False in the boxes:

a. Robotics is the study of designing, constructing, operating some intelligence that can make our tasks easy. ☐

b. REEM is a full-size humanoid service robot, created by Pal robotics. ☐

c. Machine recoginzes the languages like English, Hindi, Spanish, etc. that we speak. ☐

d. Human intelligence is implemented in modern games. ☐

e. Pepper has been given official citizenship of Saudi Arabia. ☐

4. Answer the following questions

(i) Answer each in a few lines:

a. Define artificial intelligence.

b. Write the definition of artificial intelligence given by Patterson.

c. What do you mean by creating expert systems?

d. Give two examples of digital assistants.

e. Can robots think out of box? How do they work?

f. What do you mean by computer vision?

(ii) Answer each comprehensively:

a. Explain any three goals of artificial intelligence.

b. What are the three types of artificial intelligence?

c. Give any three examples of AI in our daily life.

d. Write any three advantages and disadvantages of AI.

e. Write a few major areas of applications of artificial intelligence.

f. Write a few lines about some popular social robots in the world.

Create PowerPoint presentations on any two topics given in the chapter. Add appropriate pictures, animations, voiceover and videos.

2 Computer Memory

In this chapter, we will learn:

⇒ Introduction to Memory
⇒ Different Types of Memory
⇒ Primary Memory
⇒ Types of Primary Memory
⇒ Classification of RAM
⇒ Secondary Memory
⇒ Types of Secondary Memory

MEMORY

Memory plays a very important role in a computer. It is a temporary workplace inside the computer that stores instructions and information. Memory holds both the data that needs to be processed, and the data that has already been processed. Memory usually consists of one or more chips on the motherboard in the computer.

Memory stores three basic categories of items: (1) the operating system and other system software that control or maintain the computer and its devices; (2) application programs that carry out a specific task such, as word processing; and (3) the data being processed by the application programs and resulting information. This role of memory to store both data and programs is known as the stored program concept.

There are two categories of memory in the computer: volatile and non-volatile. When the power of the computer is turned off, volatile memory loses its contents. Non-volatile memory (NVM), by contrast, does not lose its contents when power is turned off from the computer.

Representing Character in Memory

Manufacturers state memory and storage sizes in terms of the number of bytes available within the device for storage.

A kilobyte of memory, abbreviated KB or K, is equal to exactly 1,024 bytes. A megabyte (MB) is equal to approximately one million bytes.

A gigabyte (GB) equals approximately one billion bytes. A terabyte (TB) equals approximately 1 trillion bytes.

Byte

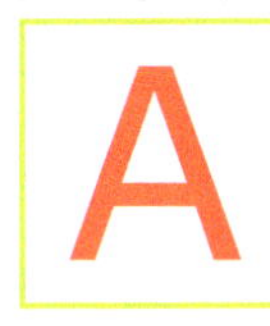

A byte is the basic storage unit in the computer memory. One byte is one character. A character can be a number, letter or symbol. One byte consists of eight bits (binary digits).

Kilobyte (KB)

One kilobyte is 1,024 characters. This is approximately equal to the one page of the text of a book.

Megabyte (MB)

One megabyte is 1,048,576 characters. This is approximately equal to one book.

Gigabyte (GB)

One gigabyte is 1,073,741,824 characters. This is approximately equal to a pile of books.

Terabyte (TB)

One terabyte is 1,099,511,627,776 characters. This is approximately equal to an entire book-stand.

TYPES OF MEMORY

Basically, the computer memory is divided into two types — Primary Memory and Secondary Memory.

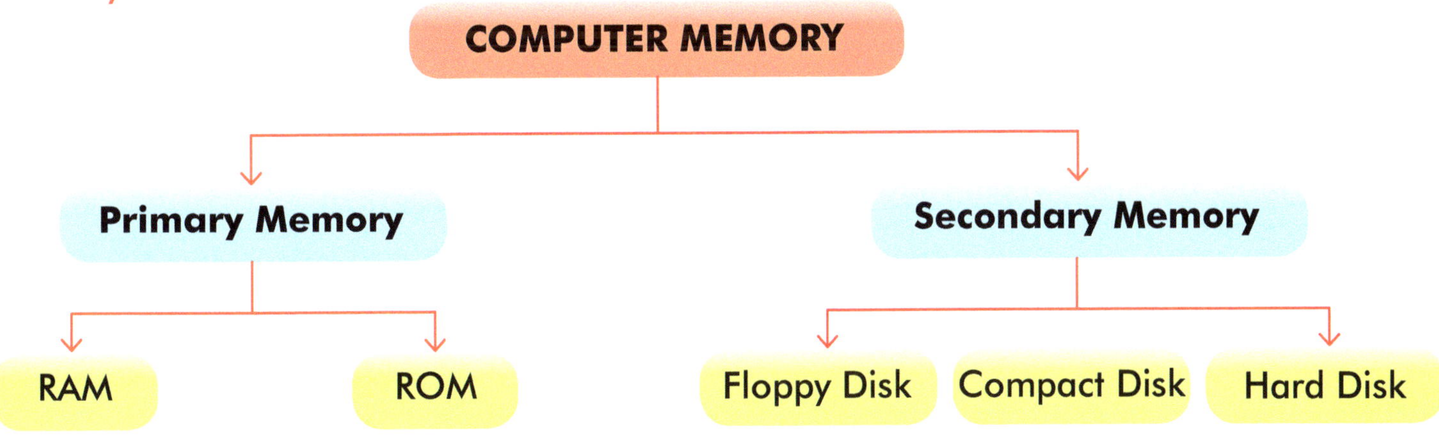

PRIMARY MEMORY

Primary or main memory can be divided into two types — RAM and ROM. The minimum size of the main memory is 256 megabytes. You can, however, increase the main memory any time.

RAM (Random Access Memory)

RAM is called the primary memory or main memory that stores data and instructions temporary in the computer.

When the power is switched On to start a computer, certain operating system files (such as files that determine how your Windows desktop displays) load from a storage device, such as a hard disk, into RAM. These files remain in RAM as long as the computer is running. Additional programs and data are also loaded into RAM from the storage.

The processor (CPU) interprets the data while it is in RAM. During this time, the contents of RAM may change. RAM can hold multiple programs simultaneously, provided the computer has enough RAM to accommodate all the programs. The program with which you are working, is usually displayed on the computer screen.

RAM is a volatile memory. It loses its contents when the power is disconnected from the computer. For this reason, you must save the items you may need in the future. Saving is the process of copying items from RAM to storage devices (hard disk).

Do you know ?

RAM is a type of memory chip that makes up the main memory in many computer systems.

Types of Memory Modules

SIMM

A Single In-Line Memory Module (SIMM) is the most common type of memory module. SIMMs can have either 30 or 72 pins, but the 72-pin module is more common in new computers.

30-pin SIMM (3.5 x .75")

72-pin SIMM (4.25 x 1")

The more RAM a computer has, the better it can carry out instructions.

DIMM

A Dual In-Line Memory Module (DIMM) is used in computers with a Pentium or compatible CPU. A DIMM is similar to a SIMM, but has 168 pins.

168-pin DIMM (5.375 x 1")

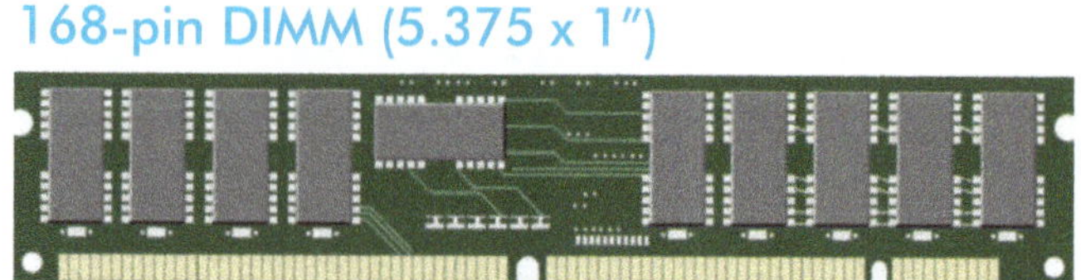

Types of Memory Chips

DRAM

Dynamic RAM (DRAM) is inexpensive and the most popular type of main memory used in computers. Many variations of DRAM chips exist; most of which are faster than the basic DRAM.

FPM DRAM

Fast Page Mode DRAM (FPM DRAM) is slightly faster than basic DRAM. It is not often used in today's computers.

EDO DRAM

Extended Data Out DRAM (EDO DRAM) is slightly faster than FPM DRAM. It is a type of dynamic RAM that keeps data available for the CPU while the next memory access is being initialized, resulting in increased speed.

Burst EDO DRAM

Burst EDO DRAM (BEDO) is a new type of EDO DRAM that is slightly faster. It is capable of processing four memory addresses in one burst. Many motherboards do not support BEDO DRAM, while SDRAM is supported by the widely popular Intel chipset motherboards.

SDRAM

Synchronous DRAM (SDRAM) is a very fast type of main memory often used in new computers. SDRAM provides a 25% speed increase over the earlier EDO technology; that is why it is used in so many latest systems.

Double Data Rate SDRAM (DDR SDRAM)

DDR SDRAM is the next-generation of SDRAM. Unfortunately, it is not backward compatible with motherboards designed for straight SDRAM, so upgrading to DDR means upgrading the motherboard as well. DDR SDRAM uses the same pin connector as plain SDRAM, although the memory modules are not interchangeable. You can't put DDR SDRAM on a motherboard unless it specifically supports it.

RDRAM

(Rambus DRAM) is yet another type of DRAM chips that are much faster than SDRAM chips because they use pipelining techniques. Most computers today use some form of SDRAM chips or RDRAM chips.

SRAM

Static RAM (SRAM) is efficient and fast, but is very expensive. The static in SRAM means that once set, the memory does not need to be constantly refreshed as dynamic RAM does. Due to the nature of its data storage, SRAM takes up more space for less memory than DRAM does. This is known as its density. SRAM is used in small amounts as cache memory in a computer. Cache memory improves the performance of a computer by storing data the computer frequently uses.

MRAM

Magnetoresistive RAM (MRAM) is a newer type of RAM which stores data using magnetic charges instead of electrical charges. Manufacturers claim that MRAM has greater storage capacity, consumes less power, and has faster access times than other RAM. Also, MRAM retains its contents after power is disconnected from the computer, which could prevent the loss of data for users.

RAM REQUIREMENTS

The amount of RAM a computer requires often depends on the types of applications you plan to use on the computer. A computer can manipulate only data that is in its memory (RAM). RAM is similar to the workspace on the top of your desk. Just as a desktop needs a certain amount of space to hold papers, pens, a stapler, your telephone and so on, similarly a computer needs a certain amount of memory to store application programs and files. The more RAM a computer has, the more programs and files it can work on at once.

The amount of RAM on the computer determines the amount of programs and data a computer can handle at one time, which affects the overall performance. The more the RAM, the faster the computer will respond.

ROM (Read Only Memory)

Read Only Memory refers to memory chips storing data that can be read only. The data on ROM chips cannot be modified—hence, the name Read only memory. ROM is non-volatile. Its contents are not lost when power is disconnected from the computer.

ROM Chip

ROM chips contain data, instructions or information that is recorded permanently. For example, ROM contains the basic input/output system (BIOS), which is a sequence of instructions the computer follows to load the operating system and other files when you first turn on the computer. Many other devices also contain ROM chips. For example, ROM chips in many printers contain data for fonts. The manufacturers of ROM chips often record the data, instructions or information on the chips when they manufacture the chip. These ROM chips, called firmware, contain permanently written data and information.

Some of the variations of the ROM chip are —

1. A programmable read-only memory (PROM) chip is a blank ROM chip on which you can place items permanently.
2. An Erasable Programmable ROM (EPROM) is another type of ROM on which its contents are erased by ultraviolet light and then reprogrammed by an RPROM programme.
3. An Electrically EPROM (EEPROM) is another type of ROM that works like flash memory in which its contents can be flashed for erasure and then written to without having to remove the clip from its environment.

SECONDARY MEMORY

Secondary memory or secondary storage devices are the units where the data or information can be stored for future use. Primary memory — RAM and ROM — has some limitations. To overcome those limitations the secondary storage devices are used. It is an auxiliary memory in which data can be stored and retrieved. Data and instructions remain for future use, even when computers have been switched off. The secondary storage has a higher storage capacity as compared to the primary memory. The different types of storage devices are: hard disk, floppy disk, compact disc, pen drive, etc.

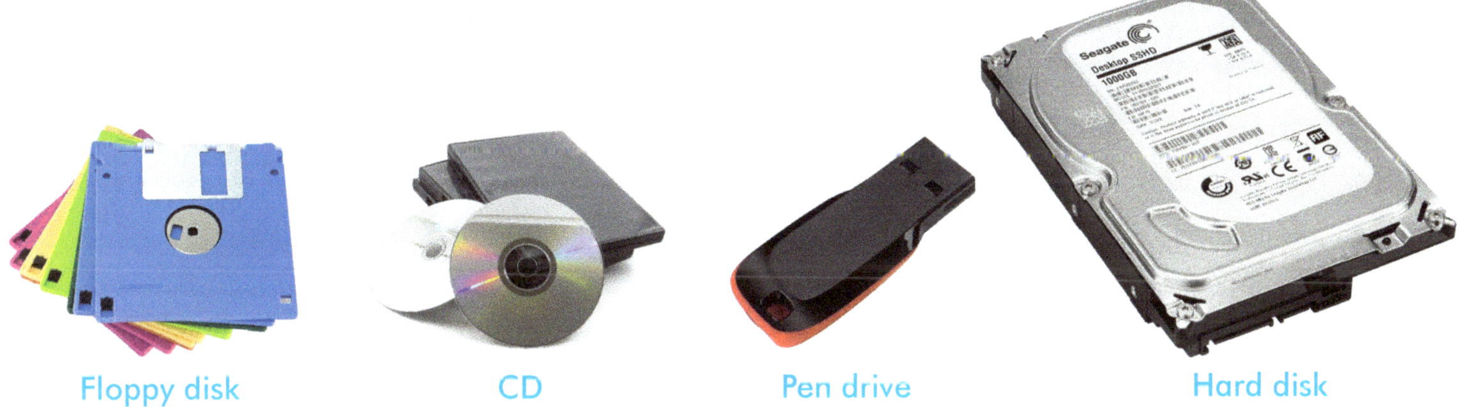

Floppy disk CD Pen drive Hard disk

Cache Memory

Cache is a temporary storage area for data and instructions that is closer to the CPU's speed. Most of today's computers improve their processing times with cache. Memory cache helps speed the processes of the computer because it stores frequently used instructions and data. Cache is built directly in the processor chip. When the processor needs an instruction or data, it first searches cache. If it cannot locate the item in cache then it searches RAM. Most modern computers have three types or layers of memory cache: Level 1, Level 2 and Level 3.

When the processor needs an instruction or data, it searches memory in this order: L1 cache, then L2 cache, then L3 cache (if it exists). If the instruction or data is not found in memory then it must search in a slower speed storage device, such as a hard disk or CD-ROM.

LET'S HAVE A LOOK

- Memory consists of electronic components that store instructions waiting to be executed and data needed by those instructions.
- There are two categories of memory in the computer: volatile and non-volatile.
- A kilobyte of memory, abbreviated KB or K, is equal to exactly 1,024 bytes.
- A megabyte (MB) is equal to approximately one million bytes.
- A gigabyte (GB) equals approximately one billion bytes.
- A terabyte (TB) equals approximately 1 trillion bytes.
- A byte is the basic storage unit in the computer memory.
- RAM is called the primary memory or main memory that stores data and instructions temporarily in the computer.
- SIMM and DIMM are two types of memory module.
- Static RAM (SRAM) is efficient and fast, but is very expensive.
- Magnetoresistive RAM (MRAM) is a newer type of RAM which stores data using magnetic charges instead of electrical charges.
- Read-only memory refers to memory chips storing data that can be read only.
- Cache is a temporary storage area for instructions and data that is closer to the CPU's speed.

Acronyms

RAM : Random Access Memory

ROM : Read Only Memory

PROM : Programmable Read Only Memory

DRAM : Dynamic Random Access Memory

SRAM : Static Random Access Memory

FPM DRAM : Fast Page Mode Dynamic Random Access Memory

EDO DRAM : Extended Data Out Dynamic Random Access Memory

RDRAM : Rambus Dynamic Random Access Memory

BRAIN TEASER

1. Multiple Choice Questions

Tick (✓) the correct answer:

a. The non-volatile memory:

i. RAM ☐ ii. ROM ☐ iii. Cache ☐

b. The Volatile Memory:
   i. RAM ☐ ii. ROM ☐ iii. PROM ☐

c. The basic storage unit in memory:
   i. Byte ☐ ii. Megabyte ☐ iii. Terabyte ☐

d. A newer type of RAM which stores data using magnetic charges:
   i. SRAM ☐ ii. MRAM ☐ iii. DRAM ☐

e. A temporary storage area for instructions and data that is closer to the CPU's speed:
   i. Cache ☐ ii. ROM ☐ iii. DIMM ☐

f. Which ROM contents are erased by ultraviolet light and then reprogrammed by an RPROM programmes?
   i. EPROM ☐ ii. EEPROM ☐ iii. PROM ☐

g. A memory module with 72 pins:
   i. SIMM ☐ ii. DIMM ☐ iii. RIMM ☐

2. Fill in the blanks:

a. The ________________ is a temporary workplace inside the computer that stores instructions and information.

b. There are two categories of memory in the computer: ________________ and ________________.

c. A gigabyte (GB) equals approximately ________________ bytes.

d. A Dual In-Line Memory Module (DIMM) has ________________ pins.

e. Static RAM chips are ________________ and more reliable than DRAM chips.

f. ________________ is a newer type of RAM which stores data using magnetic charges instead of electrical charges.

g. A ________________ is the basic storage unit in the computer.

h. The ________________ interprets the data while it is in RAM.

i. ________________ is a temporary storage area for instructions and data that is closer to the CPU's speed.

3. Write 'T' for True and 'F' for False in the boxes:

a. Memory plays a very important role in a computer. ☐

b. A megabyte (MB) is equal to approximately one billion bytes. ☐

c. One byte consists of eight bits (binary digits).

d. RAM is called the secondary memory in the computer.

e. A memory module is a circuit board that holds memory chips.

f. SRAM is efficient and fast, but is very expensive.

g. The more the RAM, the faster the computer will respond.

h. ROM is volatile memory.

i. Most modern computers have two types or layers of memory cache.

j. EEPROM is a type of ROM that works like flash memory.

4. Answer the following questions

(i) Answer each in a few lines:

a. What is byte?

b. Write the full forms of ROM and RAM.

c. Name the different types of ROM.

d. Write one difference between PROM and EPROM.

e. What is cache?

f. What is primary memory?

(ii) Answer each comprehensively:

a. Explain the term "Memory".

b. What is the difference between RAM and ROM?

c. What do you understand by Dynamic RAM?

d. Differentiate between SRAM and MRAM.

e. Explain the different types of ROM.

f. What is the requirement of RAM in the computer?

g. Explain the purpose of cache in the computer.

5. Give the full forms of:

i. RAM

ii. MRAM

iii. ROM

iv. SIMM

v. RDRAM

vi. DDR SDRAM

Formative Assessment - 1
(Chapters 1-2)

1. Use any web search engine of your choice to prepare a report/presentation on the following:

a. Types of Artificial Intelligence

b. Advantages of Artificial Intelligence

c. Major Areas where Artificial Intelligence is used

2. Open MS-Word and write a short paragraph on 'Importance of Memory in Computer'.

3. Answer the following questions:

a. What is Artificial Intelligence?

b. Define Computer Vision.

c. What is the requirement of RAM in the computer?

d. What are the special features of SRAM?

e. What is the main benefit of MRAM?

4. Complete the following:

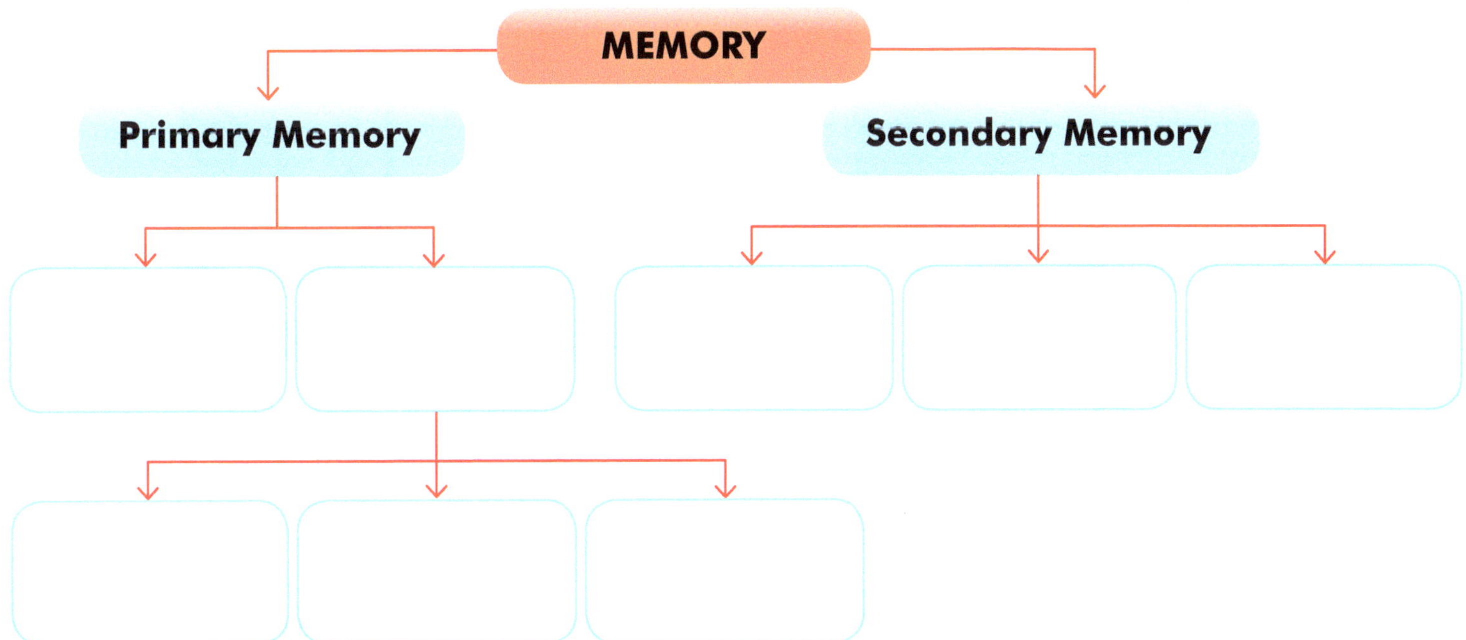

3 Access 2016

In this chapter, we will learn:

⇒ Defining Database
⇒ Access 2016
⇒ Creating a New Table in Datasheet View
⇒ Creating a New Table in Design View
⇒ Understanding Field Properties
⇒ Adding Records to a Table

DATABASE

A database is a collection of data which is organized in a manner that can be easily retrieved. It consists of field, records and files. In a manual database, you might record data on paper and store it in a filing cabinet. With a computerised database, the computer stores the data in an electronic format on a storage medium, such as a hard disk.

Manual Database

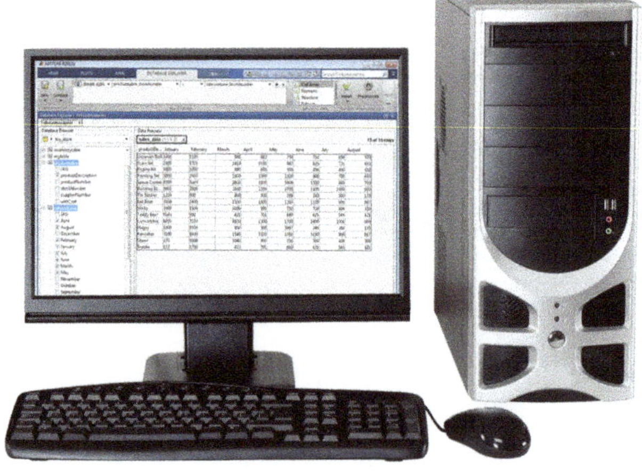
Computerised Database

In computer terminology, data is just data until it is organized in a useful manner. Then it becomes meaningful information, which is called a database. In other words, a large collection of meaningfully organised data is called a database.

Databases are maintained with the help of database management system. A Database Management System (DBMS) is a set of computer programs that controls the creation, maintenance, and the use of a database. It allows organizations to place the control of database development in the hands of database administrators (DBAs). It allows different user application programs to access the same database easily. In large systems, a DBMS allows users and other software to store and retrieve data in a structured way. Instead of having to write computer programs to extract information, a user can ask simple questions in a Query language.

The organization of a database is set in a table consisting of rows and columns having the information in them. In tables, each column consists of heading that describes the type of information it contains and each row consists of the specific information. The columns are called attributes and the rows are called records in a table. The collection of information in the form of rows and columns is called a database.

Applications of DBMS

Databases are used everywhere to ensure the smooth functioning of the organization.

a. Banks maintain customer information in databases and centralised databases enable you to have easy access with ATM cards.

b. Students' database is maintained; courses, registration, report cards, information are kept here by Schools/Universities.

c. Telecommunications to maintain the records of telephone owner, calls made and processed bills.

d. Sales invoices, sales made and inventory data are maintained.

e. Human resources information of employees, salaries, generation of pay cheques, etc.

RDBMS

In a DBMS, we cannot relate two or more tables. To avoid the duplication of data and to deal with large data and difficult application software, we need to relate tables within a database. A new concept called RDBMS offers a solution to these problems. RDBMS stands for Relational Database Management System. These days, there are sophisticated relational database software in the market, such as MS Access, Sybase, Informix, Oracle, Ingress and many more.

ACCESS 2016

Microsoft Access is a Relational Database Management System (RDBMS), designed primarily for home or small business usage; it can create two or more tables that are linked together.

Microsoft Access is a software package that is installed just like any other software packages. It is bundled as part of the Microsoft Office suite. Access provides an engine to manage database and a graphical interface to facilitate its user.

You can use Access to manage large or small collections of information. The information can be viewed, sorted, manipulated, retrieved and printed in various ways. Access gives you the flexibility to obtain this data in multiple formats.

Access stores the data in tables. Each individual entry in the table is called a record. For example, in the students' table, the information about each student is a separate record. Each record is composed of one or more fields that contain individual pieces of data. For example, student fields may include roll number, name, address and class.

Starting Access 2016

You can start Microsoft Access 2016 by following these simple steps.

1. Click on Start button. The Start menu will appear.
2. Click on Microsoft Office.
3. Click on Access 2016. Access screen appears.

Creating a Blank Database

A blank database contains only a single blank table and no other database objects, such as queries or forms. After creating a blank database, you can add tables, forms, reports and other objects in it.

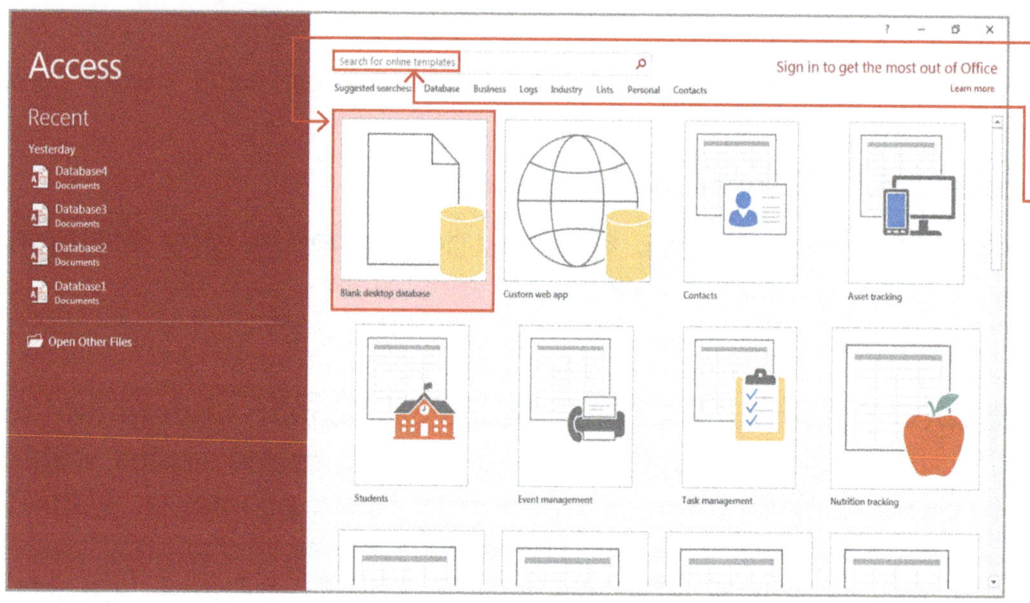

1. Click on the Blank Database option.
2. Type a name for the database.

Access automatically assigns the .accdb (Access Database) extension to all database files.

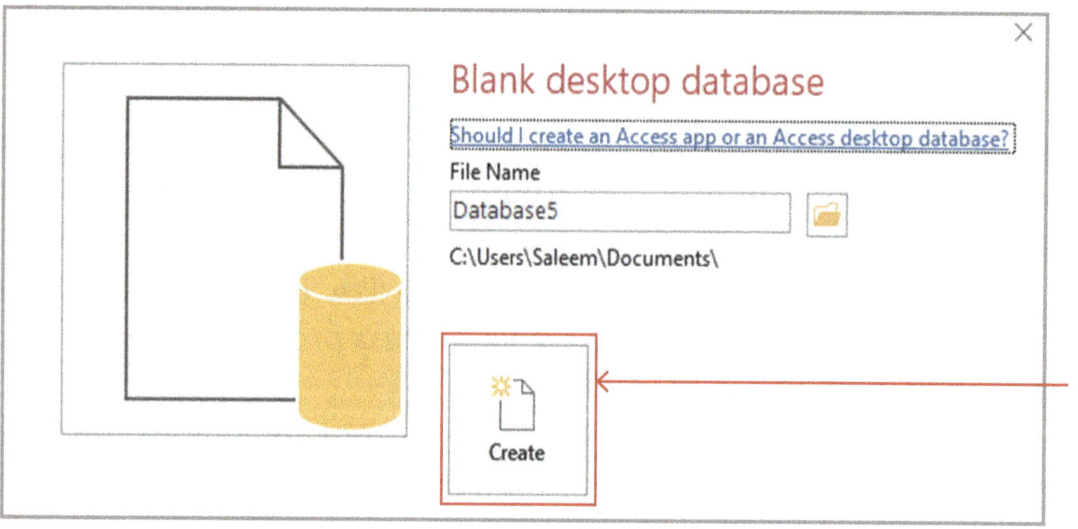

3. Click on Create.

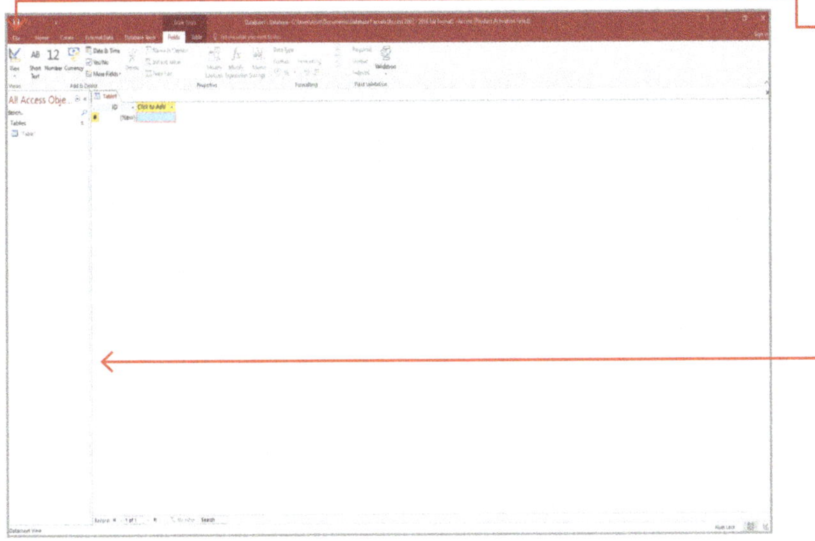

A new database opens, with a new blank table. Now you can create your own tables by entering records in it.

The Navigation pane displays database objects that you create, such as tables and forms.

Closing Database

After finishing your work, you can close a database without exiting Access 2016. Multiple databases can be opened at once, each in its own copy of the application, but after finishing your work. You can close the database to free up system resources and let your computer run other programs more quickly.

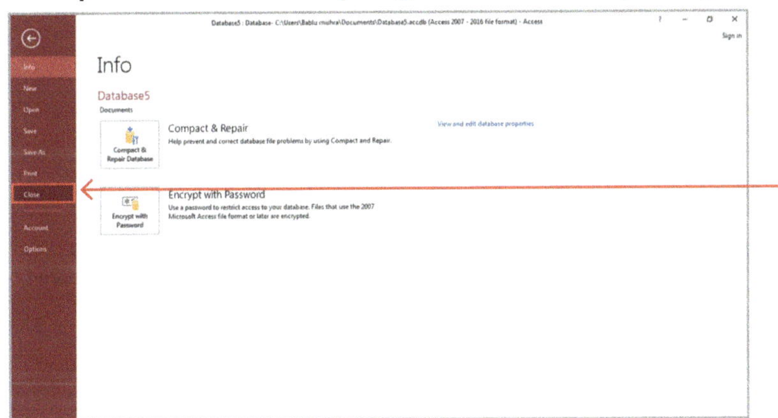

1. Click on File tab. File menu will open.
2. Click on Close Database.

The database file closes and a blank document appears there. You can open a new database by clicking on File Tab - New or you can Exit Access 2016 by clicking the Close (X) button.

Opening a Database File

A list of recently opened files appears on the left edge of the window when you click on File tab. You can either select the file you want to open from the list that appears or can click Open to display the Open dialog box and then navigate to the folder with the database you want to open.

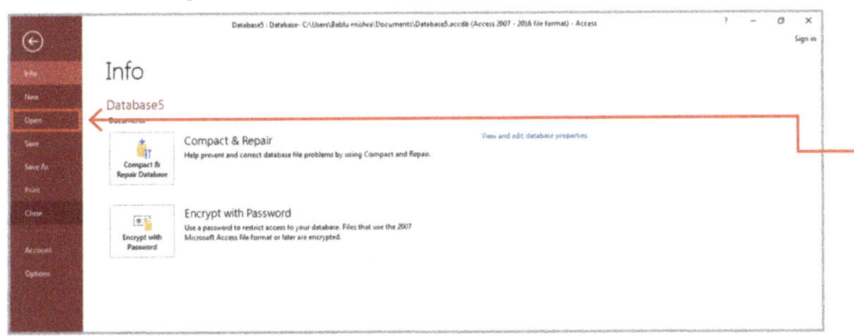

1. Click on File tab.

The backstage view appears.

2. Click on Open.

Alternatively, you can press Ctrl+O instead of performing steps 1 to 2.

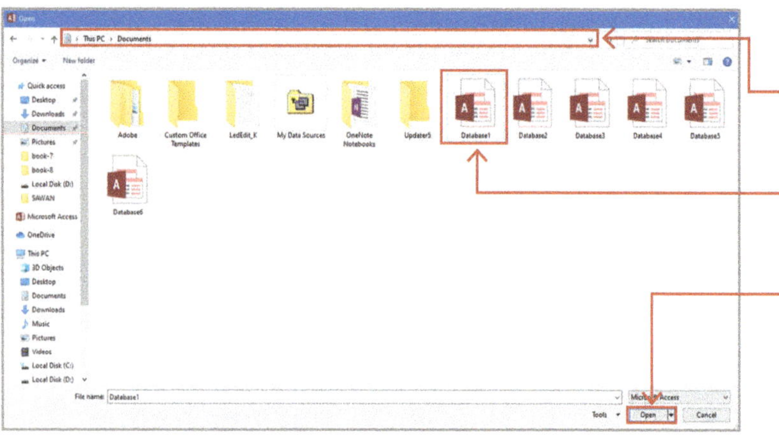

The Open dialog box will appear.

3. You can click here and navigate to a different location.
4. Click on the name of the file that you want to open.
5. Click on Open.

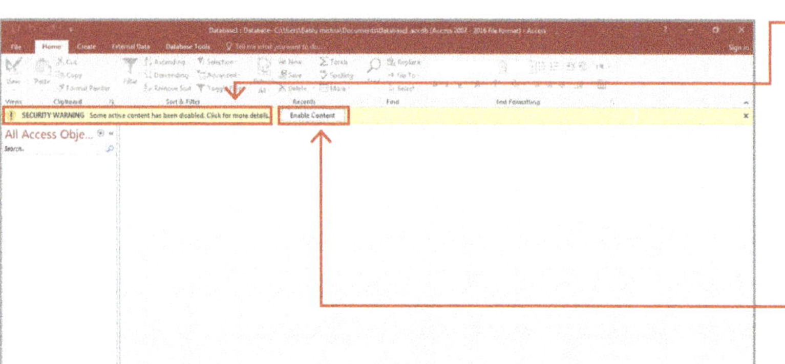

A security warning appears when you are opening a database that is stored in a location that is not trusted, such as a file you received as an e-mail attachment, or while opening a file that contains macros (sets of recorded actions).

6. Click on Enable content.
   The database file opens.

Changing the Navigation Pane View

Access 2016 organizes all the objects in the Navigation pane. You can display or hide the Navigation pane which is situated on the left side of Access window. The Navigation pane enables you to view database objects, like tables, queries, reports and forms.

1. You can press F11 key from the keyboard to display or hide the Navigation pane.

CREATING A NEW TABLE IN DATASHEET VIEW

Access 2016 assigns general names to the fields, such as Field1, Field2, and so on, in Datasheet view. You can create a table by adding new fields simply by typing the field names into the column-heading placeholders. Datasheet View is good when you need a quick table consisting of just a few fields.

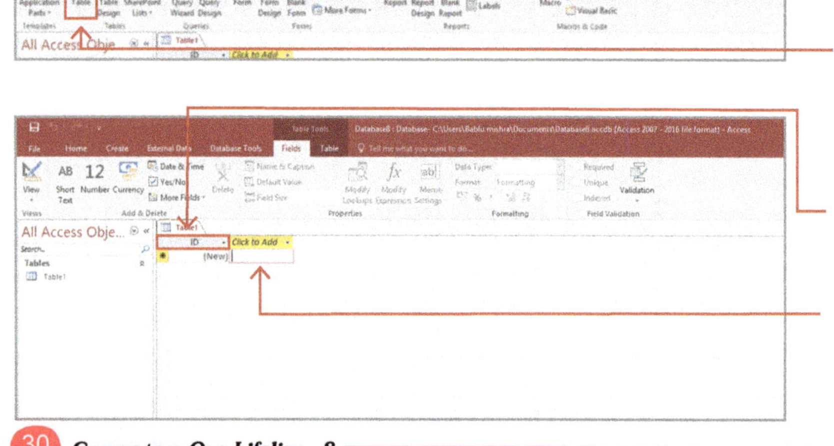

1. Click on Create tab on the Ribbon.
2. Click on Table button.

Access opens a new table in Datasheet view.

3. Double-click the column header to create a field name.
4. Type a name for the field.
5. Press the Enter key from the keyboard.

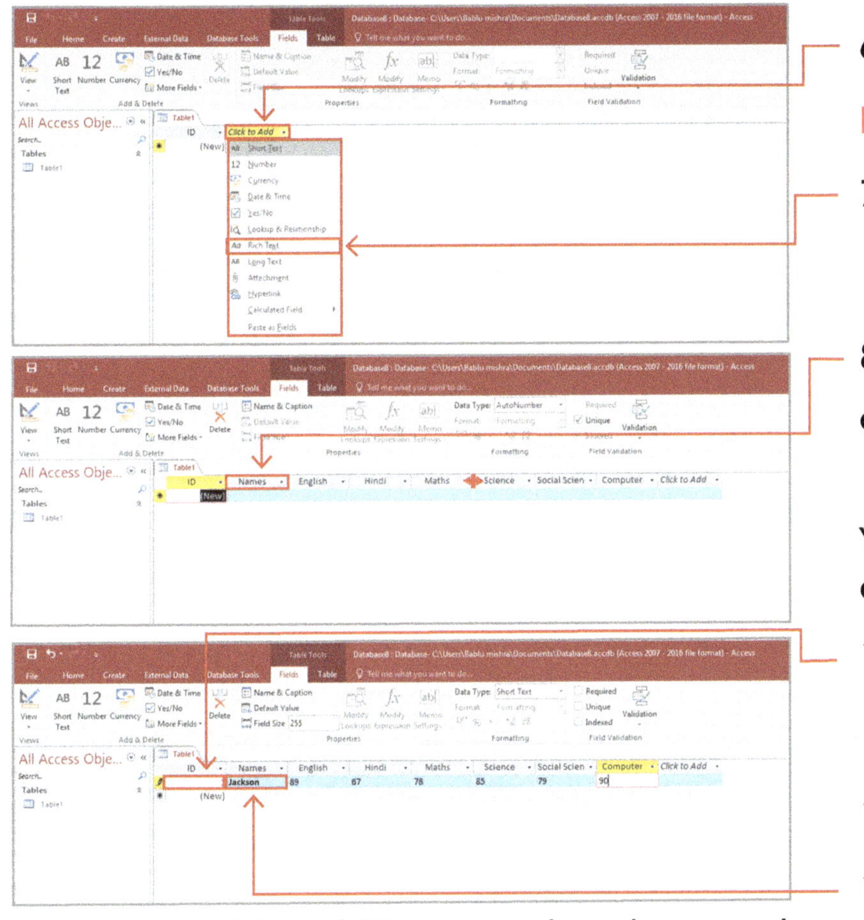

6. Click on the next column.

Data Type menu will appear.

7. Select the data type for the field, e.g., select Rich Text if you want to add Name field.

8. Type a name for the field.

9. Repeat steps 6 to 8 to create more fields for the table.

You can resize a column by dragging column border left or right.

10. Click inside the first field of the first row and type the data to enter the first record.

11. Press Tab key.

12. Type the data of the next field.

Repeat steps 11 and 12 to complete the record.

When you reach the last field, you can press the Enter to start a new record.

CREATING A NEW TABLE IN DESIGN VIEW

You can also make your table in Design View for greater control. Design View lets you first define the structure of your table before creating the table. Here, you enter your own field names and descriptions and choose your own data type to associate with each field. You can also set your own primary key. You describe the structure by describing the fields within the table. In design view, the Window is divided into two panes: top pane for creating field name, specify field types, and enter field descriptions and bottom pane for specifying field properties.

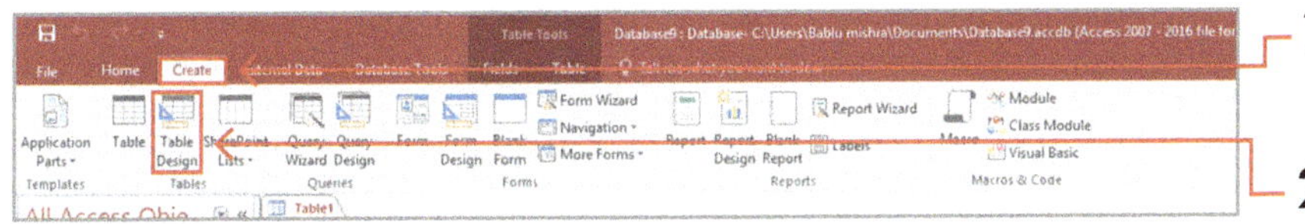

1. Open the database and click on Create tab on the Ribbon.
2. Click on Table Design button.

The Table1 Window appears.

Through Table Design view window, you can create whatever fields you like and select the data types of each field.

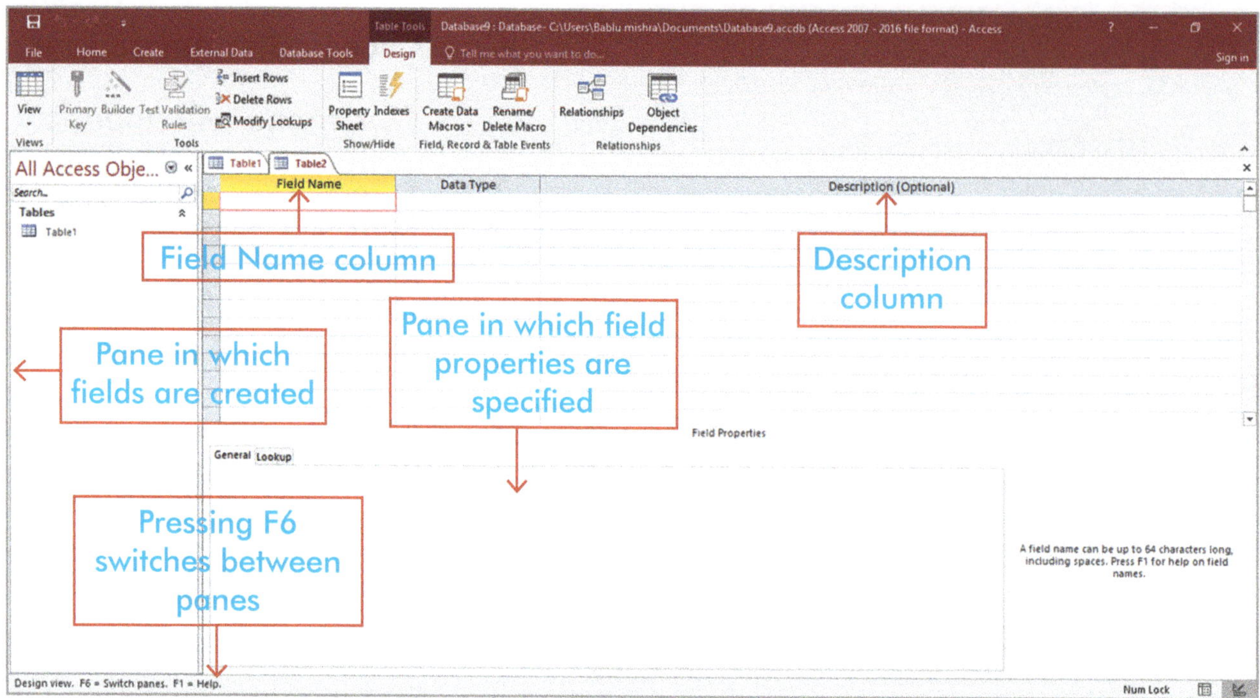

You should define the fields by specifying the required details in the table window to proceed to the next step in creating the table. You should make entries in the Field Name, Data Type and Description columns and then enter additional information in the Field Properties box in the lower portion of the Table window. Press the F6 key to move from the upper pane (portion of the screen), the one where you define the fields, to the lower pane, the one where you define field properties. You should enter the appropriate field size and then press the F6 key to return to the upper pane.

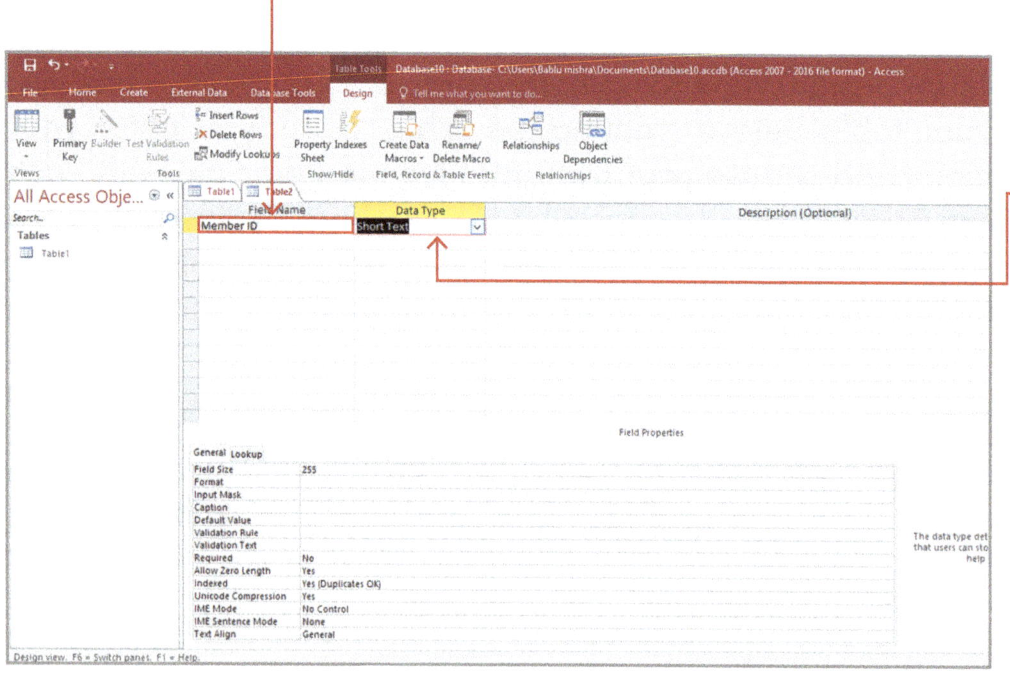

3. Type Member ID (the name of the first field) in the Field Name column.
4. Press the TAB key to bring the Insertion point to Data type field.

The words, Member ID, display in the Field Name column and the insertion point advances to the Data Type column, indicating you can enter the data type. The word, Short Text, one of the possible data types, is currently displayed.

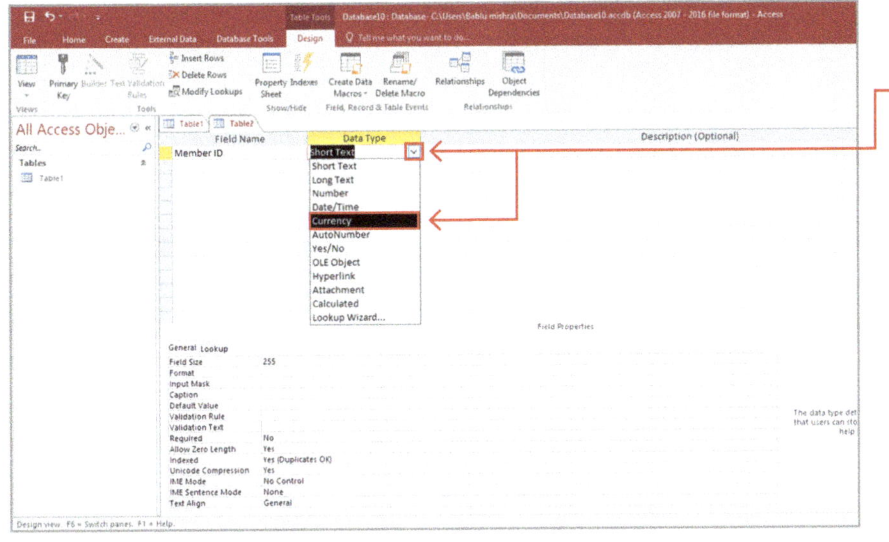

5. If you want to change the data type, click on the down arrow button and change the data type according to your need.

After selecting the data type, its properties will be displayed in the lower pane.

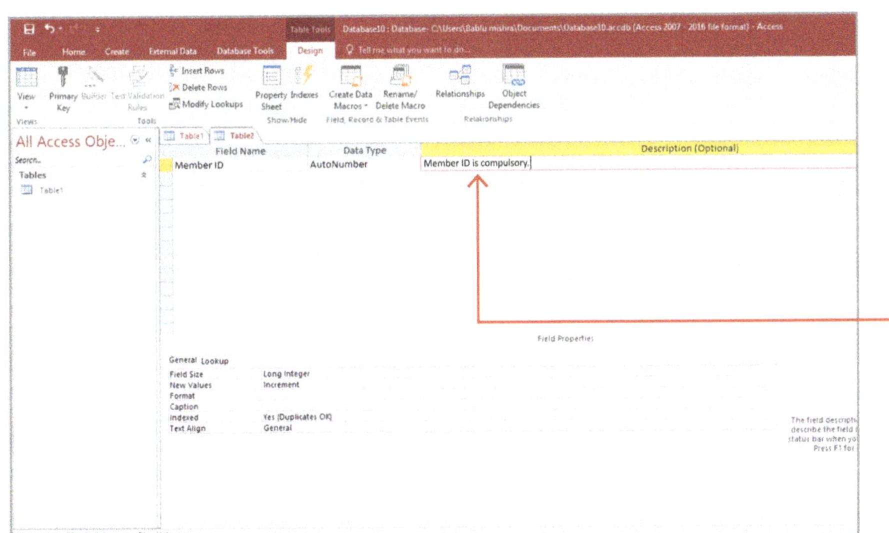

6. After selecting the Data type, press the TAB key to move the insertion point to the Description column.

7. Type your text as the description in Description column.

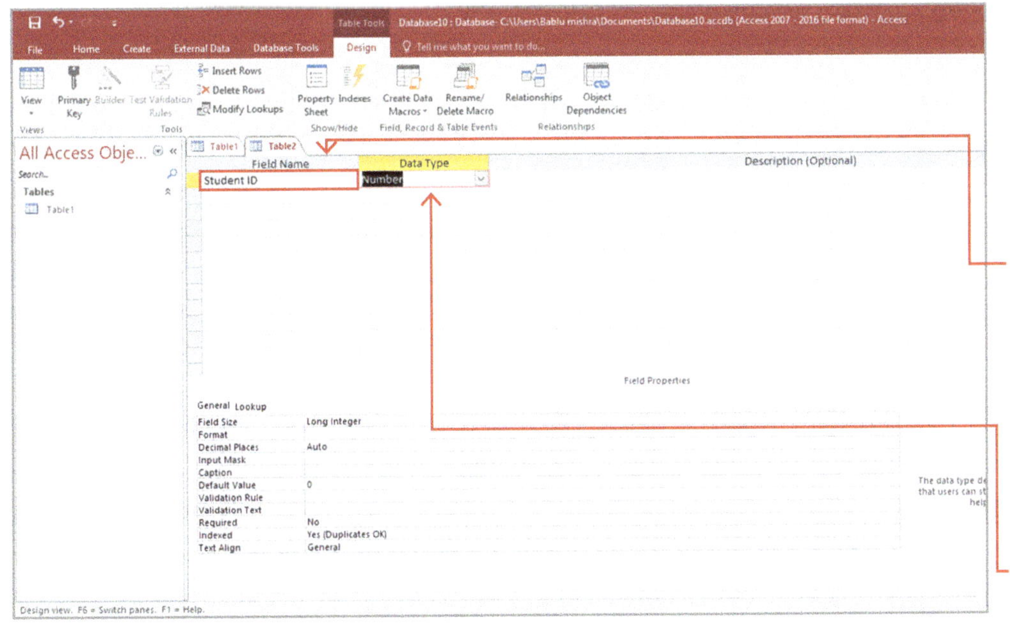

8. Press the Tab key again to move to the Field Name column in the second row.

9. Type the text (Student Name) in Field Name column.

10. Press the Tab key to move to the Data Type column.

The word 'Number' is currently displayed in that field.

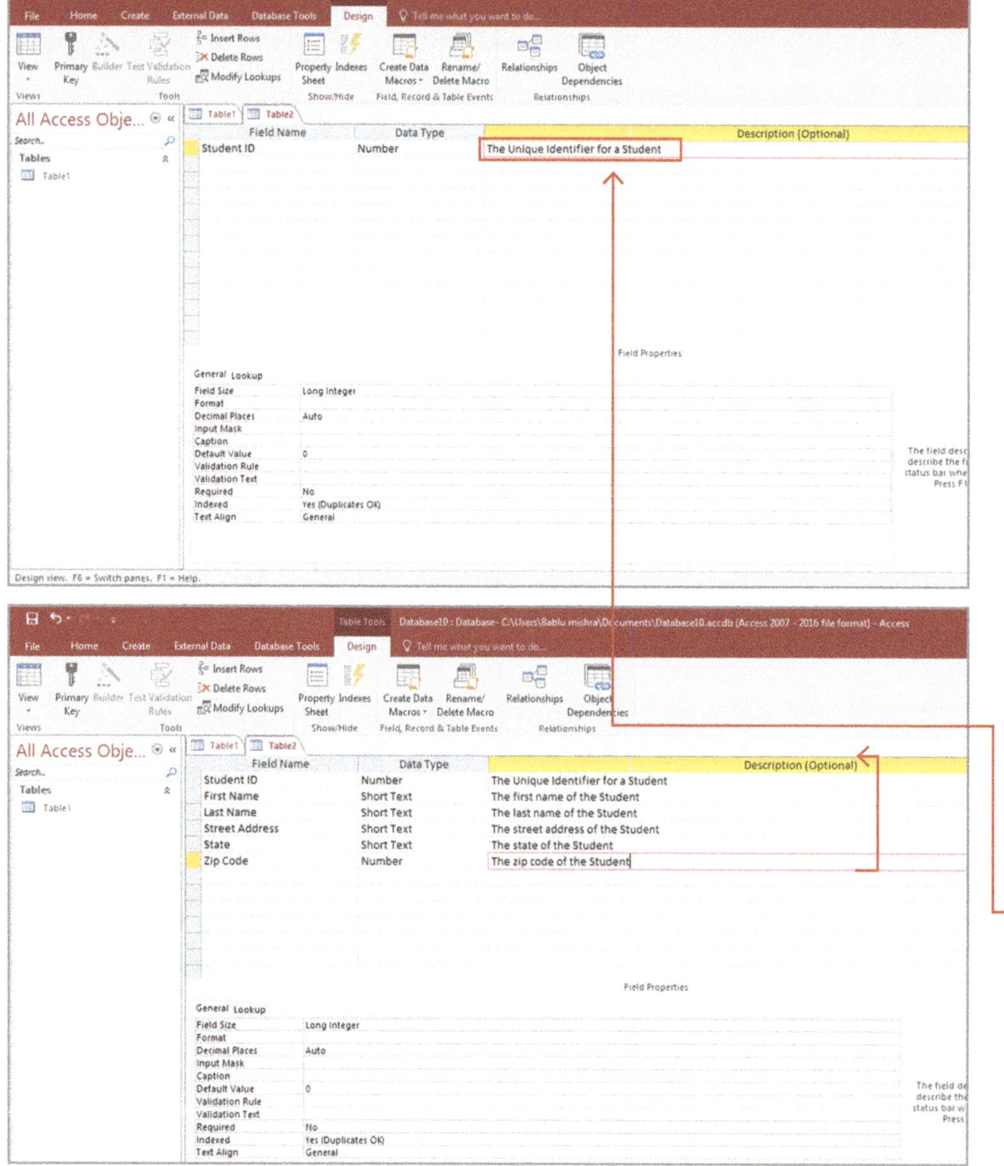

11. Press the Tab key to move the insertion point to Description column, if you want the Data Type as Text.
12. Type the text for the Description column.
13. Repeat steps 3-12 to make the remaining entries in the table to complete it.

Setting a Primary Key

A Primary key is a key that differentiates the records in a file. The data stored in a key field contains data that is unique to a specific record. In each new table that you create, you'll want to set one field as the primary key. Access uses this key to relate this table's records to those in another table. A table usually has only one primary key. When a unique combination of two or more fields' values forms the primary key, it is called a composite key.

Traditionally, the first field in the table is the primary key. Using this convention makes it easy to browse and sort records by this field. However, you may use any field you like for it. A student's record, for example, would use roll number as a key field because it uniquely identifies the student. You can use an AutoNumber field to allow Access to assign numbering for you or you can use a Number or Text field. The only limitation is that the field must contain a unique value for each record. The primary key field cannot be left blank nor can it duplicate the value of another record.

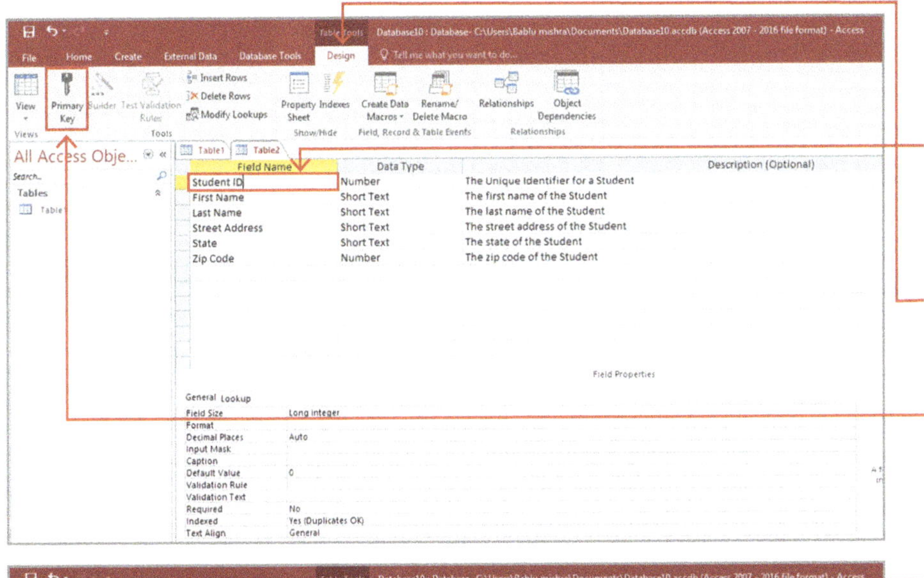

1. Choose the field that you want to set as the primary key.
2. Click on Design Tab on the Ribbon.
3. Click on the Primary Key button.

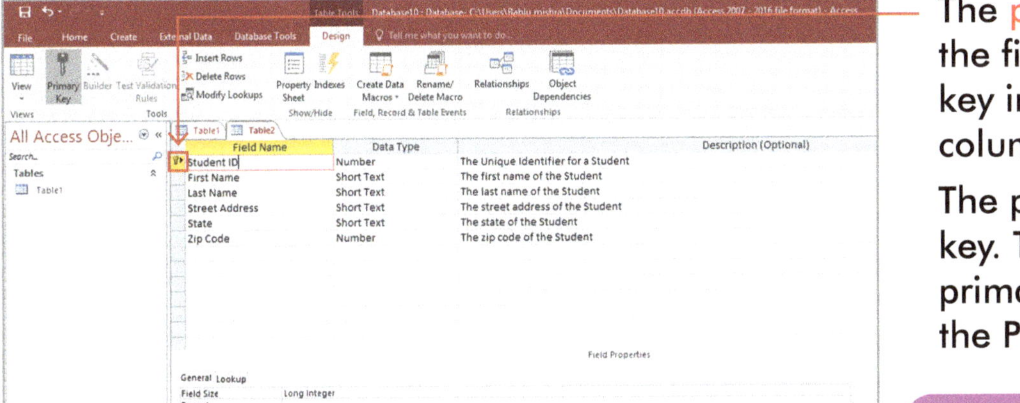

The primary key appears in the field, indicated by a small key in the field of selector column.

The primary key is a toggle key. To remove it, select the primary key field and click on the Primary Key button again.

A primary key is required for every table to identify records uniquely.

Saving and Closing a Table

Table structure is now complete. The next step is to save the table in the database. You should give a name to the table before saving it. Once you have saved the table, you can continue working in the Table window or close the window.

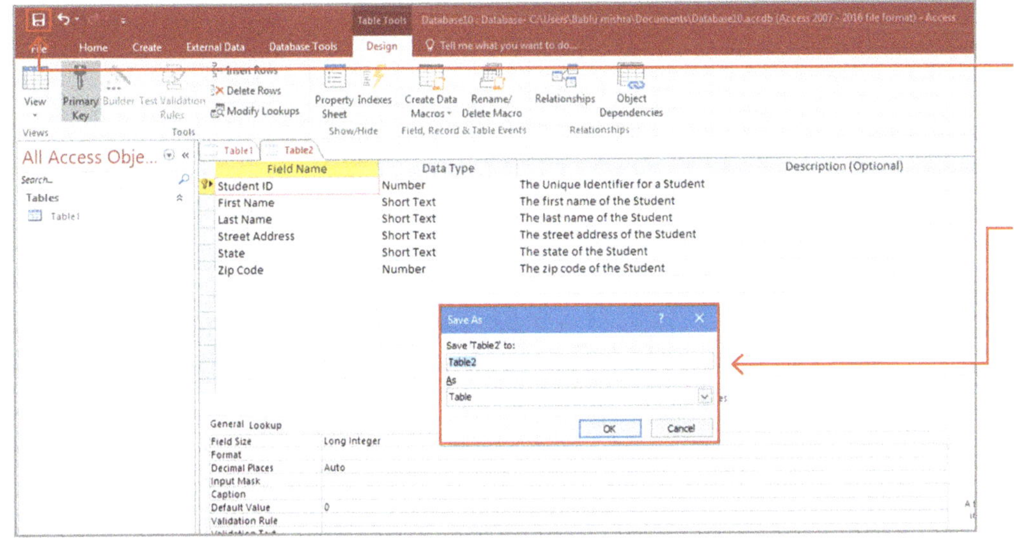

1. Click on the Save button on the Quick Access toolbar.

The Save As dialog box will appear.

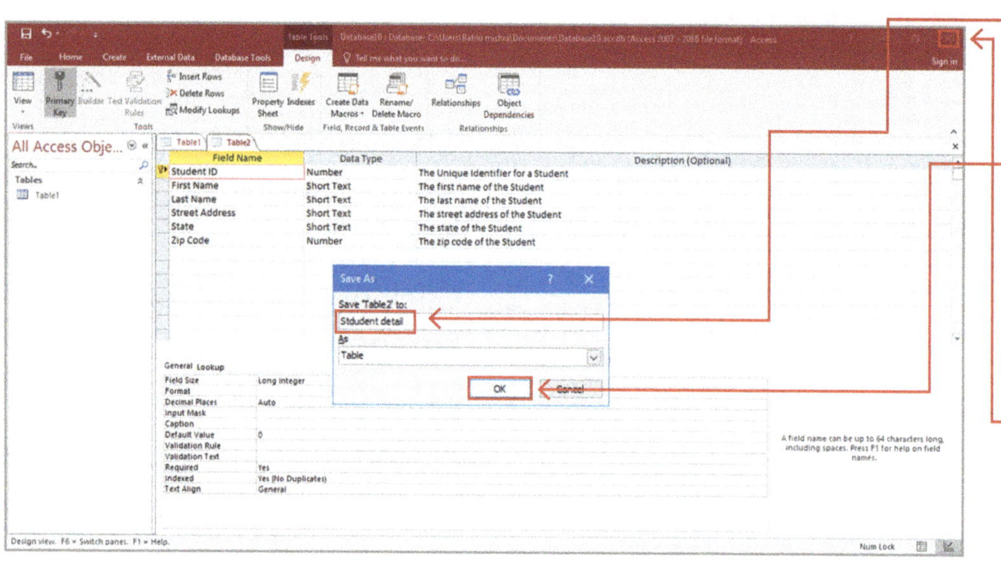

2. Type the name (Members Detail) in the Table Name box.
3. Click on the OK button.

Access saves the table and the table name appears in the Title bar.

4. Click on the Close (x) button to close the Table.

Rearranging Fields

You can change the order in which fields appear in a table. The field order in Design view from top to bottom corresponds to the order in a Datasheet view from left to right.

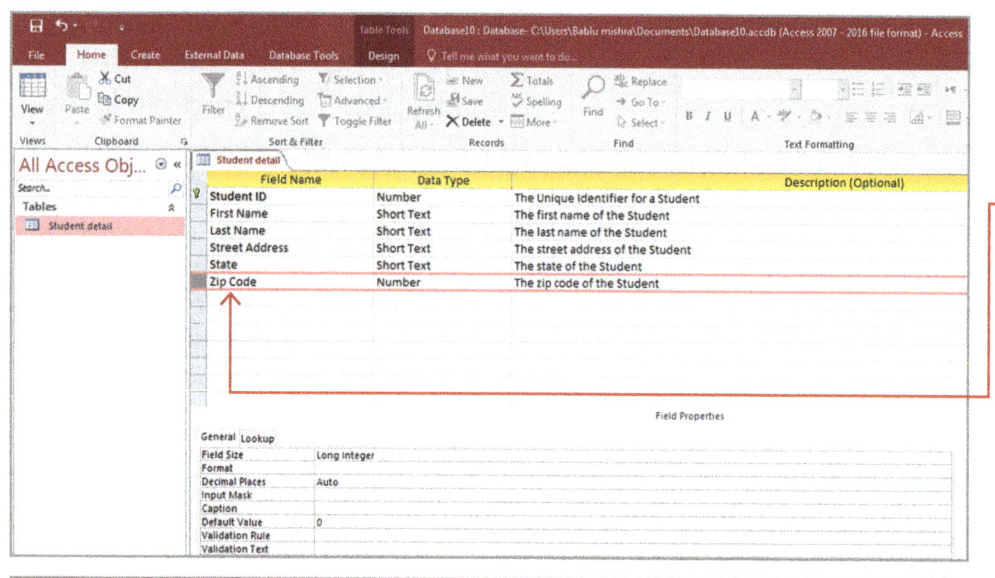

1. Click on the selector to the left of the field name. The whole row (field) will be selected.

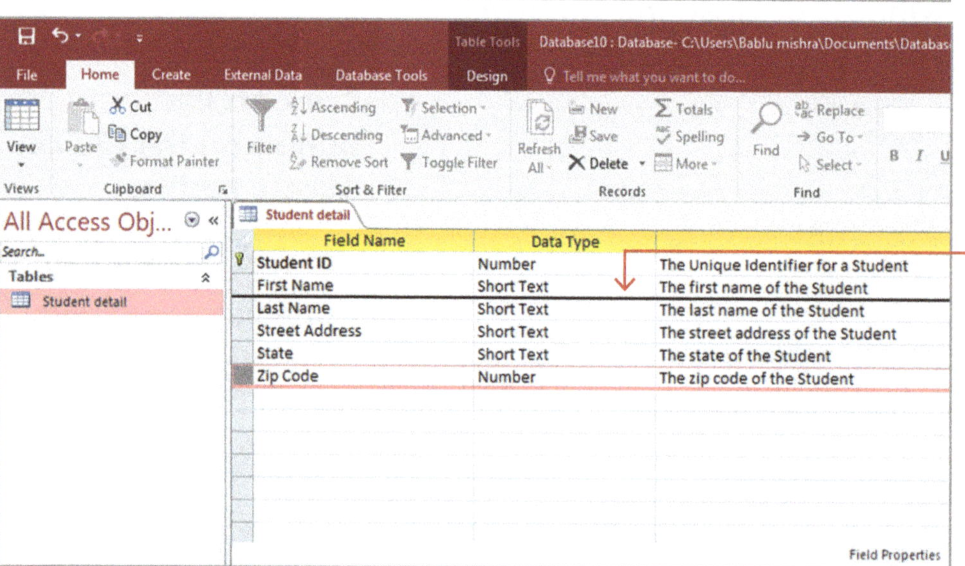

2. Drag up or down the mouse pointer on the selector to move the field.

A horizontal line shows where the field is going.

3. Repeat steps 1 and 2 to move other fields as needed.

Inserting and Deleting Fields

You can insert new fields into a field list, and you can remove existing fields from that list.

Inserting a Field

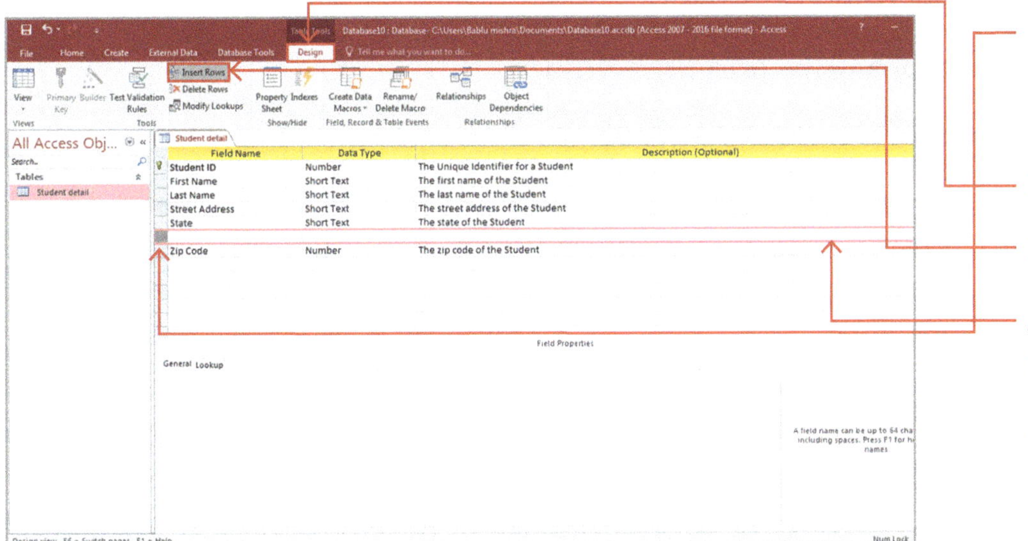

1. Select the field where you want a new field should appear above.
2. Click on Design tab.
3. Click on Insert Rows.

A new row appears above the selected row.

4. Type a field name and choose a field type.

Deleting a Field

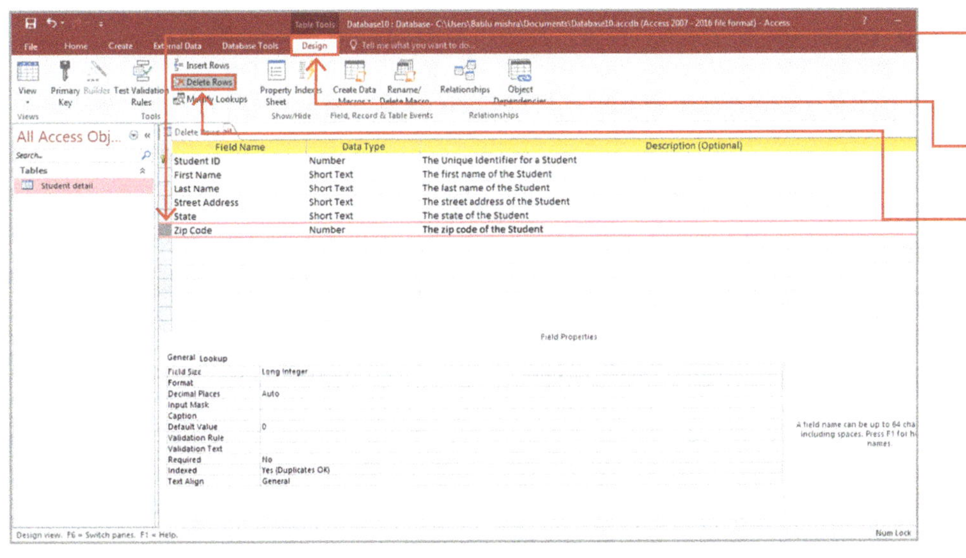

1. Select the field that you want to delete.
2. Click on Design tab.
3. Click on Delete Rows.

The row will be deleted, along with any data that the fields have.

Changing Data Type

You can change a field's data type to define each field to know what type of data you can store in it. Data entry is restricted to valid entries for the type you choose, which helps to prevent data-entry errors. For example, you cannot enter letters in a field set to Number and you must enter valid dates or times in a Date/Time field. This table lists explains possible uses for each one.

Text : To store data that contains letters, digits, spaces and special characters. It has a limit of 255 characters and cannot be used for numeric calculation.

Memo : It is used to store long text comments. This type has a limit of 63,999 characters.

Number : It is used to store numeric values. It can also hold symbols, such as decimal points and commas.

Date/time : It is used to store date and time values.

Currency : It is used to store currency values.

Auto Number : This is used when you want a sequential series of numbers to be generated automatically. The initial value is 1 and with each record the value is incremented by 1.

Yes/No : It is used for Yes/No, True/False or On/Off values.

OLE Object : It is used to store spreadsheets, word documents, drawings, photographs, etc.

Hyperlink : It can link to Web sites, e-mail addresses, files on your computer, files on a LAN, or virtually any other location.

Lookup Wizard : It is used to create a field that lets you select a value from another table or a list of values.

Attachment : This type works only in Access 2007, 2010 and Access 2016 databases. It can attach data files from word processing programs, spreadsheets, graphic editing programs and so on.

Calculated : This field type is new in Access 2016. You can use it to create calculated fields directly in a table.

It is easier to set field types before you enter data into the table, but you can change it at any time.

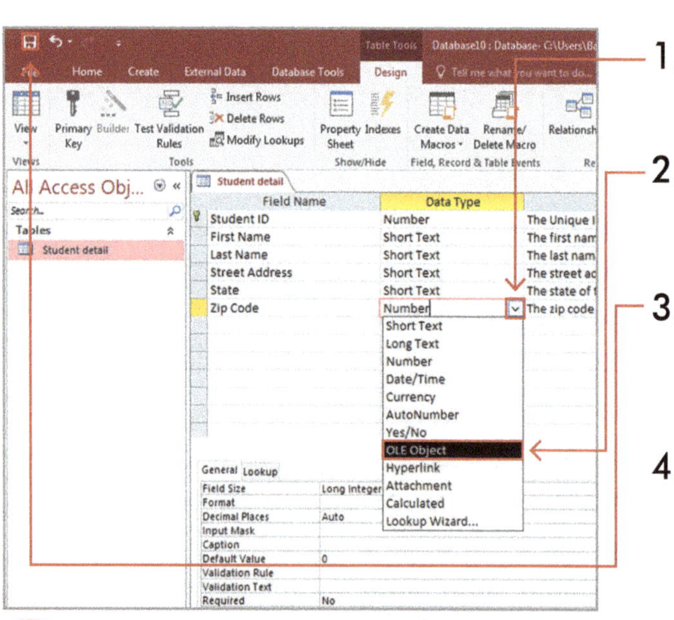

1. Click on the down arrow to open the Data Type list for the field.
2. Click on new type.

   The type changes in the Data Type column.
3. Click on Save button on the Quick Access Toolbar to save the changes to the table. A warning message may appear.
4. Click on Yes to allow the deletion of records that violate the rules of the new field type. You can also click on No to cancel the change.

UNDERSTANDING FIELD PROPERTIES

Each field has a set of properties that defines and controls it. These properties include basics, such as its size and format, as well as rules for making entries, such as specifying whether an entry is required or restricting an entry to certain values.

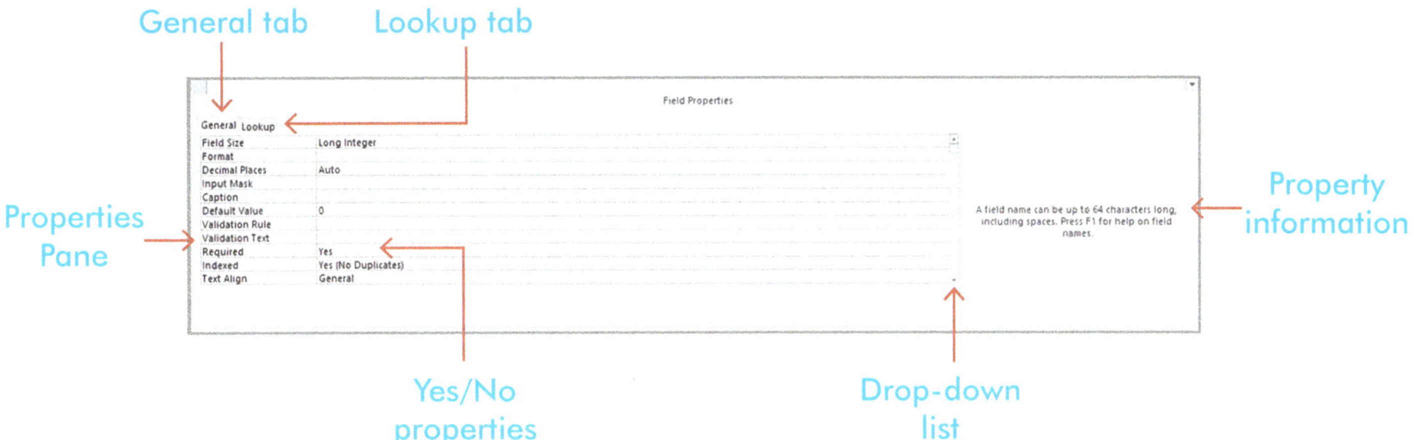

Properties pane : In Design view, the selected field appears in Properties pane.

General tab : It contains all the properties of your field in which you are working.

Lookup tab : It is primarily for setting up lookup lists.

Property information : The information about the property appears in Property information when you place mouse pointer in a property's box.

Yes/No properties : Some properties represent yes/no questions; these are typically already filled in for you with default values.

Drop-down list : Some properties have drop-down lists from which you can make a selection.

Change the Field Size

Each field has a size that limits the amount of data you can store in it. There are different ways of expressing the field size depending on the type of field.

Field Type	Field Size	Meaning
Text	255	You can specify any number of characters from 0 to 255.
Number	Long Integer	Byte, Integer, Long Integer, Single, Double, Replication ID, Decimal
AutoNumber	Long Integer	The same as Number, except there are only two choices: Long Integer or Replication ID

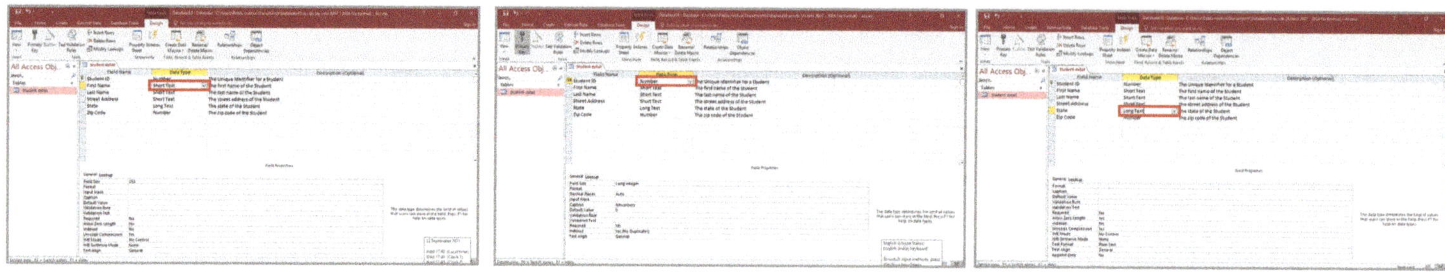

Short Text Number Long Text

Change the Field Size

You can change the Field size according to the need of your database.

For the Text Data Type

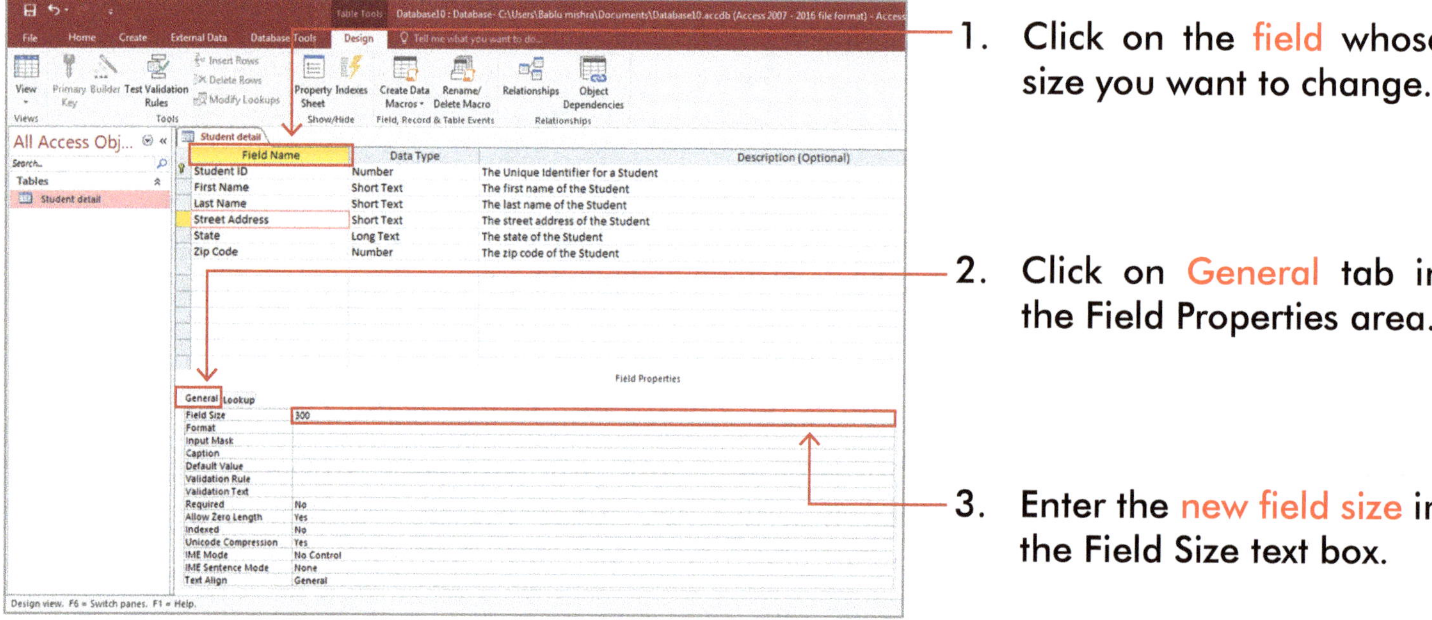

1. Click on the field whose size you want to change.
2. Click on General tab in the Field Properties area.
3. Enter the new field size in the Field Size text box.

For the Number Data Type

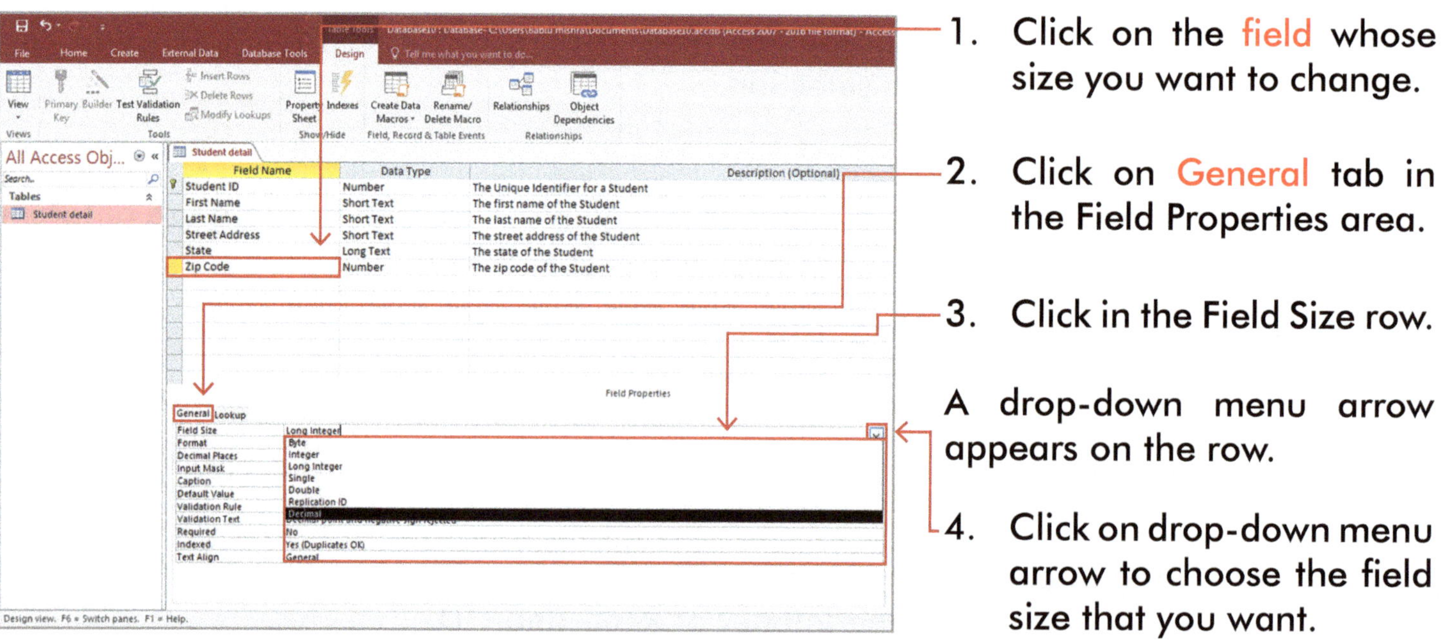

1. Click on the field whose size you want to change.
2. Click on General tab in the Field Properties area.
3. Click in the Field Size row.

A drop-down menu arrow appears on the row.

4. Click on drop-down menu arrow to choose the field size that you want.

Set the Field Caption

Captions can be specified for fields that are different from their actual names. Captions appear in datasheet headings and on labels in forms and reports.

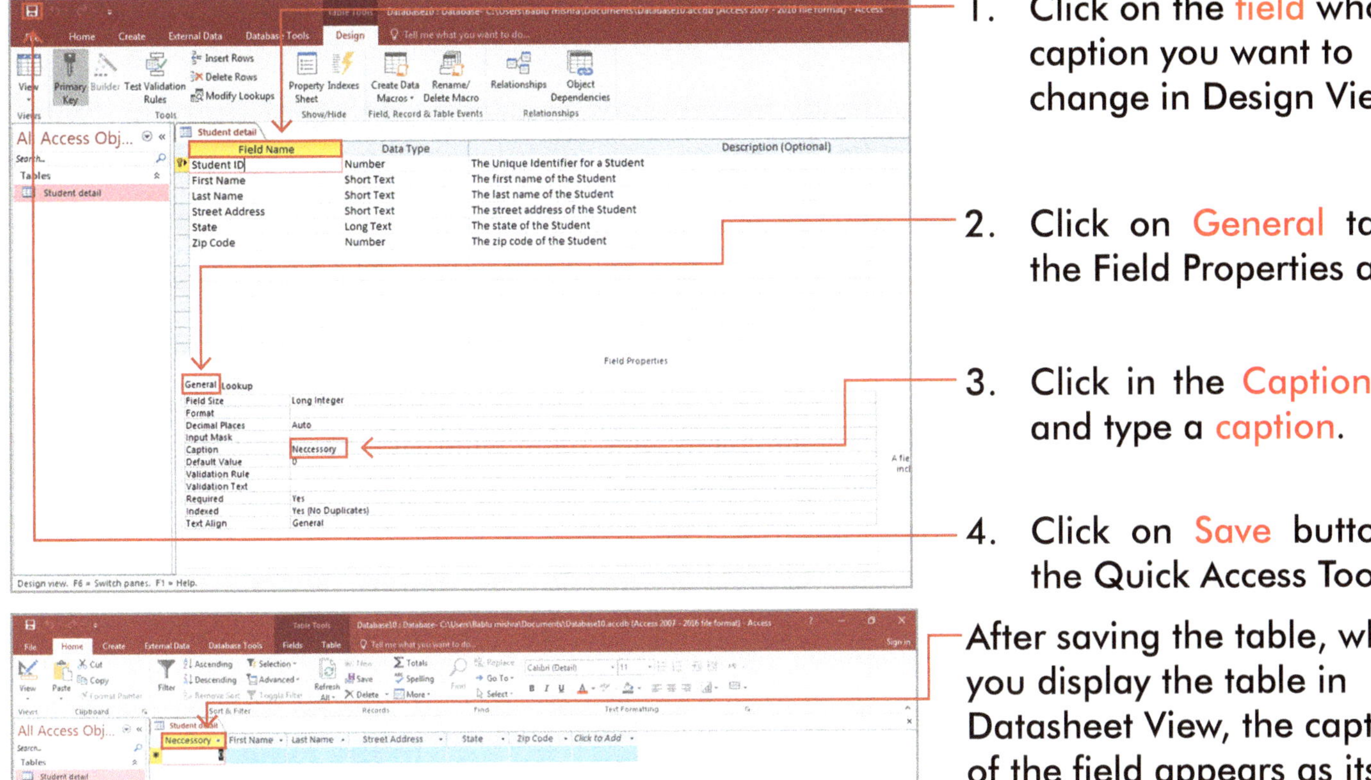

1. Click on the field whose caption you want to change in Design View.
2. Click on General tab in the Field Properties area.
3. Click in the Caption row and type a caption.
4. Click on Save button in the Quick Access Toolbar.

After saving the table, when you display the table in Datasheet View, the caption of the field appears as its column heading.

Set the format of Field

You can change the format of field to update its appearance in datasheets, forms and reports.

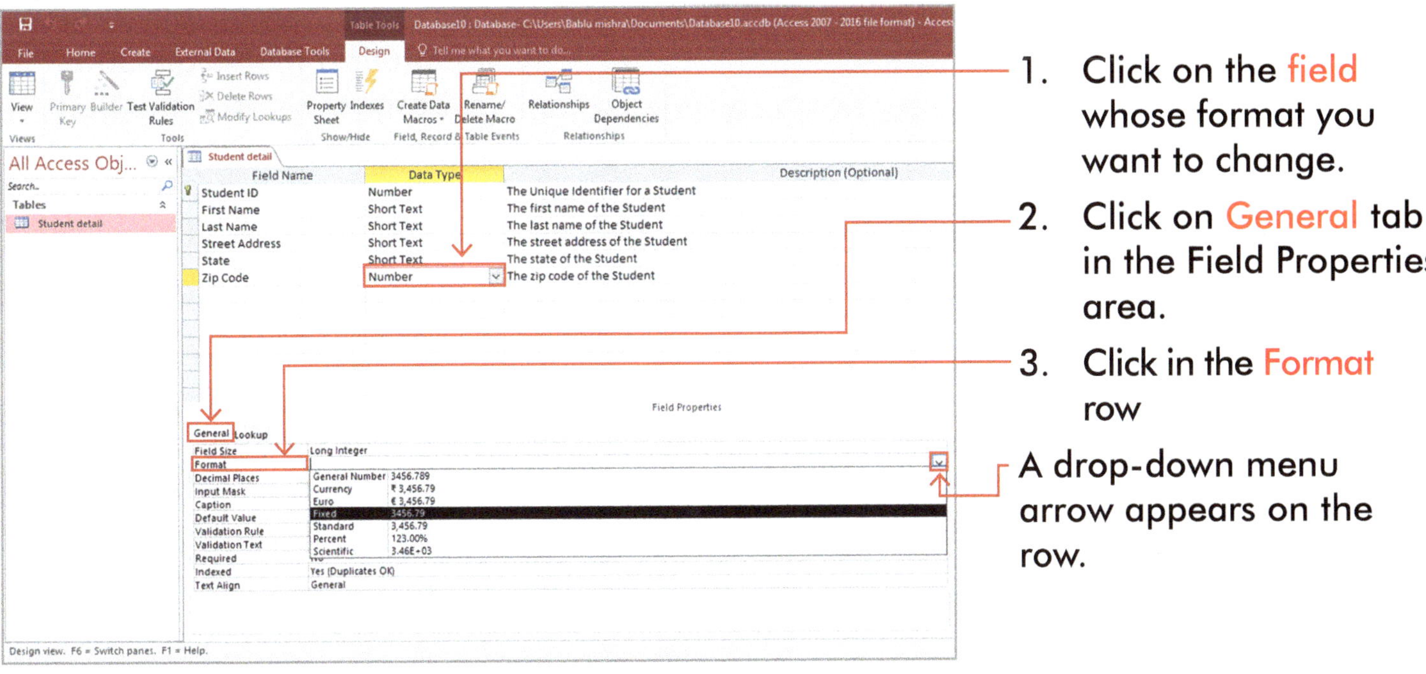

1. Click on the field whose format you want to change.
2. Click on General tab in the Field Properties area.
3. Click in the Format row

A drop-down menu arrow appears on the row.

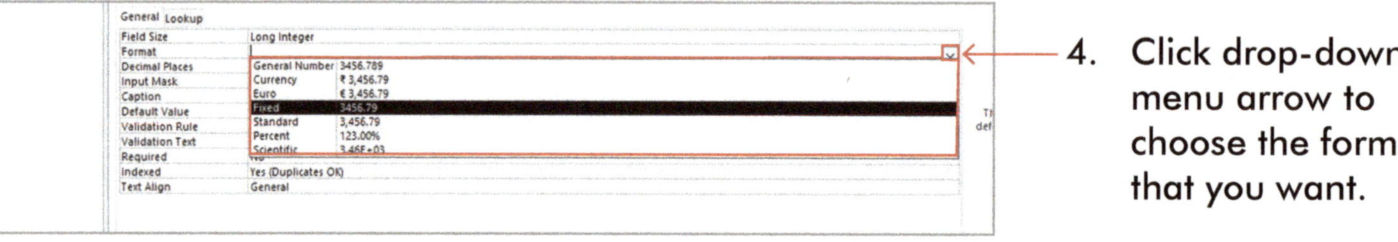

4. Click drop-down menu arrow to choose the format that you want.

⇒ For a Number or AutoNumber field, the choices represent different number types, such as General, Currency, and Percentage.

⇒ For Date/Time data types, the choices appear as date/time formats.

⇒ For Yes/No fields, the choices appear as ways of expressing yes or no.

Set a Default Value

You can speed up data entry for fields that usually contain the same value by making that value the default. For example, if 90% of members take billiards as activities, you can make billiards the default value in the Activities field.

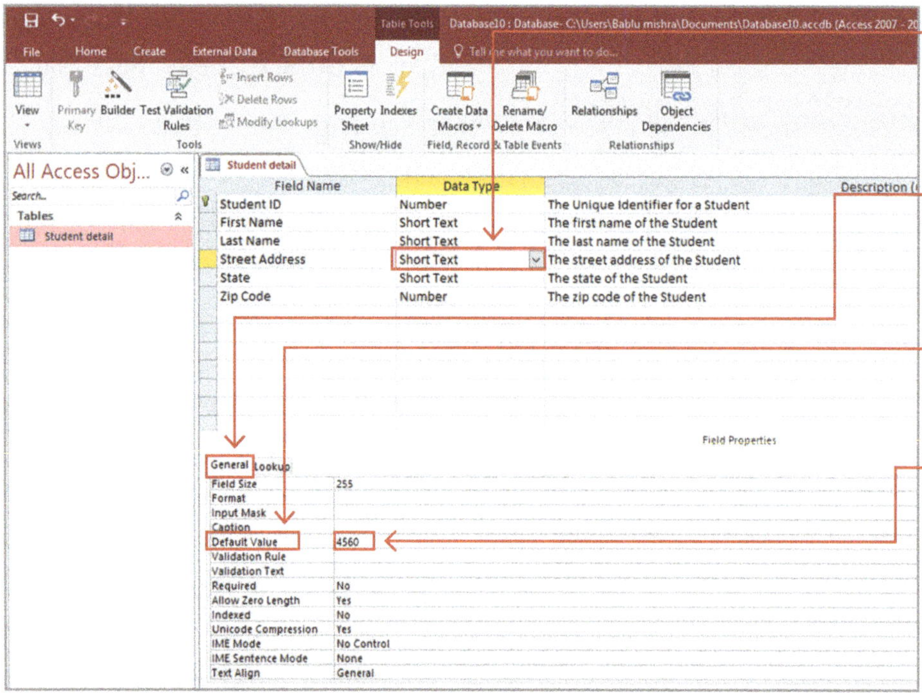

1. Click on the field whose default value you want to set.
2. Click on General tab in the Field Properties area.
3. Click in the Default Value row.
4. Type the default value.

Access automatically adds quotation marks around what you typed if the field type is Text.

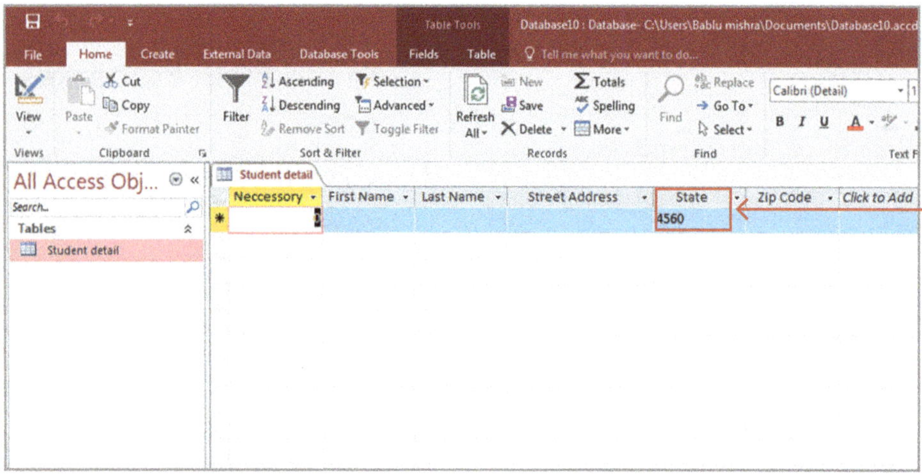

When you display the datasheet of the table, default value appears in new records.

Create Validation Rules

By performing data validation, you can make sure that data entered into fields meets certain criteria. You can ensure that the correct value is entered in the field. If the user makes an incorrect entry, error alerts can stop the user, provide a warning or just provide information.

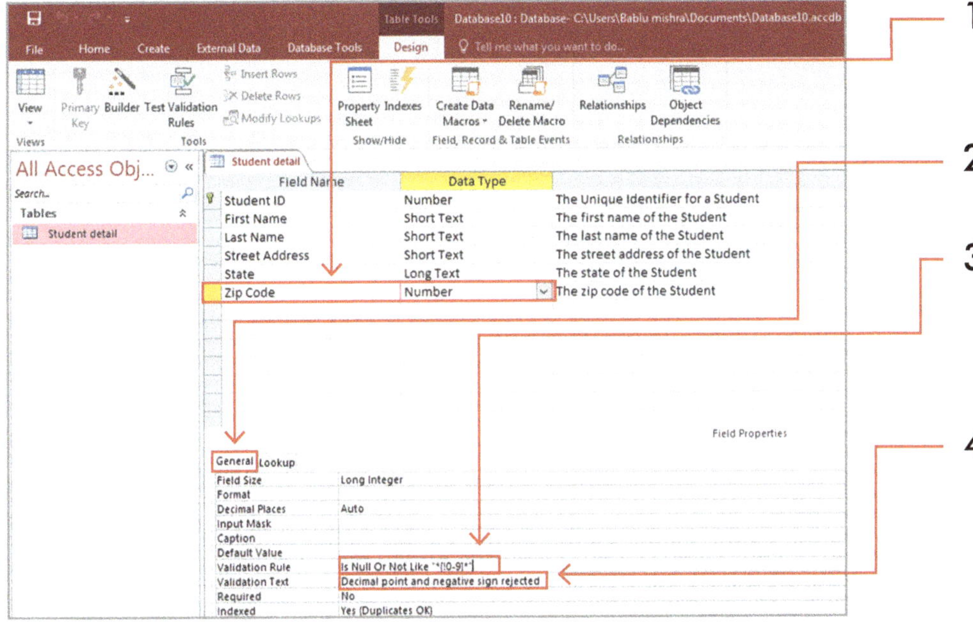

1. Click on the field where you want to create validation rule.
2. Click on General tab in the Field Properties area.
3. Click in the Validation Rule row and type the Validation Rule in that row.
4. Click in the Validation Text row and type the text for the error message.

If you enter a wrong entry or violate the rule in the datasheet view, a custom error message appears, containing the text you specified in the Validation Text row.

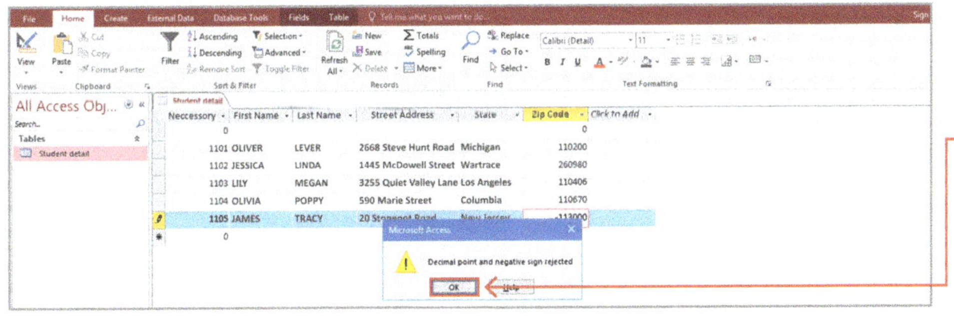

5. Click on OK and then retype the field entry.

ADDING RECORDS TO A TABLE

The first step is to create a table by building the structure and saving the table. The second step is to add records to the table. The table must be open so that the records may be added to the table. The table displays in Datasheet view. In Datasheet view, the table is represented as a collection of rows and columns called a datasheet.

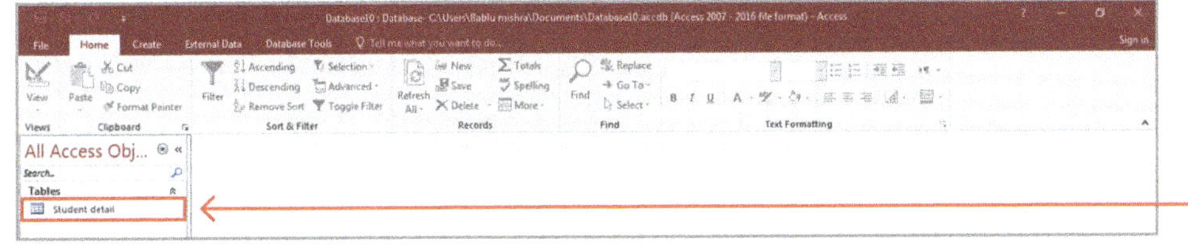

1. Double-click on student details Table.

You can close the Navigation Pane for more space.

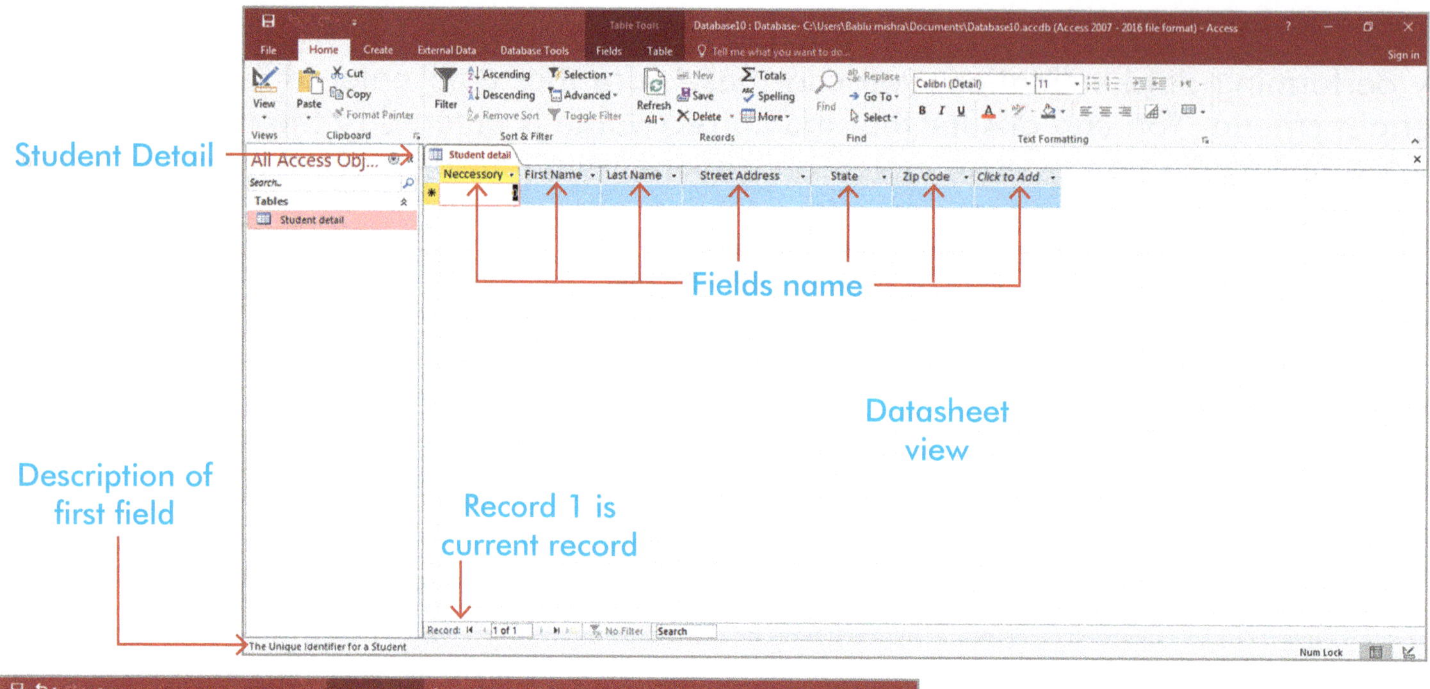

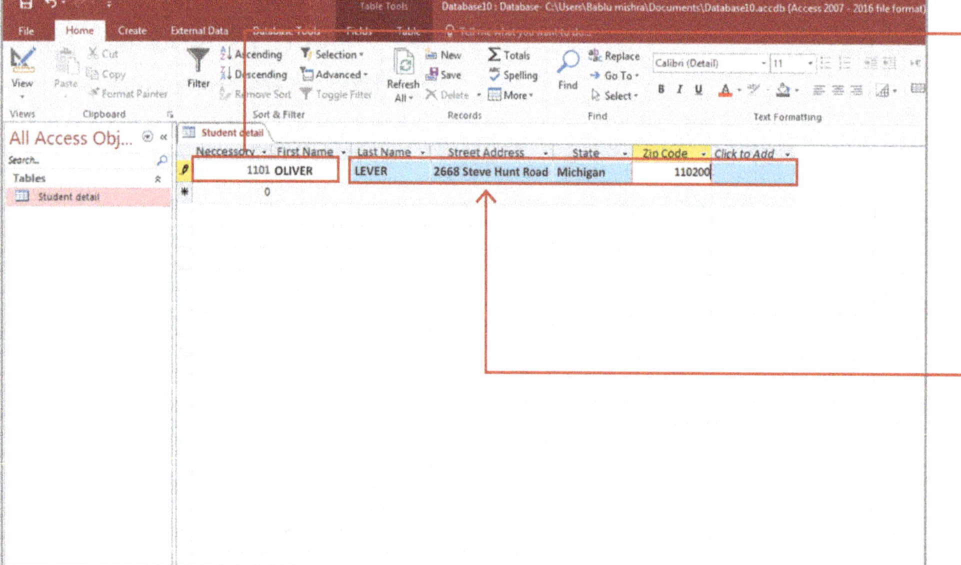

2. Type the Student ID in the first Student ID field.

3. Press the Tab key to complete the entry for the Student ID field.

Type the following entries by pressing the Tab key after each one to complete the record.

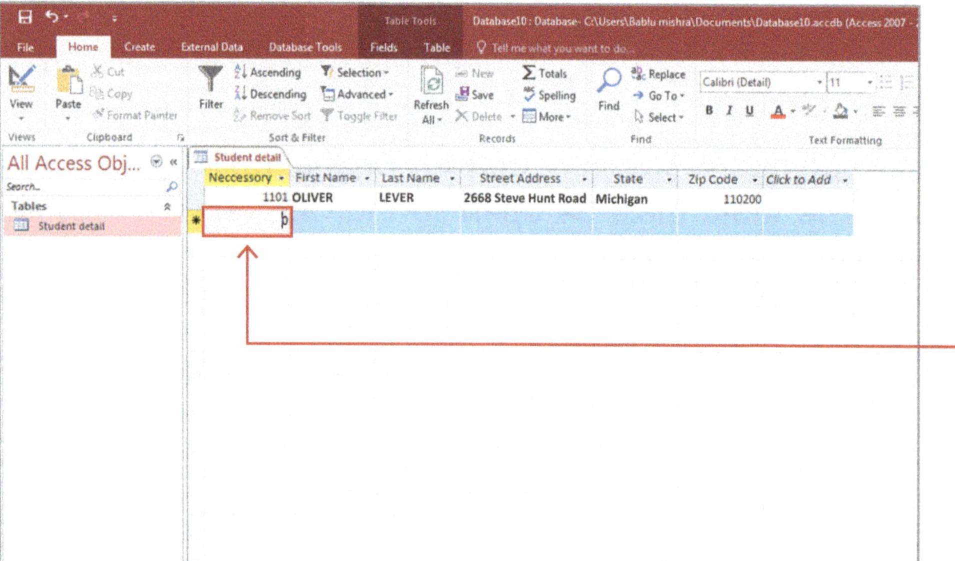

4. After typing the last entry, e.g., Zip Code, press the Tab key.

The insertion point comes to the Student ID field in the second row.

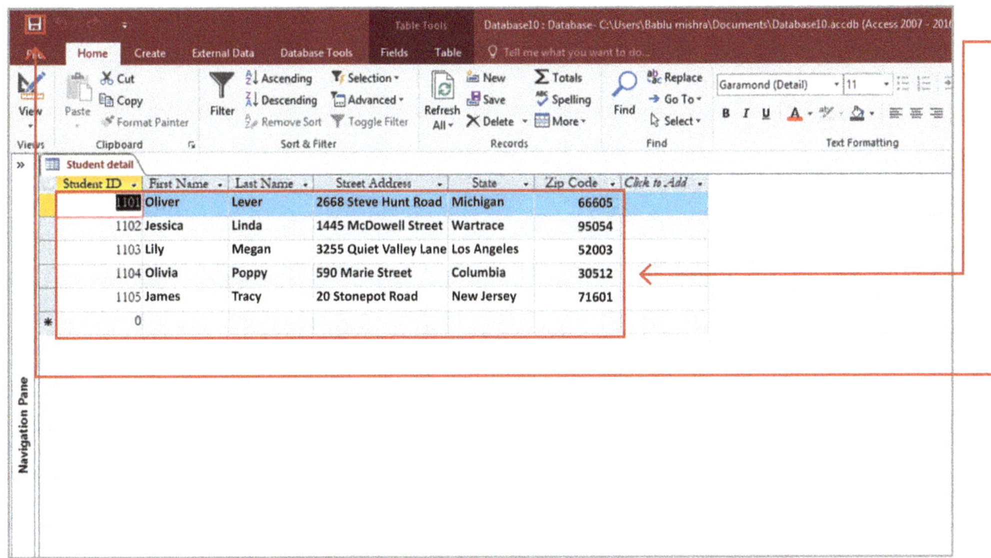

5. Add the remaining records by following the same steps you used to add the first record, as in steps 2 to 4.

6. When you have finished entering data, click on Save button under the File tab to save the changes.

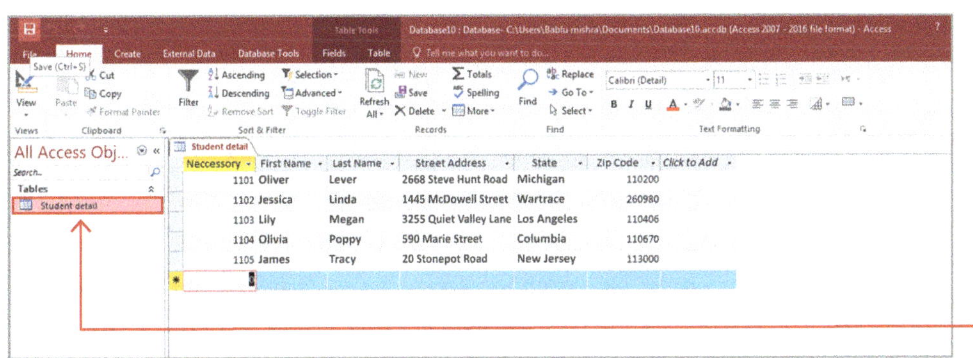

Access saves the table and you can see the name of the table in Navigational pane.

LET'S HAVE A LOOK

- A computerized database helps to store the data in an electronic format on a storage medium, such as a hard disk.
- Relational database is a tabular database in which data is defined so that it may be reorganized and accessed in a number of different ways.
- Access 2016 is a popular Relational Database Management System.
- DBMS is a software used to access, retrieve, delete, search, sort, design and print data.
- Design and Datasheet view are two views in which you create tables.
- In database table, each row is called a record and each column is called a field.
- In design view, the data fields in the table are defined before adding any data to the data sheet.
- Each field name in a table should have a unique name.
- The default field size for the text type data is up to 255 characters.
- A new record to the table in datasheet can be added by opening a table.
- After completing the table structure, the database must be saved.
- A Primary key is a key that differentiates the records in a file.
- Access has a number of data types like Text, Memo, Numbers, Date/Time, currency, AutoNumber, Yes/No, OLE Object, Hyperlink, Lookup wizard, calculation and Attachment.

1. Multiple Choice Questions

Tick (✓) the correct answer:

a. A specific piece of information:
   i. Field ☐ ii. Value ☐ iii. Record ☐

b. Access stores data in:
   i. Fields ☐ ii. Table ☐ iii. File ☐

c. Each entry in the table is called:
   i. Record ☐ ii. Data ☐ iii. Value ☐

d. Default extension of database file:
   i. .accdb ☐ ii. .abcde ☐ iii. .accab ☐

e. The key pressed to move from upper pane to lower pane:
   i. F8 ☐ ii. F1 ☐ iii. F6 ☐

f. A tabular database in which data is defined:
   i. Primary Key ☐ ii. Relational Database ☐
   iii. Flat File ☐

g. It defines the table structure before creating the table:
   i. Design view ☐ ii. Primary Key ☐ iii. Navigation Pane ☐

2. Fill in the blanks:

a. A large collection of meaningfully organised data is called a __________.

b. Access provides an __________ to manage database and a graphical interface to facilitate its user.

c. Access stores the data in __________.

d. Each individual entry in the table is called a __________.

e. A __________ key is a key that differentiates the records in a file.

f. Access automatically assigns __________ extension to all database files.

g. A __________ warning appears while opening a database which is not trusted.

h. Memo is the same as text data type with an upper limit of __________ characters.

i. __________ tab contains all the properties of our fields.

j. Design and __________ view are two views in which you create tables.

3. Write 'T' for True and 'F' for False in the boxes:

a. Access doesn't help us to add or change data in database. ☐

b. In Access, multiple databases cannot open at once. ☐

c. In design view, window is divided in three panes. ☐

d. Access has only one data type. ☐

e. Text data type has a limit up to 255 character. ☐

4. Answer the following questions.

(i) Answer each in a few lines:

a. Define Database.

b. Write the full forms of DBMS and RDBMS.

c. What is the use of navigation pane?

d. Name the two parts of window in design view.

e. Name the different views in which a table can be created.

f. What is the file extension of Access?

g. What is General tab in bottom pane?

h. What is database software?

i. Name any three data types of Access 2016.

(ii) Answer each comprehensively:

a. What is Access?

b. Explain Database.

c. What are the main functions of DBMS?

d. What are the functions of Field Properties?

e. Define a Primary Key. Why do we need a Primary Key?

f. How many data types are used in Access 2016? Explain each with its functions.

5. Write the steps for:

a. Creating a table in datasheet view.

b. Creating a table in design view.

c. Adding records to a table.

d. Setting the format of field.

e. Changing the field size.

6. Define these data fields:

a. Text:

b. Memo:

c. Currency:

d. Yes/No:

Create a table using Database View where each record contains the following fields:

Field Name	Data type	Description
First Name	Text	
Last Name	Text	
Date of birth	Number	
Address	Text	
Telephone	Number	
Qualification	Text	

a. Create a new database as 'Profile'.

b. Save the table as 'Contacts'.

c. Select 'First Name' as the primary key field.

d. Now enter the 15 records in the table.

e. Add another field named 'E-mail' before Qualification field and update the records accordingly.

f. Close the database and Access 2016.

4 More in Access 2016

In this chapter, we will learn:

⇒ Selecting Data in a Table
⇒ Find and Replace Feature
⇒ Sorting Records
⇒ Filtering Data By Selection
⇒ Filtering Data by Form, Text Value and Multiple Values
⇒ Creating Relationship between Tables
⇒ Creating Form
⇒ Changing the View of a Form
⇒ Changing the Field Formatting of Form
⇒ Apply Themes

Dear children, in the previous chapter, you learnt to change a table's structure by working with the table in Design view and adding the records in Datasheet view. Now, in this chapter, you will continue your journey of learning some important features of Access 2016.

Selecting Data In a Table

Before performing many tasks in Access, you identify the existing data on which you want to work by selecting it in a table. The selected data appears highlighted on your screen.

Selecting a Field

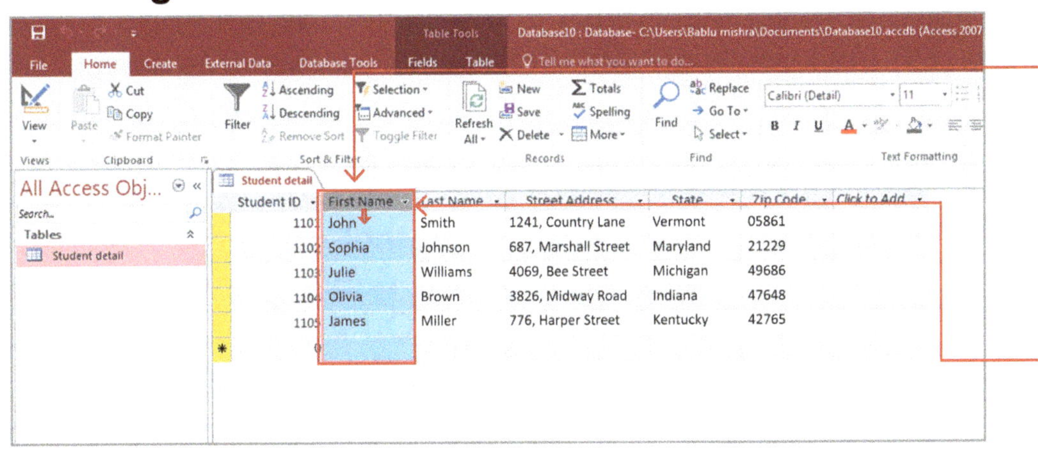

1. Take your mouse pointer over the name of the field you want to select.

The mouse pointer changes into (⬇).

2. Now click to select the field.

If you want to select multiple fields, position the mouse pointer over the name of the first field. Then drag the mouse pointer (⬇) until you highlight all the fields you want to select.

Selecting a Record

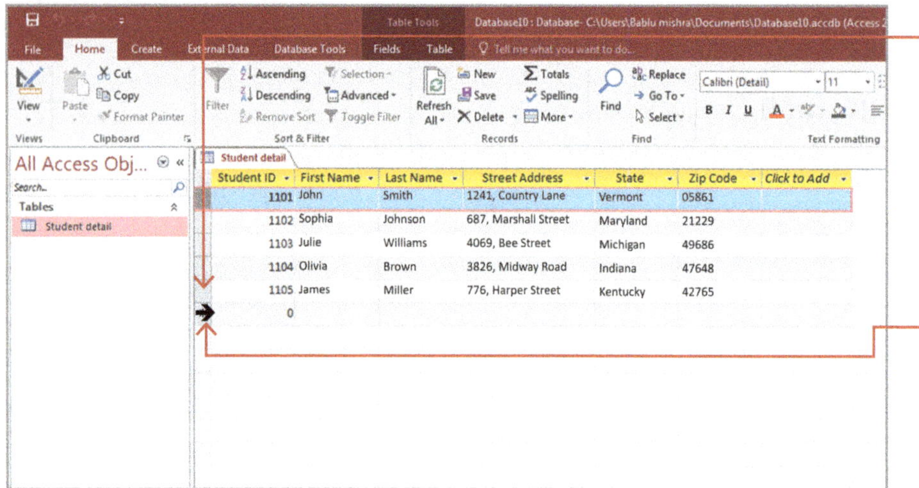

1. Take the mouse pointer over the area to the left of the record you want to select.

   The mouse pointer changes into (➔).

2. Now click to select the record.

If you want to select multiple records, place your mouse pointer over the area to the left of the first record. Then drag the mouse (➔) until you highlight all the records you want to select.

Selecting a Cell

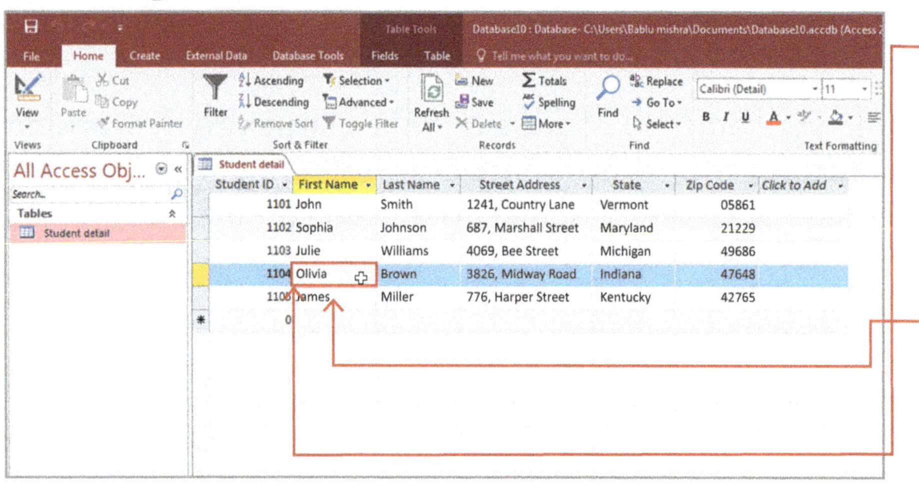

1. Take the mouse pointer over the left edge of the cell you want to select.

   The mouse pointer changes into (✜).

2. Now click to select the cell.

If you want to select multiple cells, position the mouse pointer over the left edge of the first cell. Then drag the mouse (✜) until you highlight all the cells you want to select.

Find and Replace Feature

After entering data into a table, you might need to search for a particular record or might need to replace some record in a large database. You can do that using the Find and Replace tools in Microsoft Access 2016. Find and Replace is a single feature with two parts. On the Find tab, you can find text strings within records. On the Replace tab, you can do the same thing, except you can also replace the found data with some other text that you specify.

Find Tab

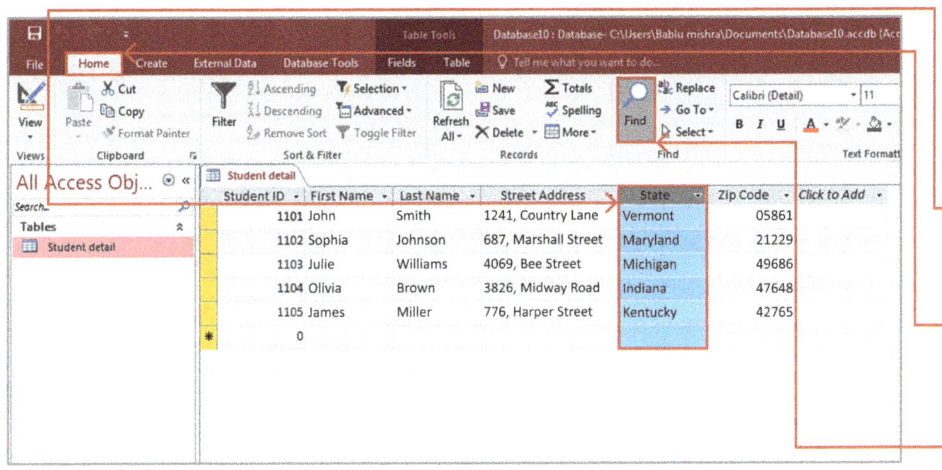

1. Open the table that you want to find.
2. Select the field (column) that you want to search.
3. Click on the Home tab on the Ribbon.
4. Click on Find.

The Find and Replace dialog box appears with the Find tab in front.

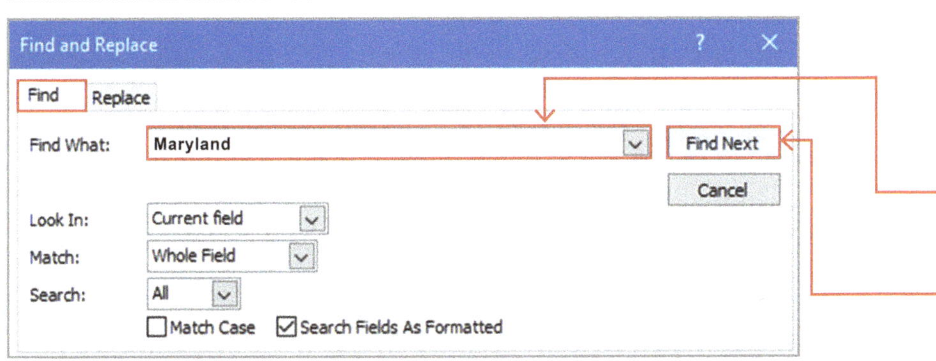

5. In the Find What text box type 'Maryland'.
6. Click on the Find Next button.

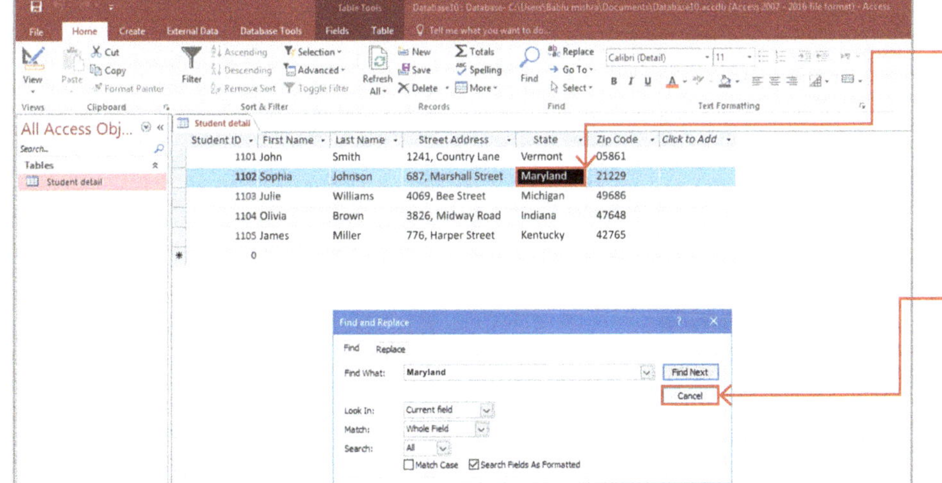

Access jumps to the first occurrence of the word Maryland that it finds in the table.

7. To close the dialog box, click on Cancel. Now, you can also replace information in a database.

Replace Tab

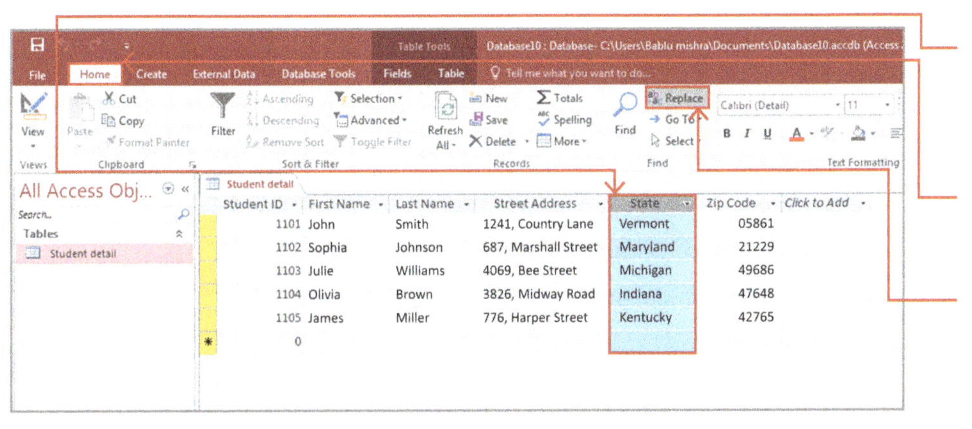

1. Select the field (column) that you want to search for and then replace.
2. Click on the Home tab on the Ribbon.
3. Click on Replace from the Find group.

The Find and Replace dialog box appears with the Replace tab in front.

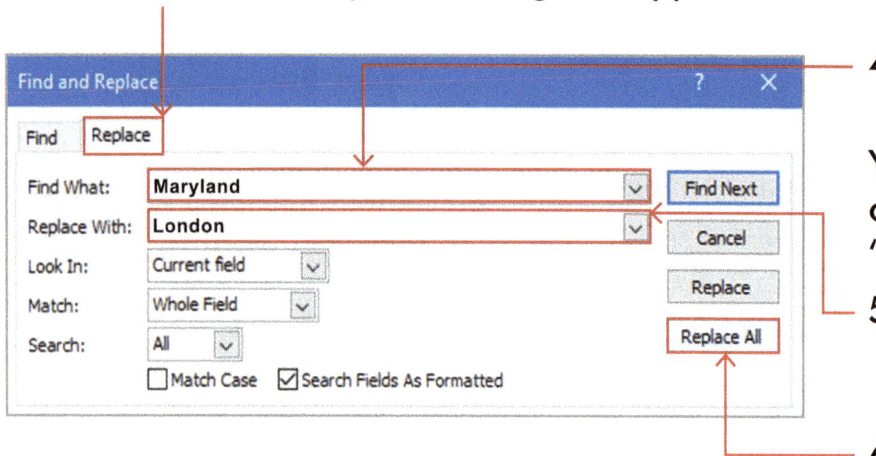

4. In the Find What text box, type "Maryland".

You want to replace every occurrence of the phrase "Maryland" with the phrase "London".

5. Select the Replace With text box by clicking it and type "London".
6. Click on Replace All.

A warning dialog box will appear telling you that you won't be able to Undo the replace operations if you replace the entry.

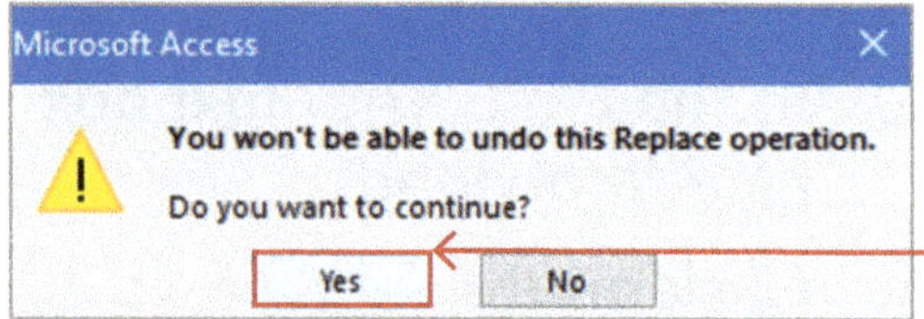

7. Click on Yes to continue.

Access finds all the occurrences of the phrase "Maryland" in the table and replaces them with the words "London".

8. To close the dialog box, click on Cancel.

Sorting Records

You can arrange the records of table either in ascending or descending order, which can help you find, organize and analyze data.

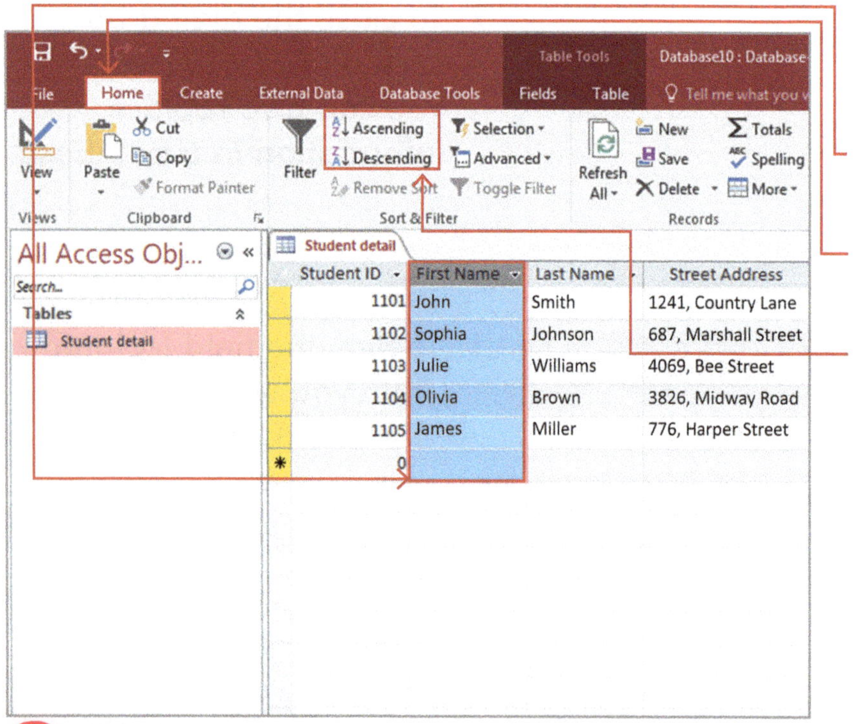

1. Open the table that you want to sort.
2. Click on the column header for the field that you want to sort.
3. Click on the Home tab on the Ribbon.
4. Click on the following Sort buttons:

⇒ Click on Ascending (A↓Z) to sort the records in ascending order.

⇒ Click on Descending (Z↓A) to sort the records in descending order.

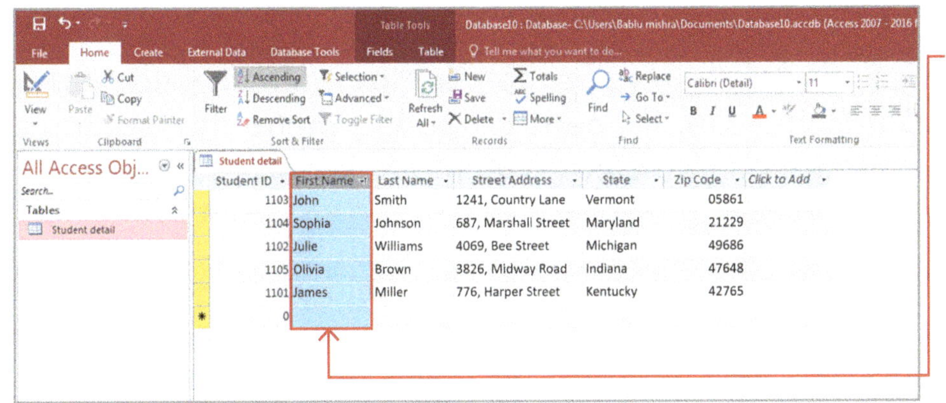

The records appear in the new order.

In this example, the records are sorted by Ascending order according to the names of the members.

Filtering Data by Selection

In the large database, you can filter for any specific value in any field. For example, you may want to find all the members whose Zip Code of payment is cash.

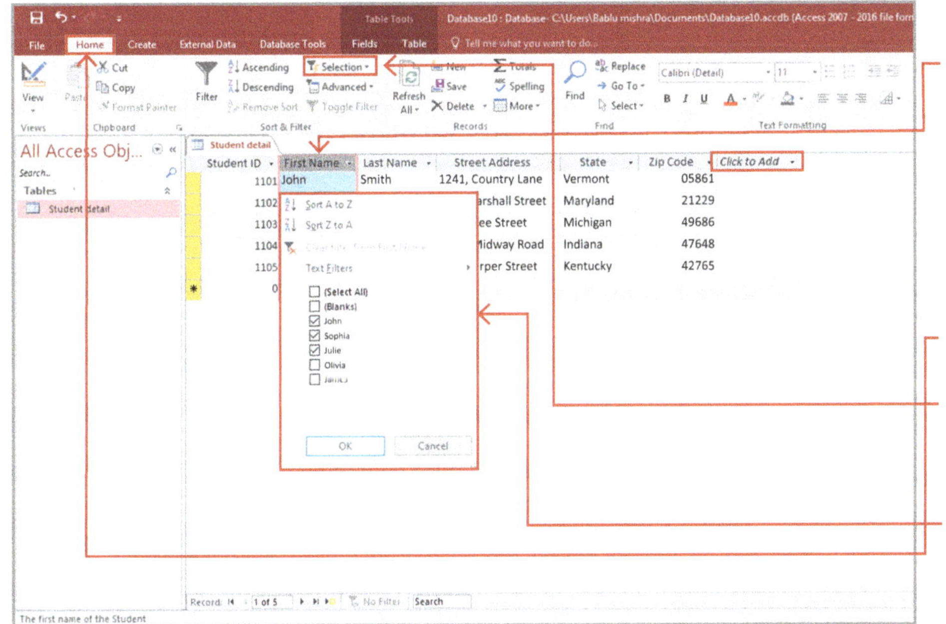

1. Click the data you want to use to filter the records.

Access will display only records that contain exactly the same data.

2. Click on Home tab.
3. Click on Selection (▼) to filter the records.
4. Click on your choice of criterion.

Access displays only the records containing the data that you have selected in step 1.
All other records are hidden.

The word Filtered appears in this area to indicate that you are viewing filtered records.

5. When you have finished reviewing the filtered records, click on Toggle Filter to display all the records once again.

Filtering for Multiple Value

Filter by Selection works well, but it finds only one value. To filter for multiple values, you can use the Filter button on the Datasheet tab. It opens a floating menu that contains check boxes for each value in that field, and you can select multiple values to filter.

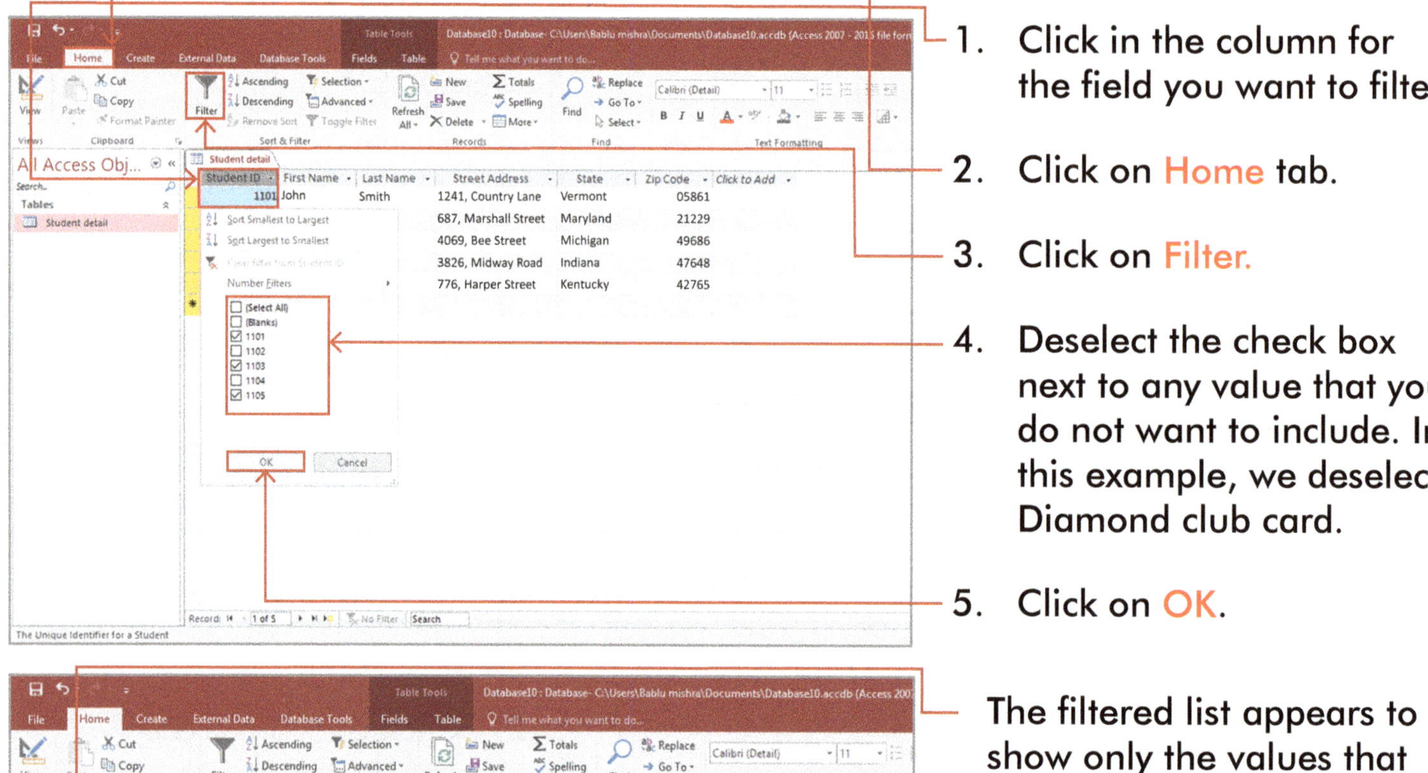

1. Click in the column for the field you want to filter.
2. Click on Home tab.
3. Click on Filter.
4. Deselect the check box next to any value that you do not want to include. In this example, we deselect Diamond club card.
5. Click on OK.

The filtered list appears to show only the values that you chose.

6. Click on Toggle Filter to remove the filter when finished.

Filtering for Text Value

Access provides a special set of filters for working with text values. Text value filter is used to filter text strings. For example, if you want to filter the member from the same city, you can use a text filter to find all the forms of the name of the city.

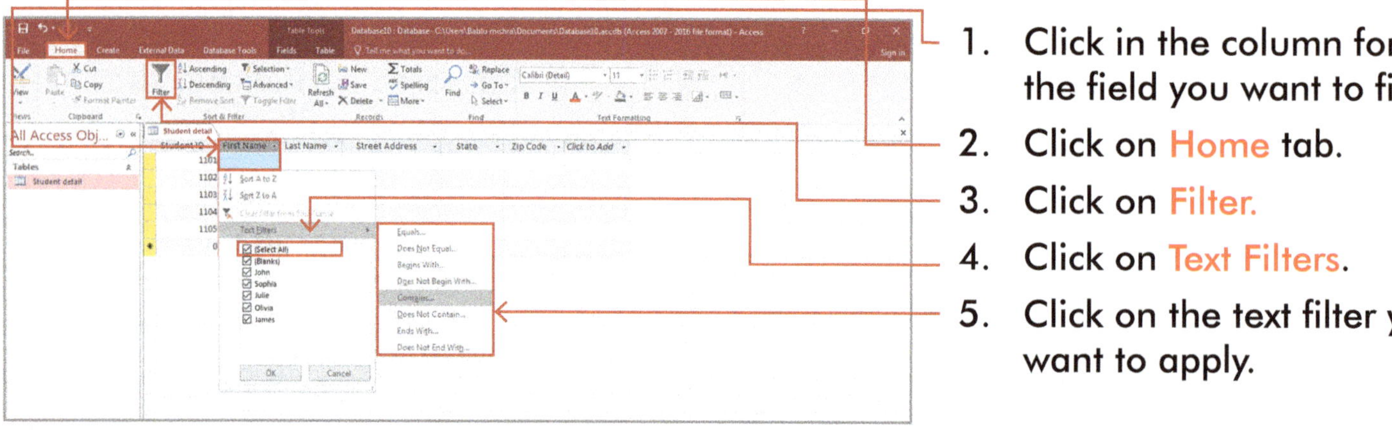

1. Click in the column for the field you want to filter.
2. Click on Home tab.
3. Click on Filter.
4. Click on Text Filters.
5. Click on the text filter you want to apply.

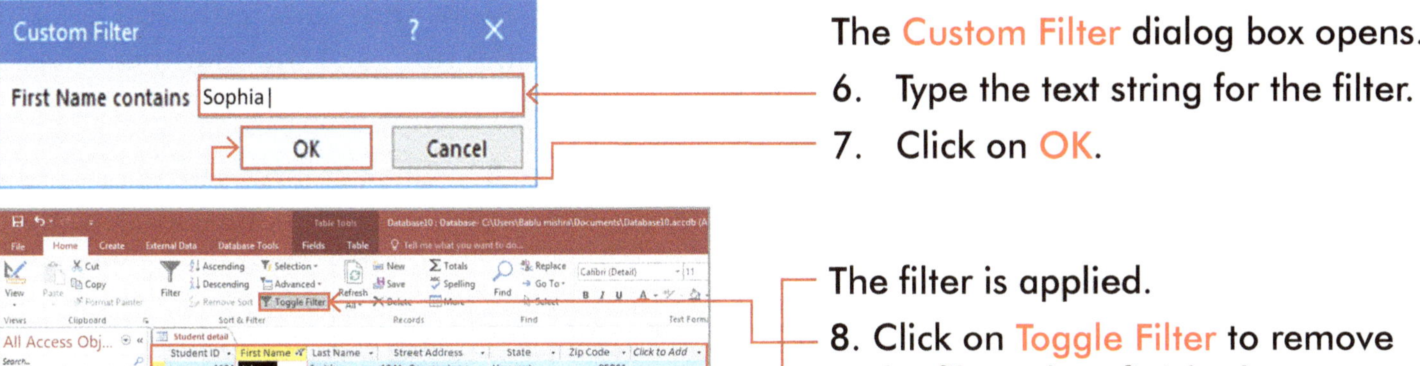

The Custom Filter dialog box opens.

6. Type the text string for the filter.
7. Click on OK.

The filter is applied.

8. Click on Toggle Filter to remove the filter when finished.

Filtering Data By Form

You can filter by multiple fields and specify criteria for as many fields using AND, OR, or a combination of the two. An AND combination finds records where both criteria are met; an OR combination finds records where at least one criterion is met.

Using AND

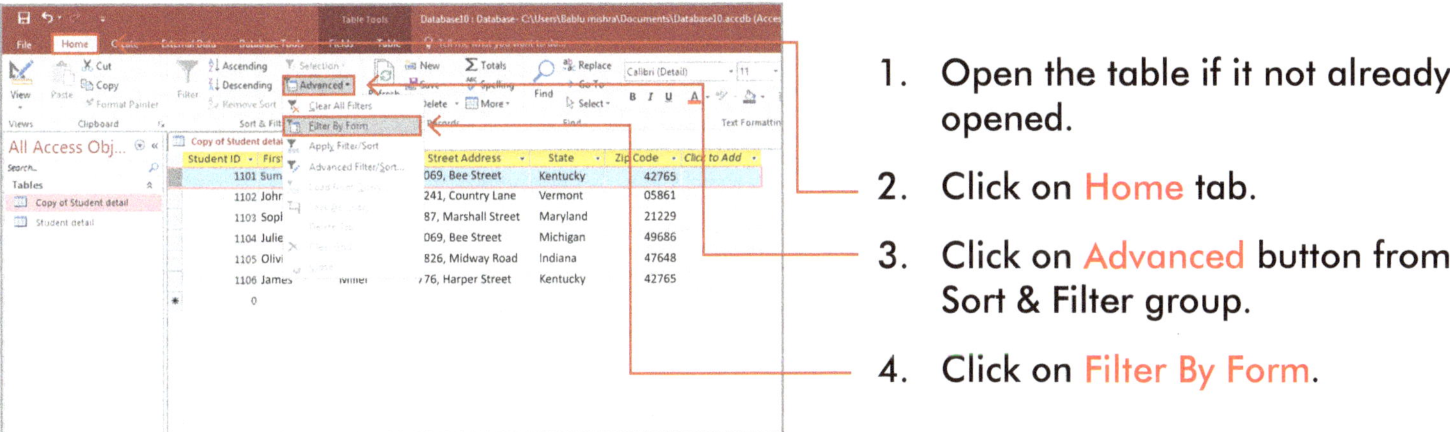

1. Open the table if it not already opened.
2. Click on Home tab.
3. Click on Advanced button from Sort & Filter group.
4. Click on Filter By Form.

The Filter by Form window appears, which looks like an empty table. Next, you have to select the field and value you want to use as your criteria.

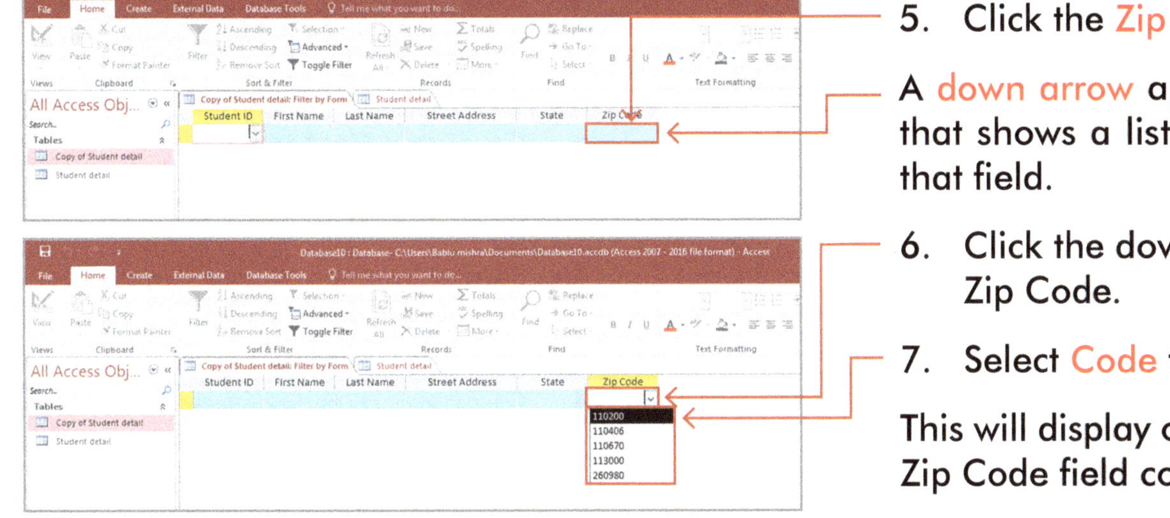

5. Click the Zip Code field.

A down arrow appears in the field that shows a list of values used in that field.

6. Click the down arrow button of Zip Code.
7. Select Code from the list.

This will display only records whose Zip Code field contains that code.

You can create an AND criteria statement by specifying more than one criterion on the same Filter By Form tab. For example, you could filter for the name of the member whose payment Zip Code is 110200 and Street Address is Country Lane.

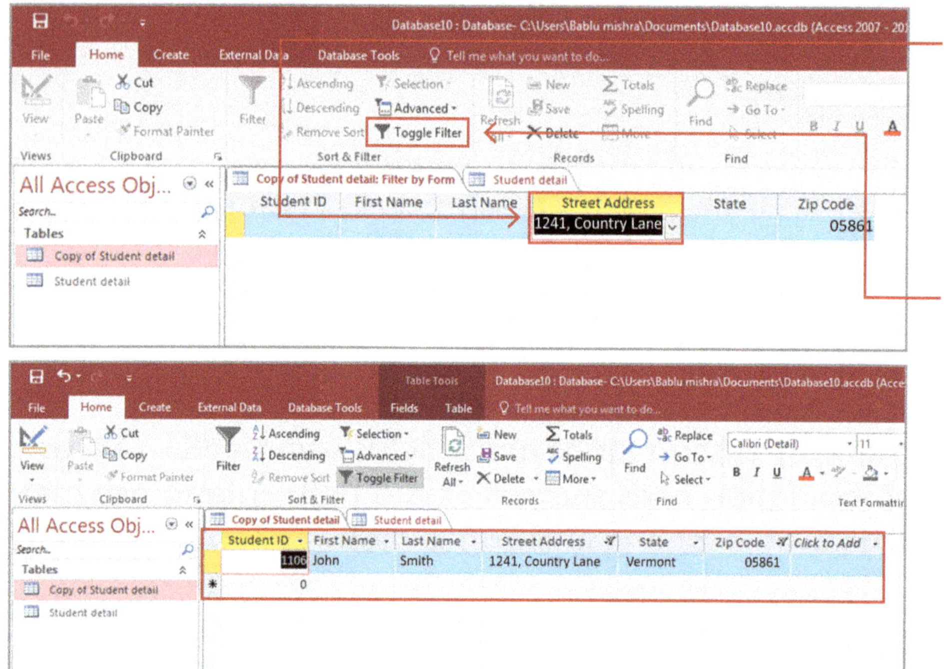

8. Click on the Street Address field; click on the down arrow and select the Country Lane from the list.
9. Click on the Toggle Filter button.

Access applies Street Address is "Country Lane" filter and displays only those records whose Street Address is "Country Lane" AND whose Zip Code is "110200"." Only one record meets the filter criteria.

Using OR

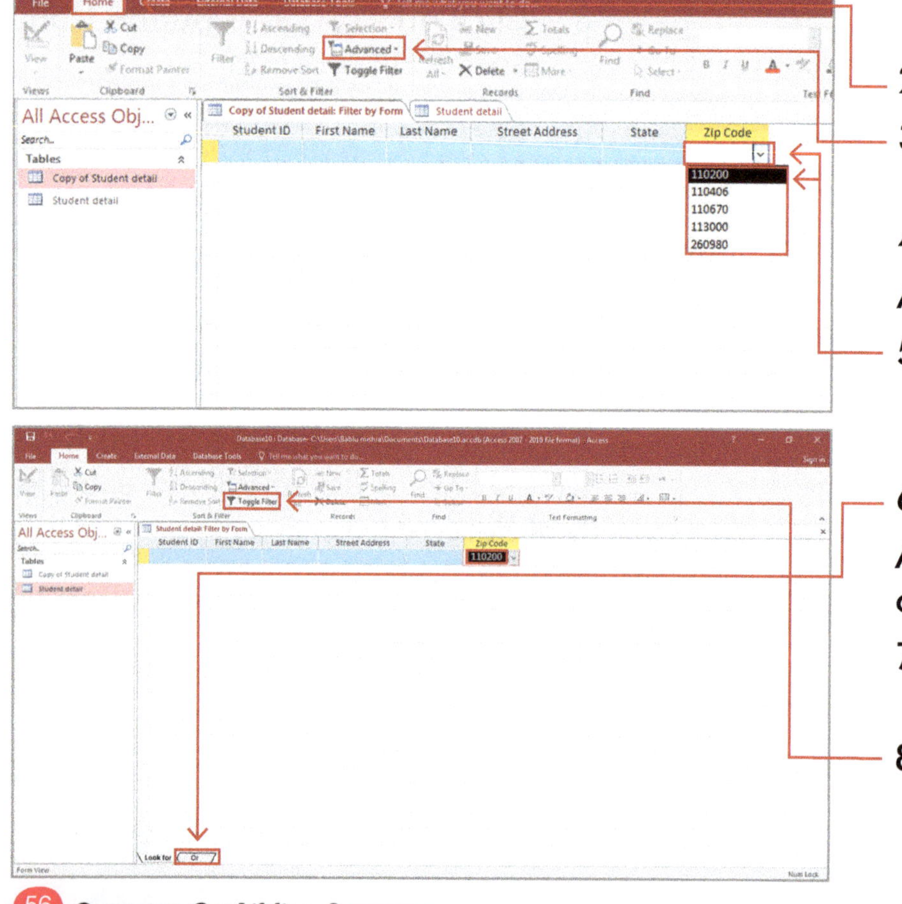

1. Open the table if it is not already opened.
2. Click on Home tab on ribbon.
3. Click on Advanced button from Sort & Filter group.
4. Click on Filter By Form.

A Filter by Form sheet opens.

5. Open the list for a field and select the value that you want.
6. Click the Or tab.

A blank Filter by Form page opens.

7. Repeat step 5 to select another criterion.
8. Click on Toggle Filter to apply the filter.

CREATING RELATIONSHIP BETWEEN TABLES

Relational databases like Access can contain multiple related tables. You can create relationships between tables directly in the Relationships window. You can connect tables by creating relationships between them based on a common field that they share.

These relationships make it possible to create forms, queries and reports that include fields from multiple tables.

Common Field: For a relationship to exist between two tables, they must have a common field. For example, the Student table may have a StudentID field, and the Marks table may also have a StudentID field. The two tables could be joined or related by that field. The field type must be the same in both tables for a relationship to exist. One exception is that an AutoNumber field can be related to a Number field.

Primary Key: In most relationships, the primary key field in one table is related to a field in the other table that is not its primary key. In one table, the field contains unique values, whereas in the other table, it does not. The related field in the other table is called the foreign key.

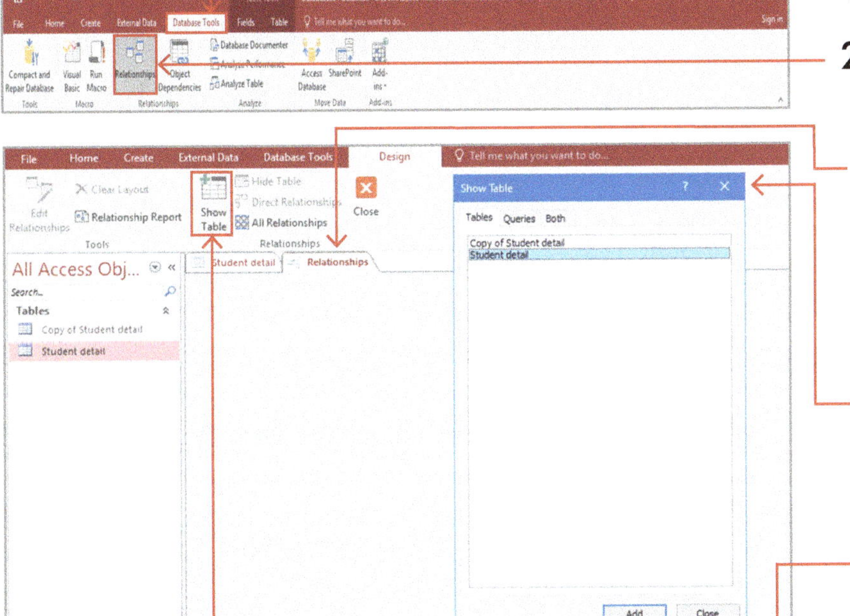

1. Click on Database Tools tab.
2. Click on Relationships button to display the Relationships window.

The Relationships window appears. If any relationship already exists between the tables in your database, a box for each table appears in the window.

The Show Table dialog box may also appear, listing all the tables in your database.

3. If the Show Table dialog box does not appear, click on Show Table button on the ribbon to display the dialog box.
4. Click on a table you want to add to the Relationships window.
5. Click on the Add button to add the table to the window.
6. Repeat the steps 3 and 4 for each table that you want to add.
7. When you have finished adding tables to the Relationships window, click on the Close button to remove the Show Table dialog box.

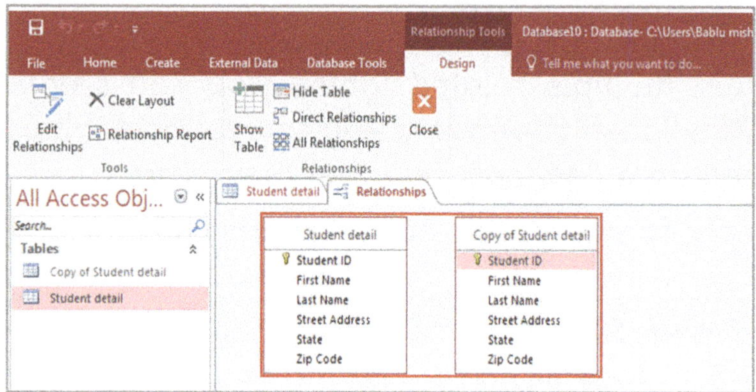

The Relationships window displays a box for each table.

The Primary key for each table appears highlighted. The primary key uniquely identifies each record in a table.

Now you can create a relationship between tables by identifying the matching fields in the tables.

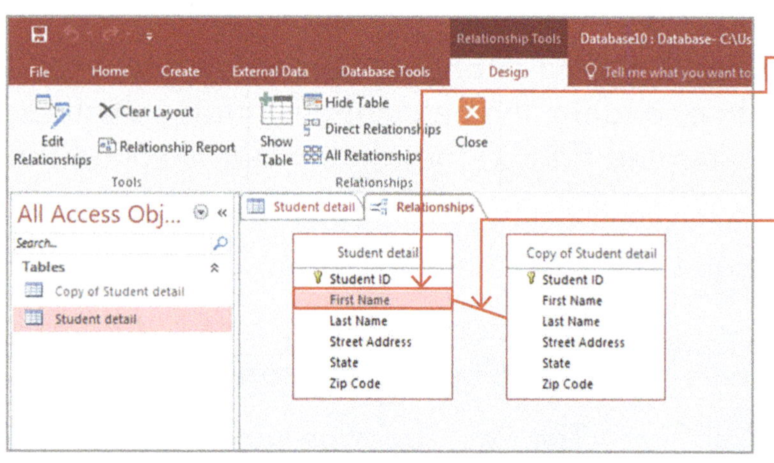

8. Place your mouse pointer over the field you want to use to create a relationship with another table.

9. Drag the field with mouse over the other table until a small box appears over the matching field.

The Edit Relationships dialog box will appear.

Table/Query and Related table/Query area displays the names of the tables you want to create a relationship between and the names of the matching fields.

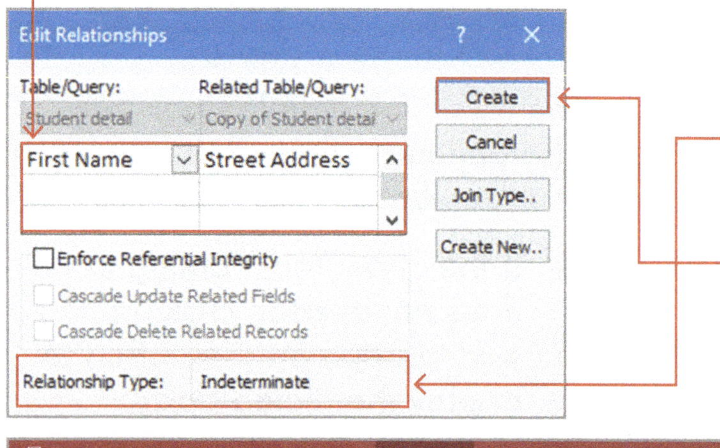

Relationship Type displays the type of relationship.

10. Click on the Create button to create a relationship.

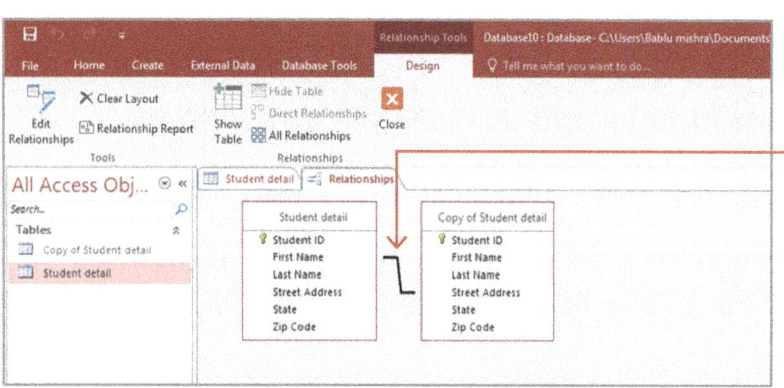

A line connects the fields in the two tables to show that the relationship is created.

Edit A Relationship

You can change your mind about the nature of a relationship after creating it. For example, you may choose to change the referential integrity options or the join type.

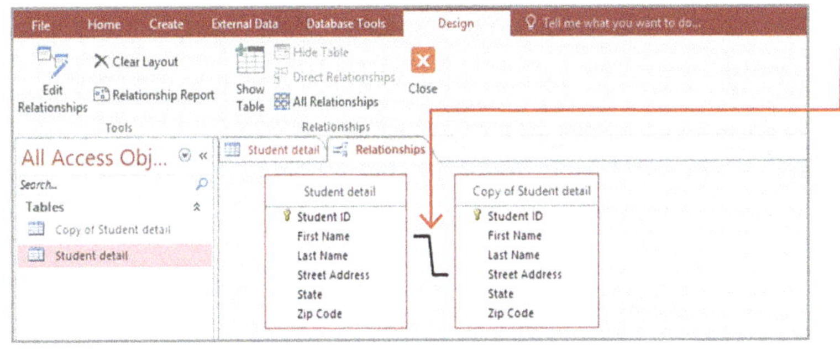

1. Double-click the connector line between two tables in the Relationships window.

The Edit Relationships dialog box opens.

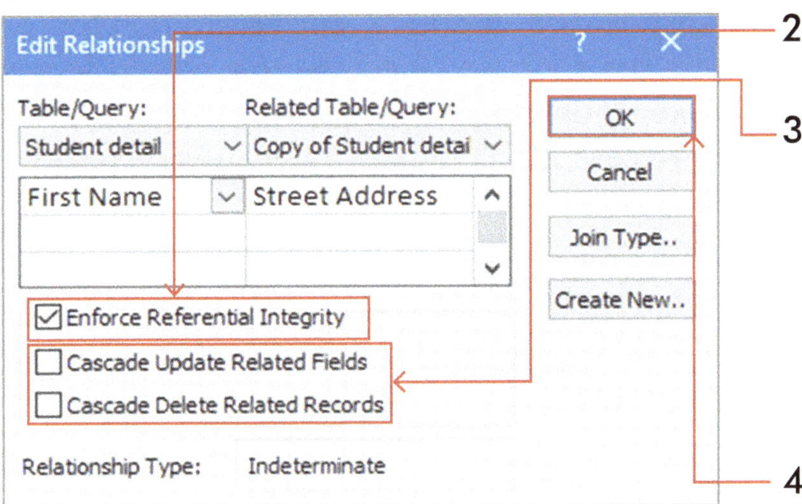

2. Select or deselect the check box of Enforce Referential Integrity.
3. If you click the Enforce Referential Integrity check box, you can click the following:
   ⇒ Select or deselect the Cascade Update Related Fields check box.
   ⇒ Select or deselect the Cascade Delete Related Records.
4. Click on OK.

Cascade Update : When referential integrity is enabled, you can also enable Cascade Update and Cascade Delete. With Cascade Update, when a primary key entry changes, the foreign key entry in the related table also changes. For example, if a customer's CustomerID changes in the Customers table, all the orders in the Orders table reflect the new ID number.

Cascade Delete : With Cascade Delete, when a record is deleted from the table containing the primary key part of the relationship, all corresponding records in the table containing the foreign key are deleted. For example, if a customer's record is deleted from the Customers table, then all of that customer's orders are deleted from the Orders table. Use this feature with caution.

Remove a Relationship

If you no longer want the relationship between tables, you can delete it.

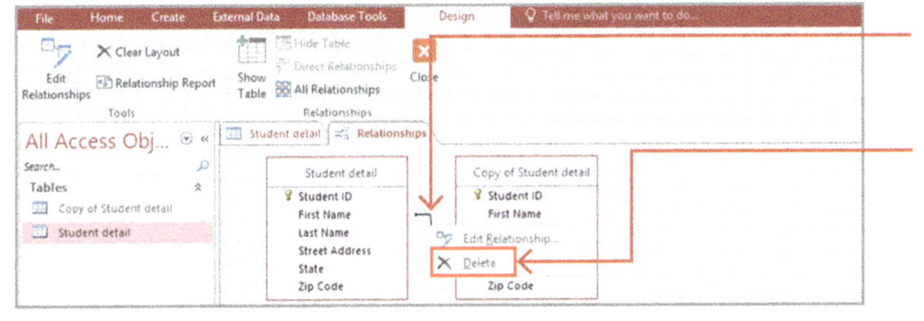

1. Click on the connector line for the relationship you want to delete.
2. Click on Delete option or press the Delete key from the keyboard.

You can also right-click on the connector line between the two tables and then click on Delete from the menu that appears.

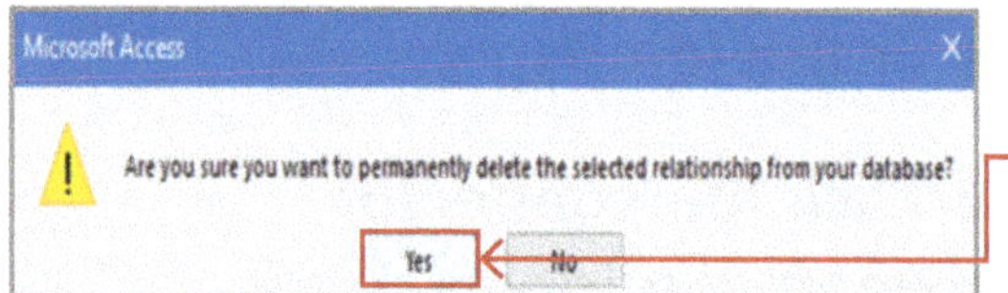

A warning dialog box appears, confirming the deletion.

3. Click on the Yes button to delete the relationship permanently.

Be sure while deleting the relationship because you cannot undo a relationship deletion. You have to re-create the relationship if you want it back.

CREATING AND SAVING SIMPLE FORMS

For data entry and editing, forms provide an easy-to-use interface. Forms are helpful for databases that will have less experienced users assisting you because on-screen forms can mimic familiar paper forms. You can make your database more user-friendly for users who need to enter and edit records in it. Access 2016 makes it very easy to create several simple types of forms based on a table.

Creating a Basic Form

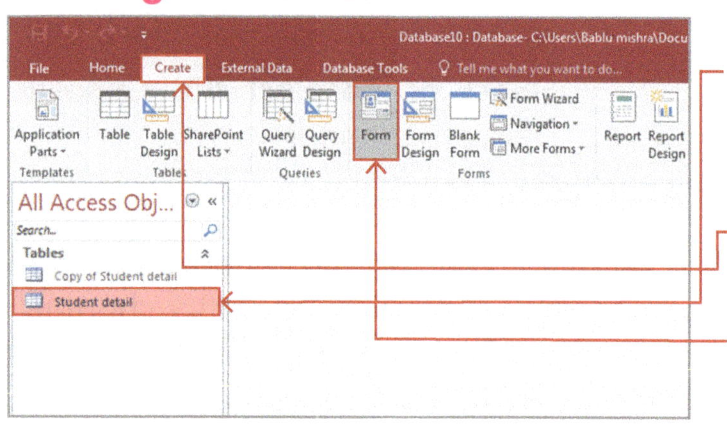

1. In the navigation Pane, click on the table you want to use as a form.
2. Click on the Create tab.
3. Click on Form.

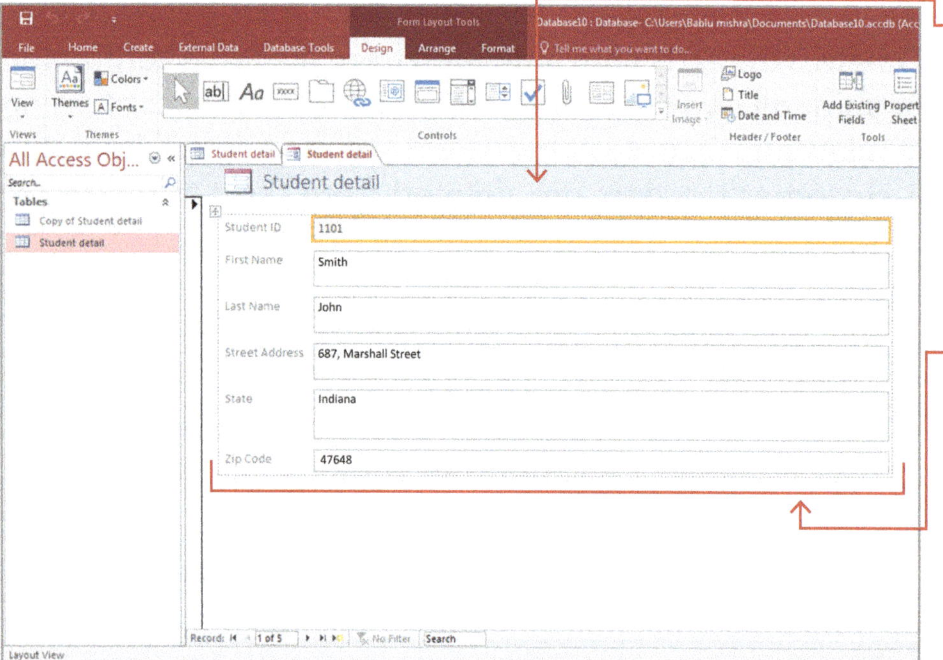

The form appears.

Understanding Form

A form is a view of one or more tables that is designed to be used for data entry and editing.

One Record at a Time : The default form shows the fields as fill-in boxes for one record at a time. This makes it easier for users to enter a new record without becoming confused by the multiple rows and columns of a datasheet.

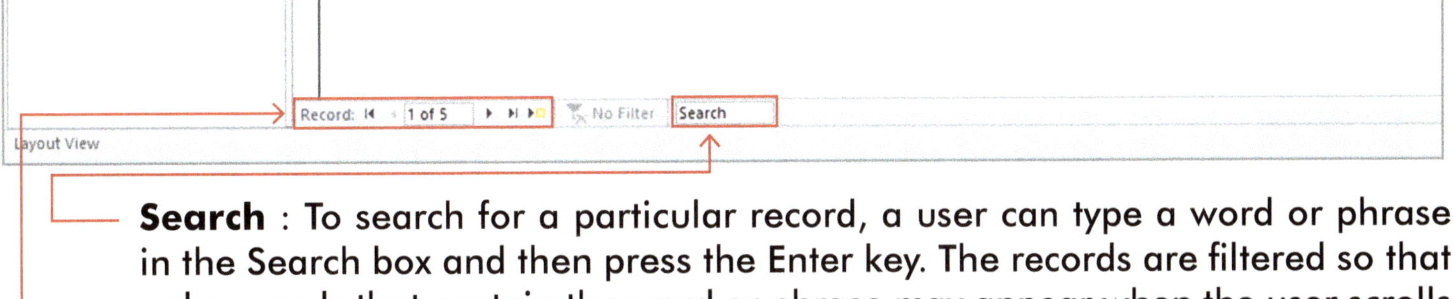

Search : To search for a particular record, a user can type a word or phrase in the Search box and then press the Enter key. The records are filtered so that only records that contain the word or phrase may appear when the user scrolls through them with the record navigation controls. Click on Filter to remove the filter.

Record Navigation : To move between records, users can use the Record Navigation buttons. These are the same as in a datasheet, but they are more useful here because you cannot see other records without them.

Creating a Split Form

There are two parts in Split Form. The upper part shows the Form and the lower part shows datasheet for the table.

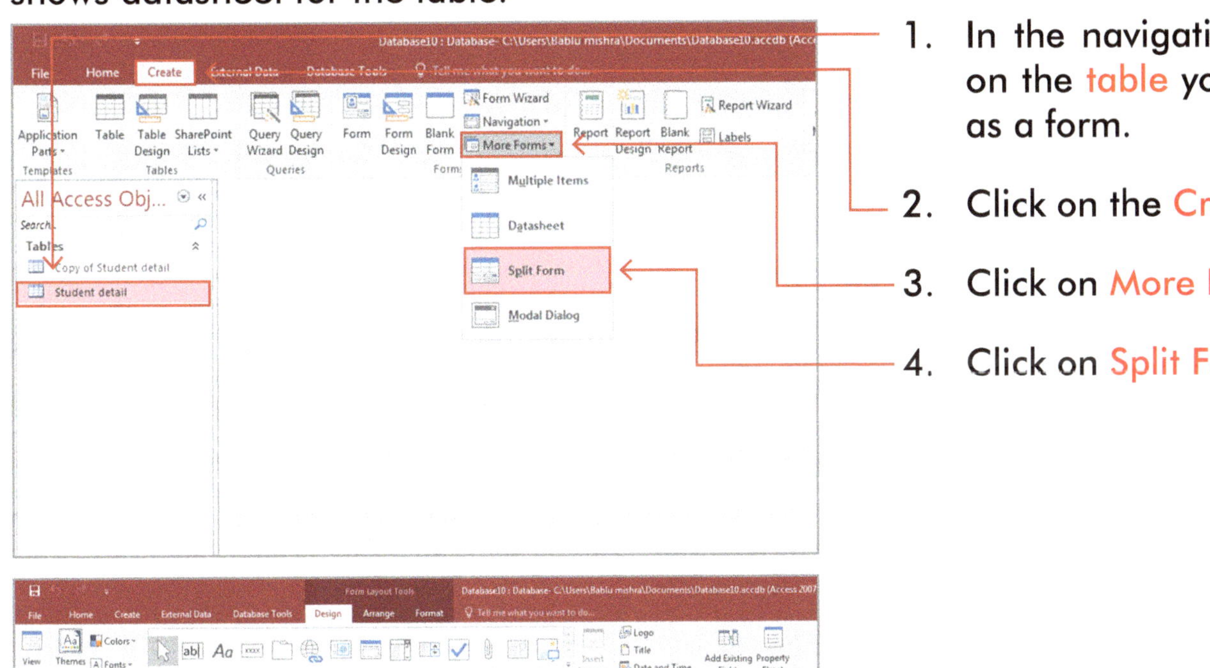

1. In the navigation Pane, click on the table you want to use as a form.
2. Click on the Create tab.
3. Click on More Forms.
4. Click on Split Form.

Student detail

Student ID	1101	Street Address	1241, Country Lane
First Name	John	State	Vermont
Last Name	Smith	Zip Code	05861

The upper part of the screen shows the Form.

Student ID	First Name	Last Name	Street Address	State	Zip Code
1101	John	Smith	1241, Country Lane	Vermont	05861
1102	Sophia	Johnson	687, Marshall Street	Maryland	21229
1103	Julie	Williams	4069, Bee Street	Michigan	49686
1104	Olivia	Brown	3826, Midway Road	Indiana	47648
1105	James	Miller	776, Harper Street	Kentucky	42765

The lower part of the screen shows the datasheet for the table.

Some Other Types of Basic Forms

There are some other types of basic forms in Access 2016.

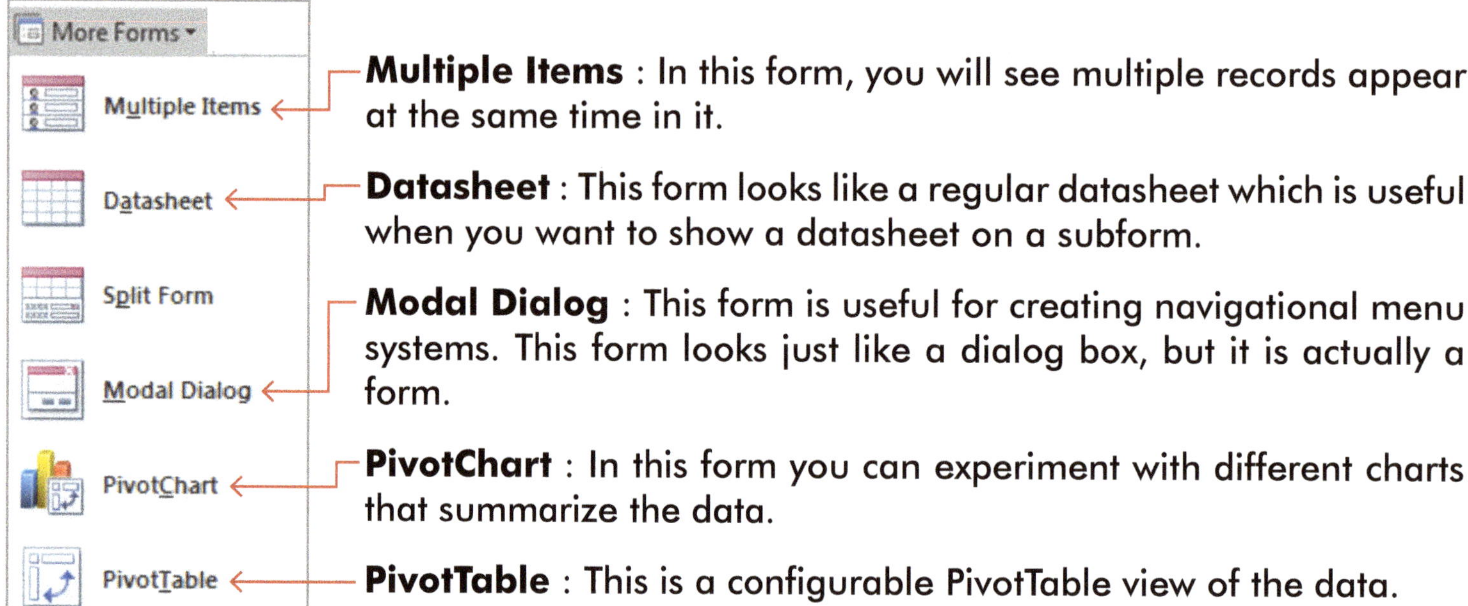

Multiple Items : In this form, you will see multiple records appear at the same time in it.

Datasheet : This form looks like a regular datasheet which is useful when you want to show a datasheet on a subform.

Modal Dialog : This form is useful for creating navigational menu systems. This form looks just like a dialog box, but it is actually a form.

PivotChart : In this form you can experiment with different charts that summarize the data.

PivotTable : This is a configurable PivotTable view of the data.

Saving a Form

You can save the form to give it a name and use it in future.

1. Click on Save button on the Quick Access Toolbar. The Save As dialog box opens.
2. Type a new name for the form.
3. Click on OK to save the form.

The name of the form appears in Form tab and the Navigation Pane.

Changing the Views of Form

Design and Layout view are two views of forms. Design view shows that each object appears as a separate, editable element in the form. Layout view lets you re-arrange the form controls and adjust their sizes on the form.

In Design View

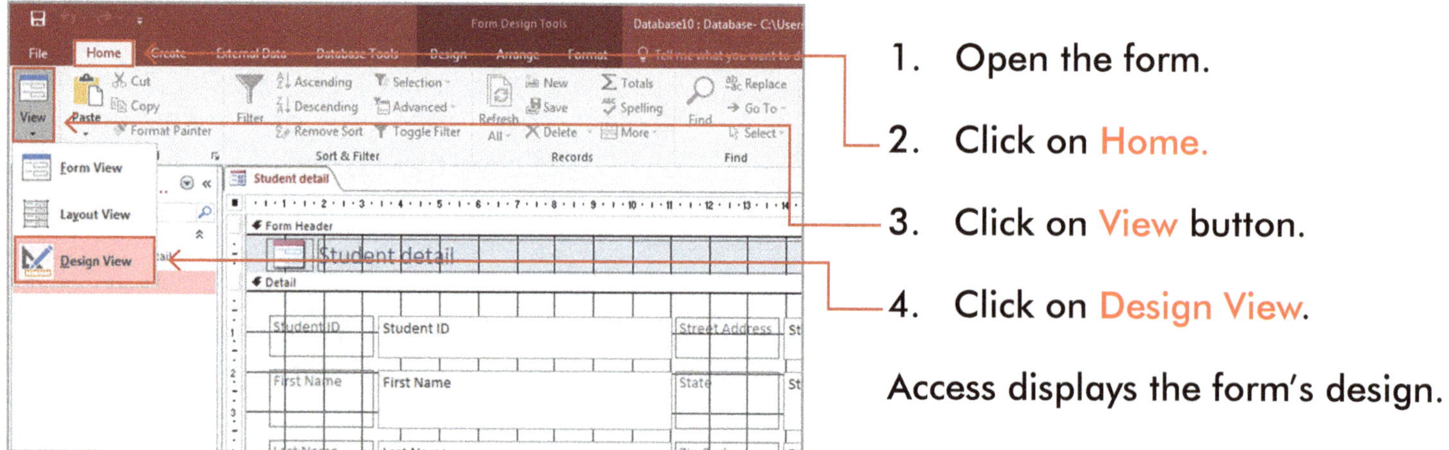

1. Open the form.
2. Click on Home.
3. Click on View button.
4. Click on Design View.

Access displays the form's design.

In Layout View

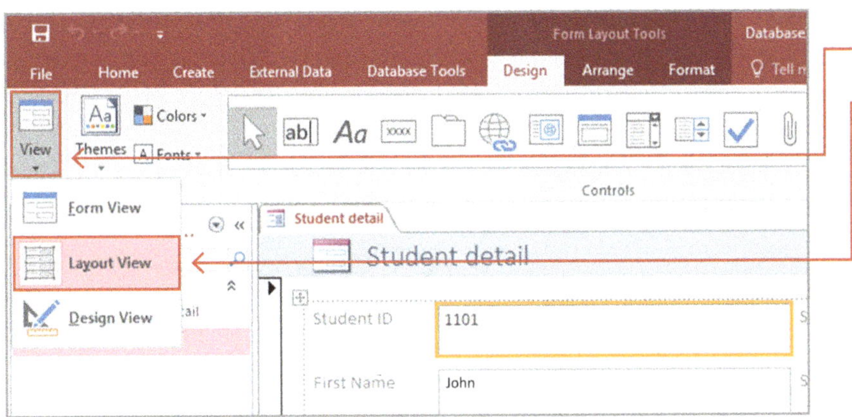

1. Click on View button.
2. Click on Layout View.

Access displays the form as it originally appears, but each element is editable.

To return to Form view, you can click on View button and then click on Form View.

Create a Form in Layout View

You create a form by dragging and dropping fields onto a blank page in Layout view.

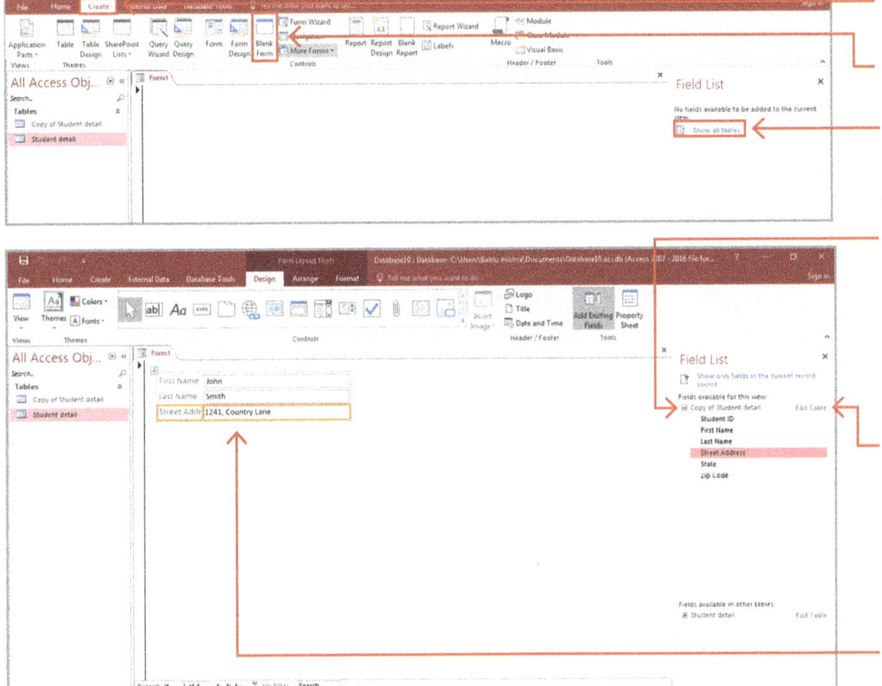

1. Click on the Create tab.
2. Click on Blank Form.
3. Click on Show All Tables.

A list of all the tables appears.

4. Click on Plus sign next to a table.

A list of the fields appears in the table.

5. Double-click a field you want to add it to the form.
6. Repeat step 5 to add more fields.

Continue with the following steps to complete the form.

Adjust the Spacing

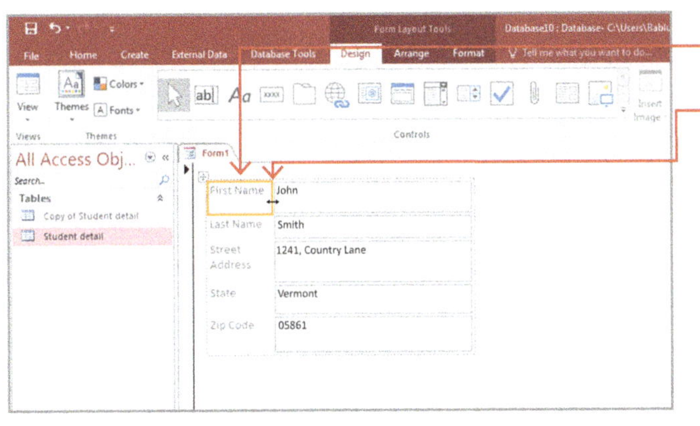

1. Click a label to select it.
2. Position the mouse pointer between the field and its label. The mouse pointer changes into (↔).
3. Drag to the left or right to change the spacing. When you drag, its change affects all fields in the form, not just the one.

Create a Form in Design View

You can create a form in Design view that arranges the fields and labels in exactly the way you want them. Fields and labels are not restricted in their placement as they are in Layout view. But it can be time-consuming.

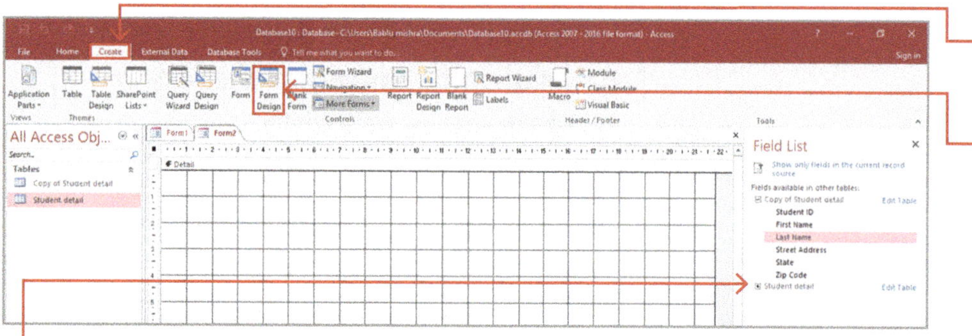

1. Click on the Create tab.
2. Click on Form Design.

A blank form appears, along with a Field List pane.

If the Field List does not appear, click on Add Existing Fields on the Design tab.

A list of tables appears.

3. Click on Plus sign next to a table.

A list of the fields in the table appears.

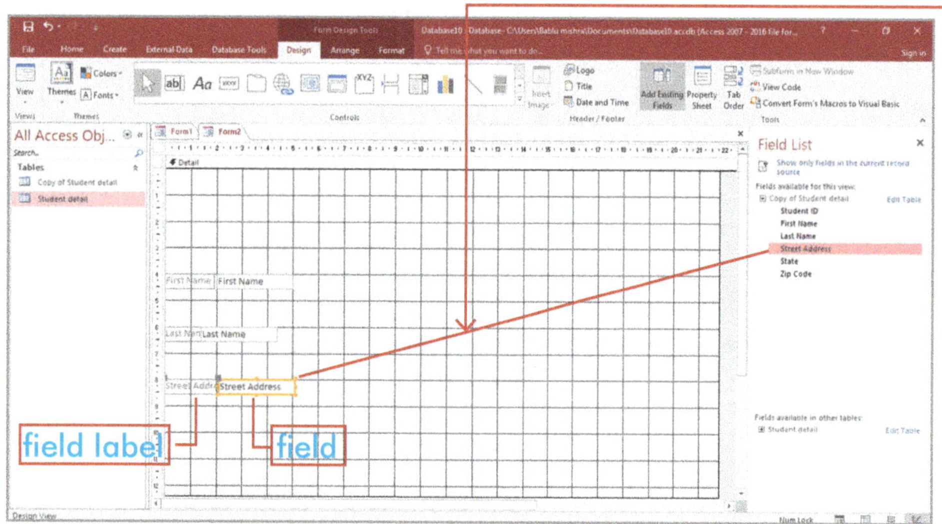

4. Click and drag a field onto the design grid.

Both the field and an associated label appear.

5. Drag and drop more fields onto the form.

You can freely drag a field around on the grid or make a field align or conform in size to other fields.

Change Field Formatting of Form

You can change the font, size, style, alignment or colour of the text from the Formatting tab. The Formatting tab appears only when you view the form in Layout view.

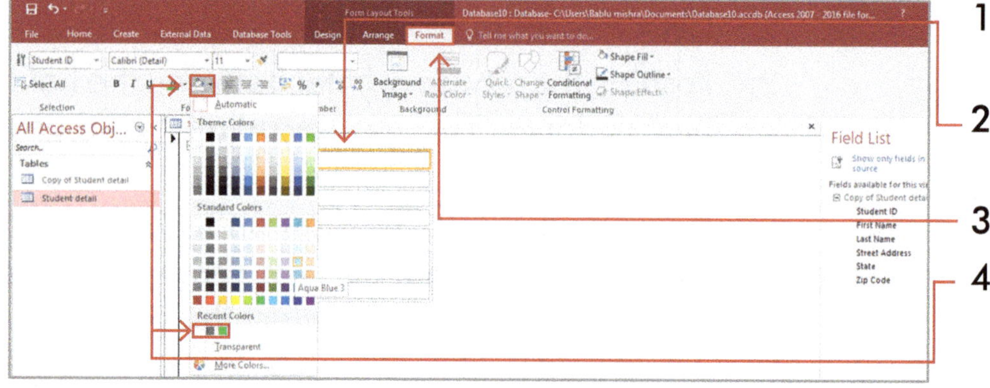

1. Open the form you want to format in Layout view.
2. Click on the field or label you want to format.
3. Click on Format tab.
4. Click on the formatting that you want to apply, such as a fill color.

You can also apply another formatting in this field.

Access applies formatting to the field.

Apply Theme

By using preset designs, you can change the theme of a form to give it a different look.

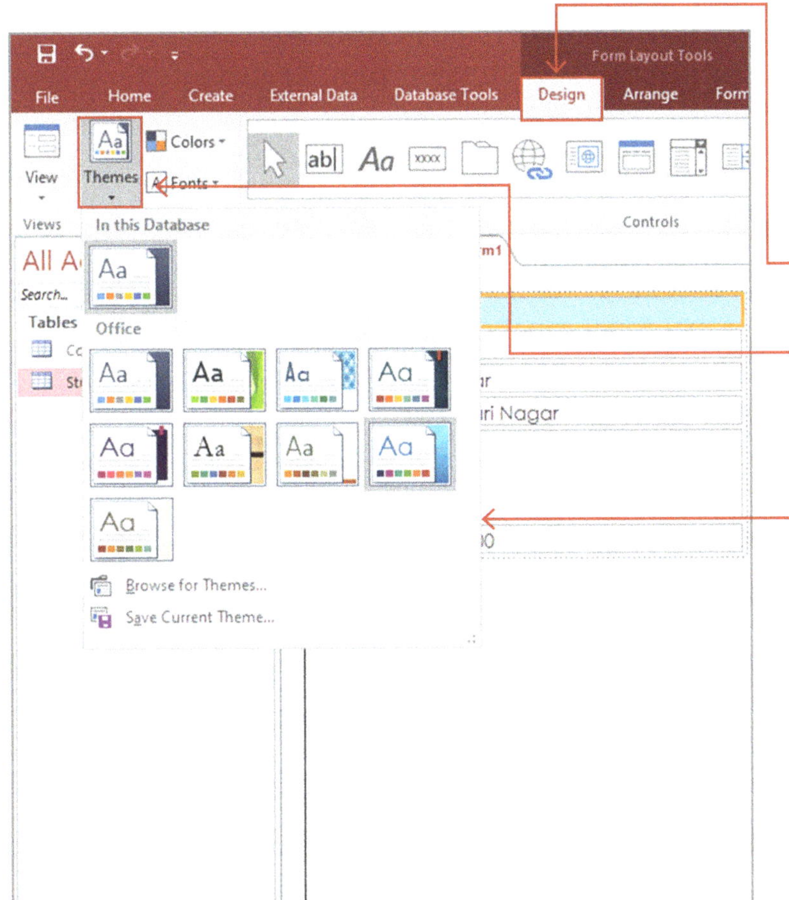

1. Open the form that you want to format in Layout view.
2. Click on Design tab.
3. Click on Themes button.

The full palette of theme appears. You can point to a theme without clicking it to see a preview of it on the form.

4. Click on a new theme.

Access applies new format to the form.

LET'S HAVE A LOOK

- Selecting data in a table is necessary before performing any tasks in Access.
- Find and Replace is one of the important features used to find and replace the specific records in a large database.
- On the Find tab, you can find text strings within records.
- On the Replace tab, you can do the same thing, except you can also replace the found data with some other text that you specify.
- Sorting can arrange the records of table either in ascending or descending order.
- MS-Access can create a relationship between two tables when the primary key from one table is present in another table.
- Form can be customized by using Design and Layout Views.
- A form is a view of one or more tables that is designed to be used for data entry and editing.

BRAIN TEASER

1. Multiple Choice Questions:

Tick (✓) the correct answer:

a. One can easily search tables, queries and forms with the help of:
   i. Replace option ☐ ii. Find Option ☐ iii. Filter Option ☐

b. Option for arranging the records in ascending or descending order:
   i. Find ☐ ii. Data ☐ iii. Sorting ☐

c. Display only records the containing data of interest:
   i. Sorting ☐ ii. Report ☐ iii. Filter ☐

d. A form appears in two parts - Upper part and Lower Part:
   i. Split ☐ ii. Basic ☐ iii. Datasheet ☐

e. If we want to find records where both criteria are met, we should use:
   i. AND ☐ ii. OR ☐ iii. NOT ☐

2. Fill in the blanks:

a. The selected data appears ______________ on your screen.

b. On the ______________ tab, you can find text strings within records.

c. On the ______________ tab, you can also replace the found data with some other text that you specify.

d. ______________ option is used to display records containing the data of interest.

e. In Filtering by form, you can filter by multiple fields and specify criteria for as many fields using ______________, ______________ or a combination.

f. Relational databases like Access can contain ______________ related tables.

g. ______________ and ______________ area display the names of the tables you want to create a relationship between and the names of the matching fields.

h. In split form, the upper part shows the ______________ and the lower part shows the ______________.

i. In forms, to move between records, users can use the ______________ buttons.

3. Complete the following:

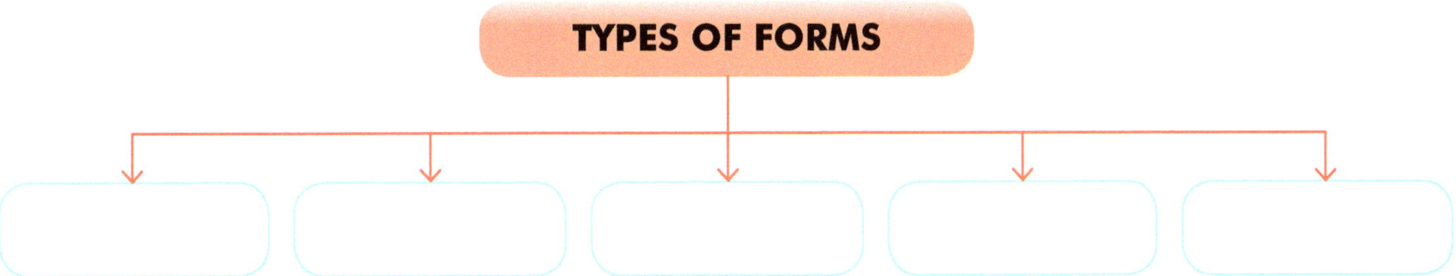

4. Answer the following questions

(i) Answer each in a few lines:

a. What is the use of selecting data?

b. What is the use of Find and Replace option?

c. On which tab is Find and Replace tab present?

d. What is the benefit of sorting records?

e. How is filtering helpful?

f. Name the key which helps to make relationship among different tables.

g. Name the different types of Basic forms in Access 2016.

(ii) Answer each comprehensively:

a. Explain with steps to show the Find and Replace feature in Access 2016.

b. Explain changing the views of forms in Access 2016.

Open Access and create a new Database named 'Student'.

a. Create a table using Datasheet view, containing the following fields in it:

Roll No.	First Name	Last Name	Address	Date of Birth	Phone No.	Postal code

b. Add 15 records in the above table and save by the name 'Student Detail'.

c. Select the Roll Number as the primary key field.

d. Create a simple form by using the above table.

e. Save the form by the name 'Student Form'.

f. Close the window and quit MS-Access.

Queries & Reports in Access

In this chapter, we will learn:

⇒ Defining Query
⇒ Types of Queries
⇒ Creating a Query
⇒ Running a Query
⇒ Using Criteria In Query
⇒ Sorting Data in Query
⇒ Deleting Field in a Query
⇒ Report in Access 2016
⇒ Creating a Report

QUERIES

In a very simple term, a Query means a question. The word 'Query' comes from the Latin word 'quoerere'. The meaning of 'quoerere' is 'inquiry'. In datadase, a query is simply a question represented in a way that Access can understand. It is a powerful tool which helps to use database in the real sense. Queries are like costumes that tables wear. They display the data from the table in some modified way, such as sorted by a certain field or filtered to show certain values in a field.

A query is used to extract information from the table. Suppose you want to search for some information to satisfy certain criteria from a large table with thousands of records stored in it. This type of problem can be handled by a query very easily. You can use the Query feature in these types of situations.

a. Students passed with > 80% marks.

b. Number of centuries made by Sachin Tendulkar from 1/1/2000 to 1/1/2013.

A query can be a handy tool for these types of situations. Each query functions like a question that can be asked immediately or saved to be asked later.

Types of Queries

To view, change and analyze data in different ways, the queries can be used. There are several types of queries in MS-Access.

Select Queries : The select query is the most common type of query that retrieves data from one or more tables and displays the result in datasheet.

Parameter Queries : Parameter query displays its own dialog box prompting you for information, such as criteria for retrieving records or a value you wish to insert in a field.

Crosstab Queries : Crosstab query is used to create the summary view of data for easier analysis.

Action Queries : An action query uses just one operation to make changes to or move many records. Its categories are Append Queries, Update Queries, Delete Queries and Make Table Queries.

Creating a Query in Design View

In Design view, a query appears as a grid at the bottom of the window, into which you drag fields from the table or tables. When you run a query, the results appear in Datasheet view, just like a table.

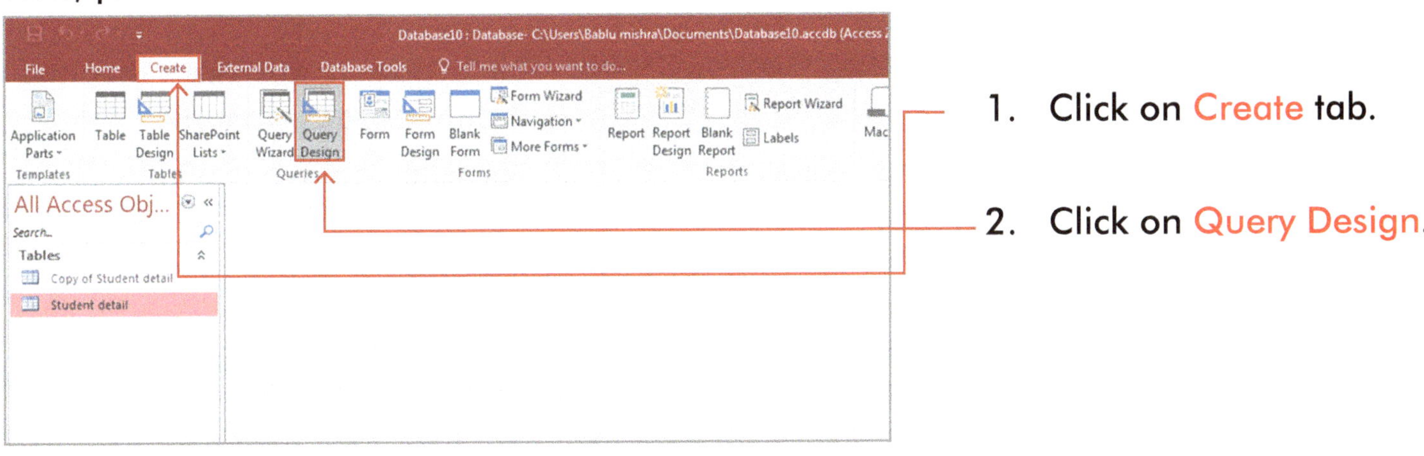

1. Click on Create tab.
2. Click on Query Design.

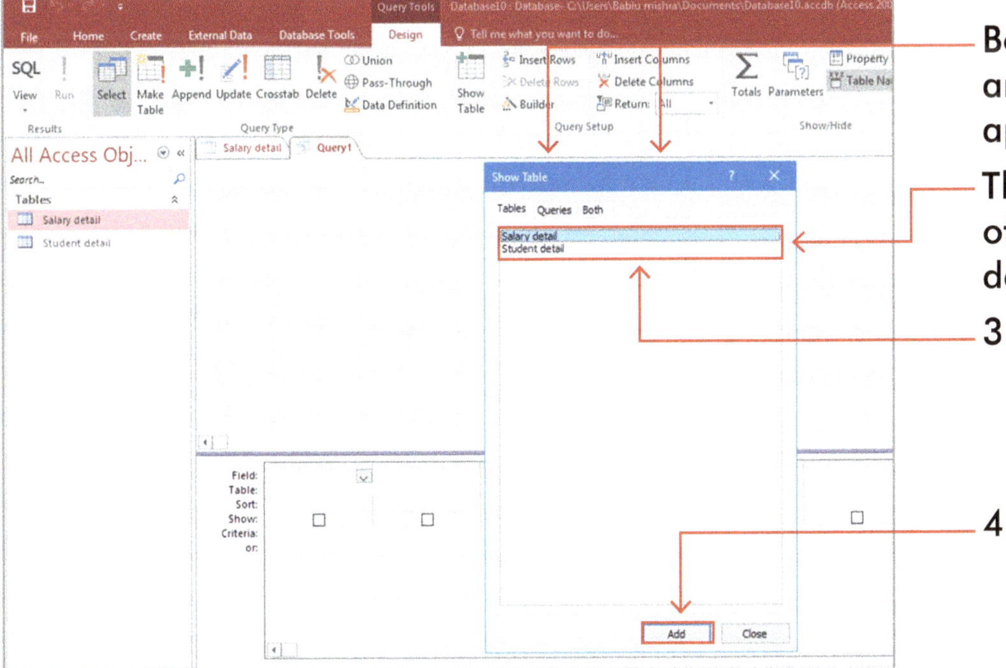

Both Select Query window and Show Table dialog box appear.

This area shows the lists of all the tables in your database.

3. Click on a table that contains information you want to use in your query.
4. Click on Add button to add the table to your query.

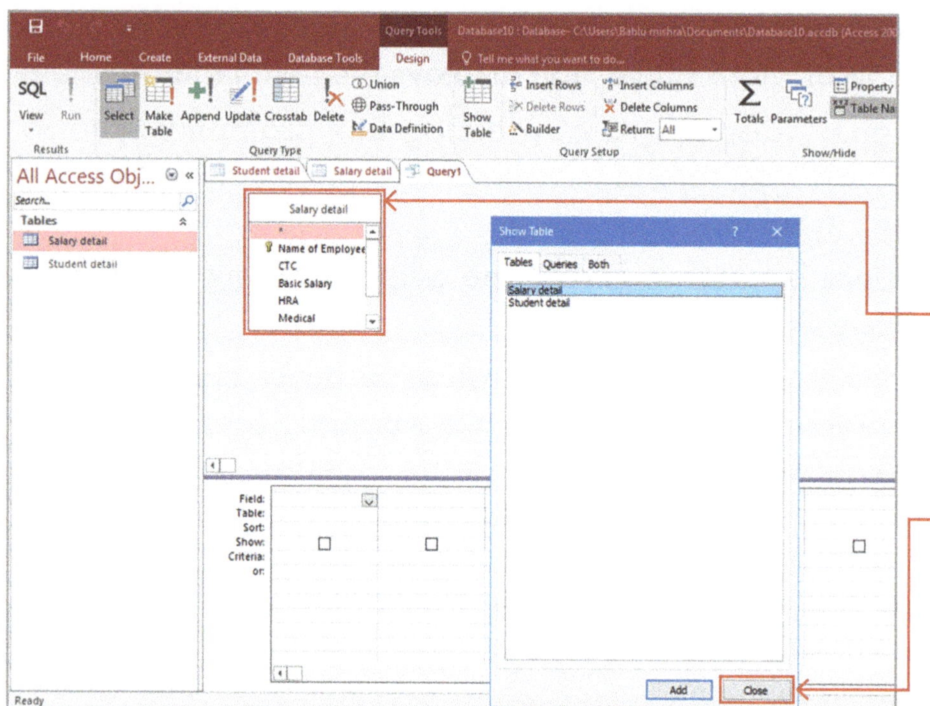

A box appears in the Select Query window, displaying the fields for the table you selected.

5. Repeat steps 3 and 4 for each table you want to use in your query.

6. Click on Close button to hide the Show Table dialog box.

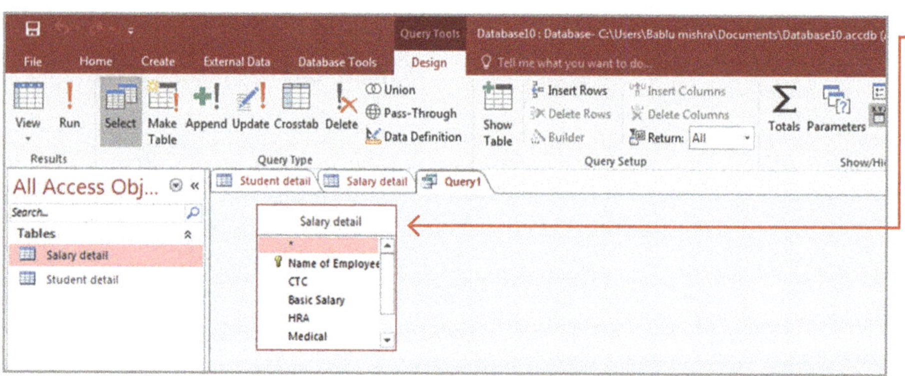

Each box in this area displays the fields for one table.

You can remove the table from the query by just clicking on the table and then press on the Delete key. This removes the table from the query, but not from the database.

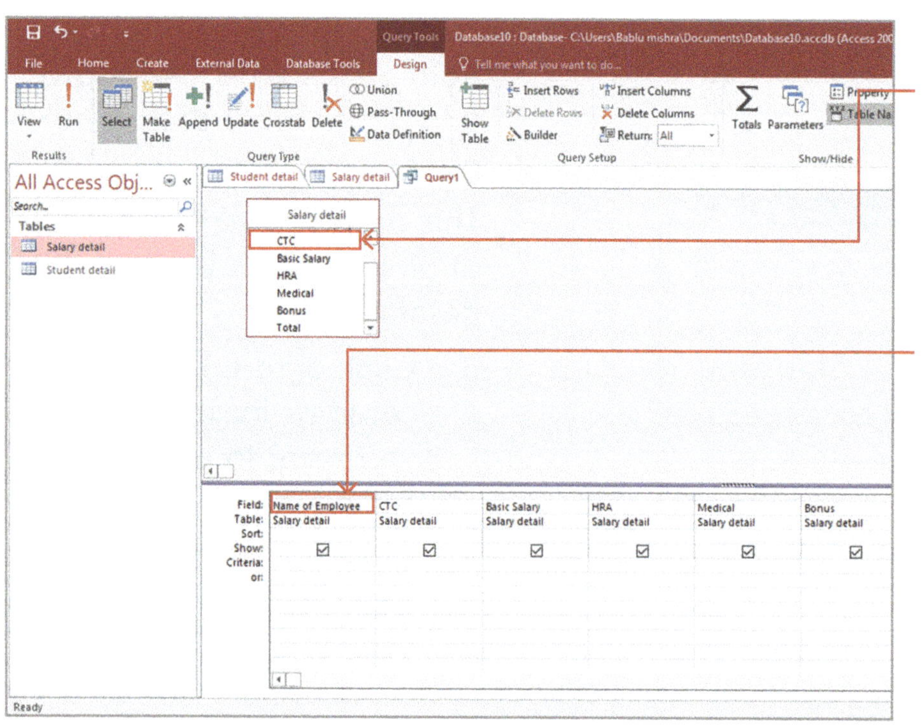

7. Double-click with the left mouse button on a field you want to include in your query.

The field you selected and the table that contains the field, are displayed in this area.

8. Repeat step 7 for each field you want to include in your query.

Running a Query

After creating a Query, the query has to be run to produce the result by clicking on the Run button in the database toolbar. When you run a query, the results appear in Datasheet view, just like a table.

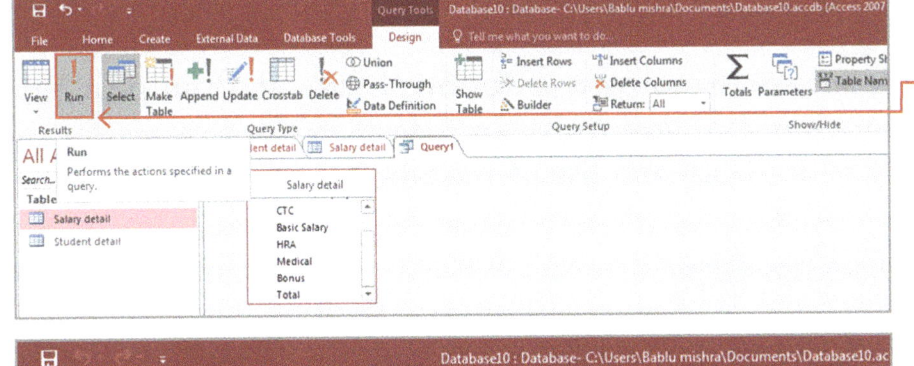

1. Click on Run button (Run) in the result group from Design tab to run the query.

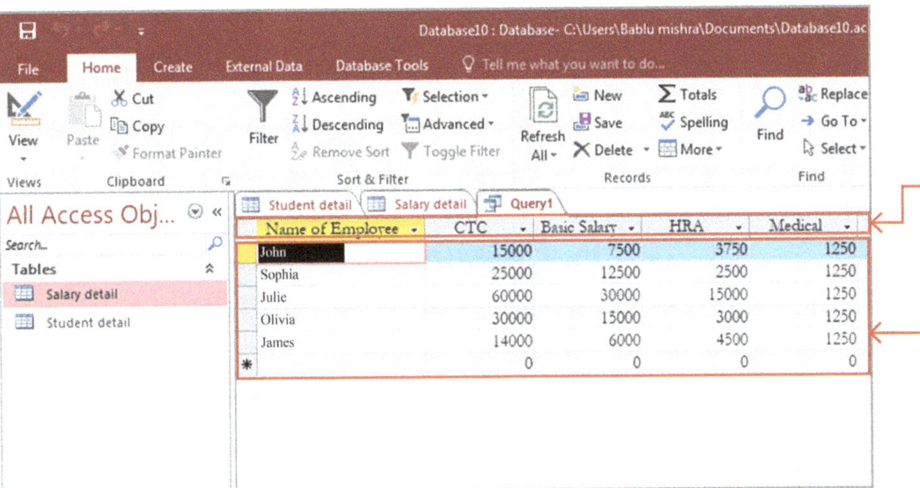

Name of Employee	CTC	Basic Salary	HRA	Medical
John	15000	7500	3750	1250
Sophia	25000	12500	2500	1250
Julie	60000	30000	15000	1250
Olivia	30000	15000	3000	1250
James	14000	6000	4500	1250
*	0	0	0	0

The results of the query appear in Datasheet View.

This area displays the names of the fields you included in the query.

The records that meet the conditions you specified appear in this area.

Saving a Query

You can save the query to use the query result in the future. To save the result of the query as a new table, follow the steps.

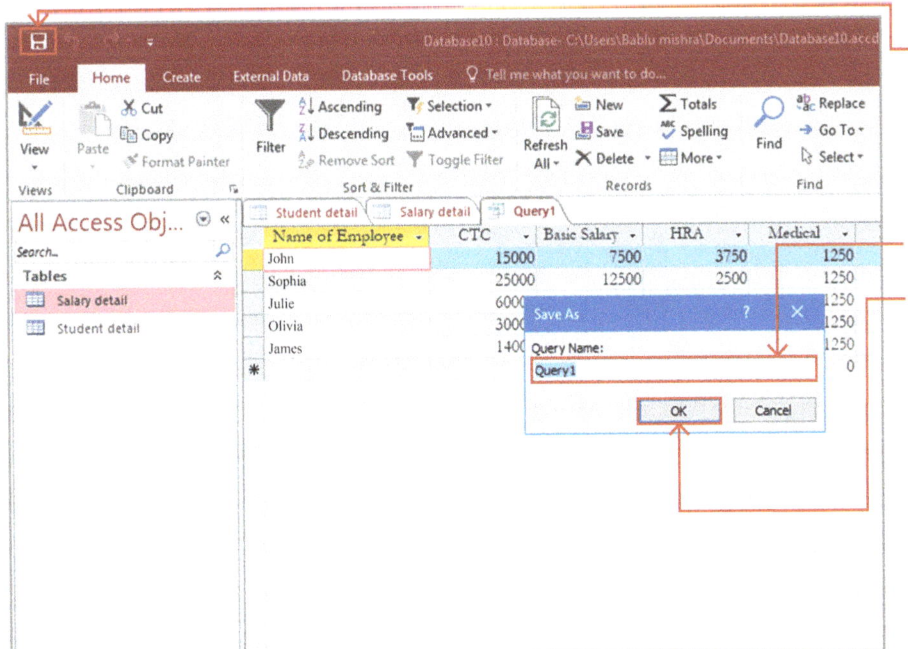

1. Click on Save button or Press Ctrl+S from the keyboard.

The Save As dialog box appears.

2. Type a name for your query.
3. Click on OK button to save your query.

When you have finished viewing the results of your query, click on Close button (x) to close the query and return to the Database window.

Using a Criteria in Query

To filter the query results, you can create criteria. Criteria are specifications that dictate which records will be included. A criterion acts like a filter option that filters out certain records. If the records meet that criterion, that is included in the results.

Using Text Data

While using criteria, you can specify a text string as a criterion. It can contain multiple words, including punctuation and spacing, but you must enclose it in quotation marks. For example, you can use the query to find out the list of members who are paying by credit card.

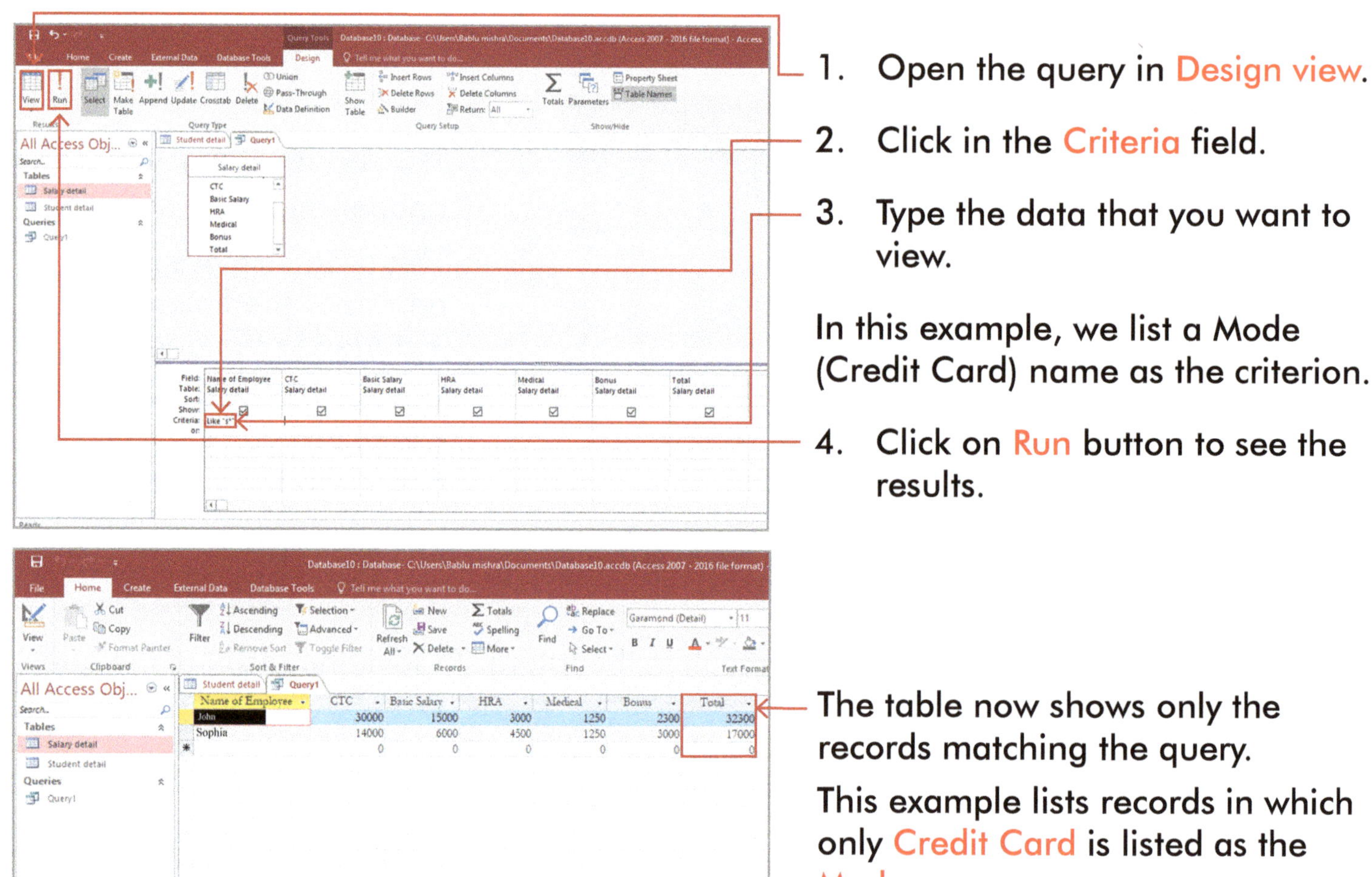

1. Open the query in Design view.
2. Click in the Criteria field.
3. Type the data that you want to view.

In this example, we list a Mode (Credit Card) name as the criterion.

4. Click on Run button to see the results.

The table now shows only the records matching the query.

This example lists records in which only Credit Card is listed as the Mode name.

Using Wild Cards in Query

In query, the symbols that represent any character or a combination of characters are wildcards. The two special wild cards are Asterisk (*) and question mark (?). The asterisk (*) represents all characters followed after a specified letter. Thus S* represents the letter S followed by any collection of characters. Question mark (?) represents only one character. Thus H?rvey represents a letter followed by any single character that follows the letter, such as in Harvey.

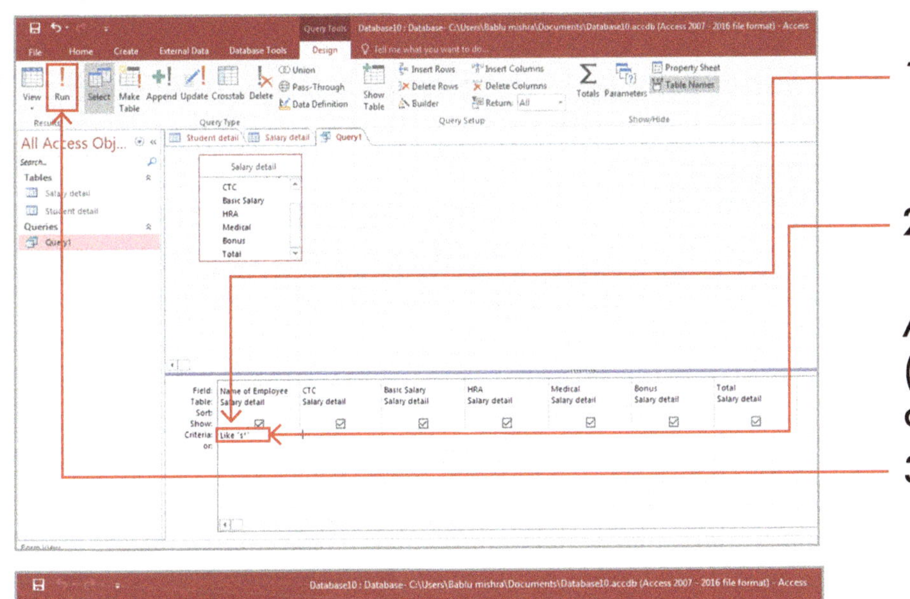

1. Click on the Criteria area for the field you want to use to find specific records.
2. Type the criteria S* and then press the Enter key.

Access may add quotation marks (" ") or number signs (#) to the criteria you type.

3. Click on Run button.

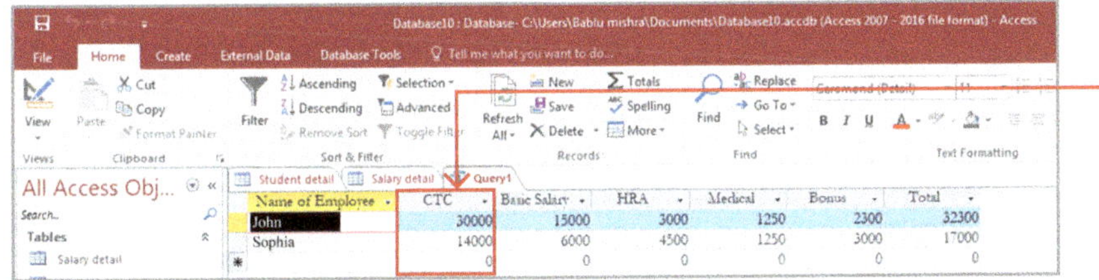

The result is displayed.

Only the members whose names start with S are included.

Using Comparison Operator

It is often useful to specify a range of values for a criterion instead of one specific value. You can accomplish this with comparison operators and special keywords. You must enter the appropriate comparison operator if you want something other than an exact match. The comparison operators are > (greater than), < (less than), >= (greater than or equal to), <= (less than or equal to), and <> (not equal to).

Let us find the members whose charges are more than or equal to 20000.

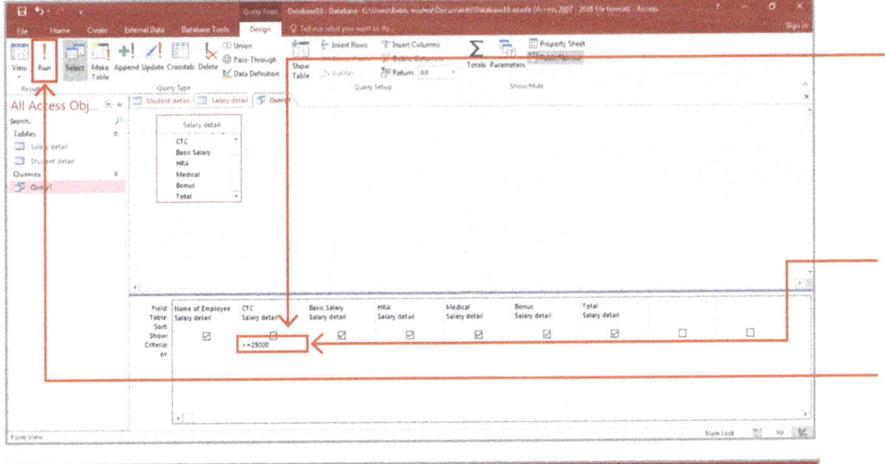

1. Click the Criteria area for the field you want to use to find specific records.
2. Type the criteria (>= 20000).
3. Click on Run button.

The results of the query appear.

In this example, Access found members whose total charges for club are more than or equal to 20000.

Sorting Data in Query

You can set a query to sort the results alphabetically by a certain field, either in ascending or descending order. You can specify sorting for more than one field if you like.

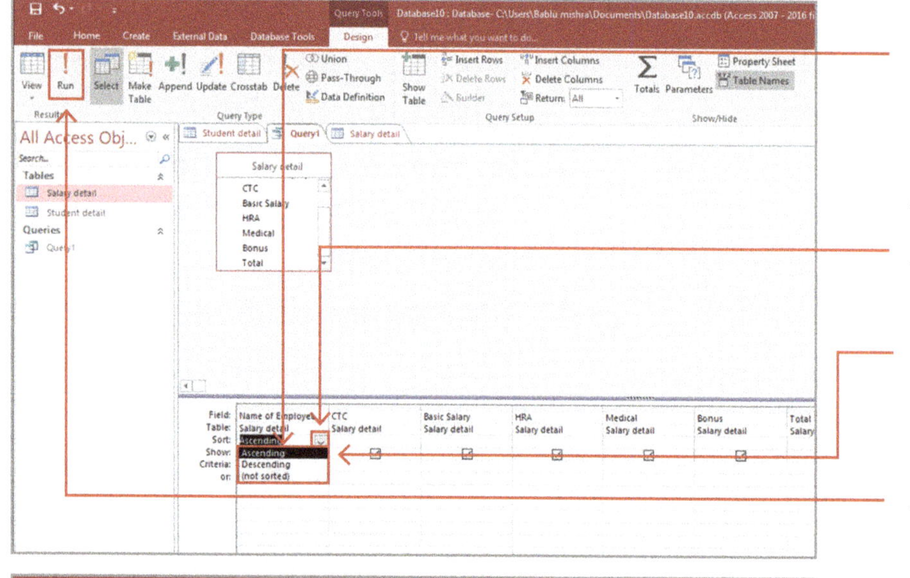

1. Click on the Sort area for the field you want to use to sort the results of your query.

A down arrow appears.

2. Click on the down arrow button.
3. Click the way you want to sort the results (Ascending, Descending, Not Sorted).
4. Click on Run button.

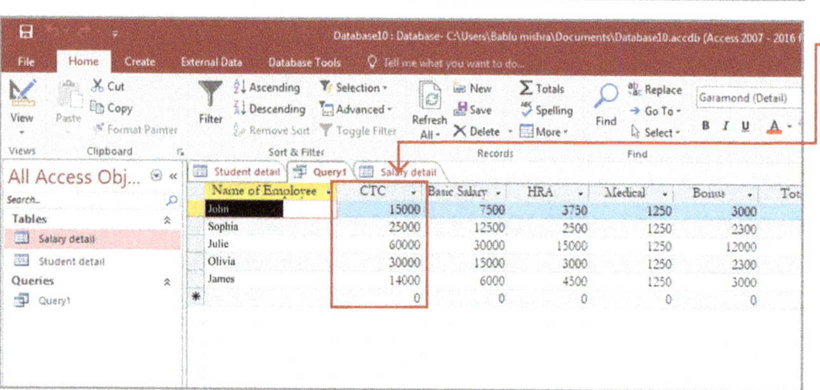

The records appear in the order you specified. In this example, the Members names are sorted in ascending order.

To cancel the sorting, repeat steps 1 to 3, selecting (not sorted) in step 3.

Deleting a Field in a Query

You can delete the unwanted field from your query. Deleting a field from a query does not delete the field from the table.

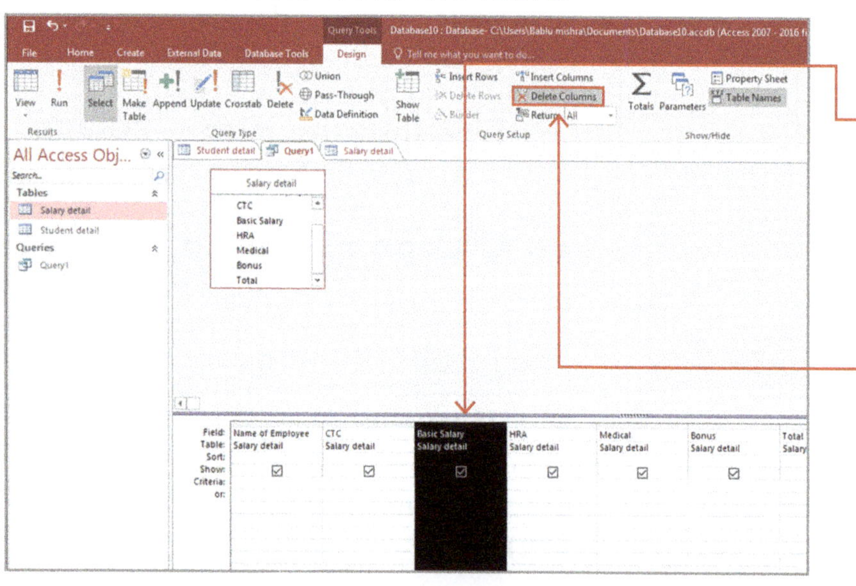

1. Position the mouse directly above the field you want to delete. The mouse pointer changes into (⇩) and then click to select the field.
2. Click on Delete Columns.

The field disappears from your query.

Hiding a Field in a Query

You can hide a field without removing it from the query grid.

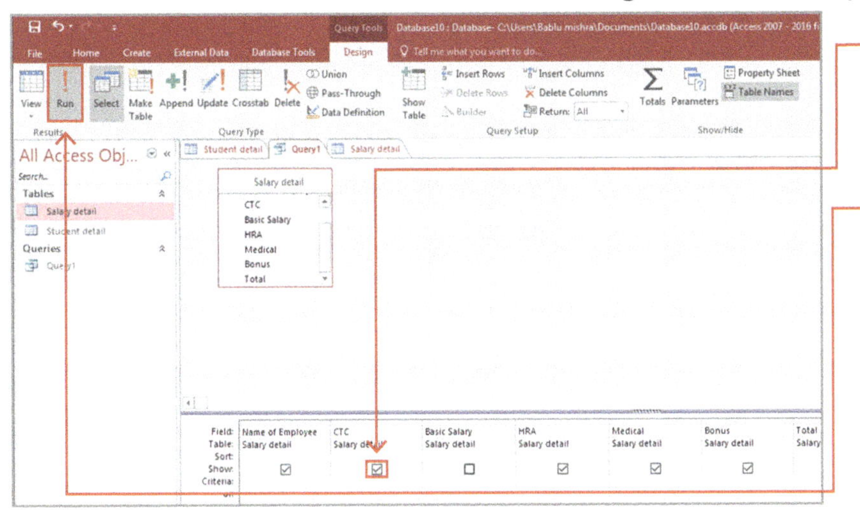

1. In the Show row, deselect the check box for the field you want to hide.
2. Click on Run.

The datasheet opens, showing the query results. The field you hide does not appear.

REPORT IN ACCESS 2016

In Access, reports are designed to be printed. They give you the ability to present your table and query data in a printable format. A report can have more elaborate formatting and layouts than other objects you can print. It is the way for you to display data from a query and table in appealing way, *i.e.* presentable. You can create basic reports with default settings or you can create custom layouts by using the exact settings that work best for your situation.

You have several choices of views for working with reports. Each has a specific function for which it is best suited.

When a report is opened in Access, it is opened in Print Preview. Print Preview shows the report exactly as it will be printed. It shows page margins by simulating the edges of the paper on-screen.

Report view shows the report approximately as it will be printed, but it does not simulate the edges of the paper on-screen, so you cannot see the actual margins that will be used.

Layout view enables you to configure the overall formatting and layout of the report but not to change individual elements, such as text boxes.

Design view is where you can fine-tune the fields and labels to be included on the report.

Creating a Simple Report

You can create a simple report very quickly by using the default settings of tools.

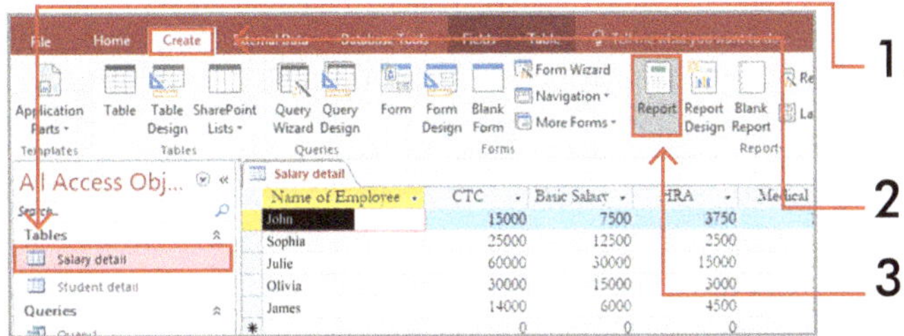

1. Click on the table or query on which you want to base the report from the Navigation Pane.
2. Click on Create tab.
3. Click on Report tool from Reports group.

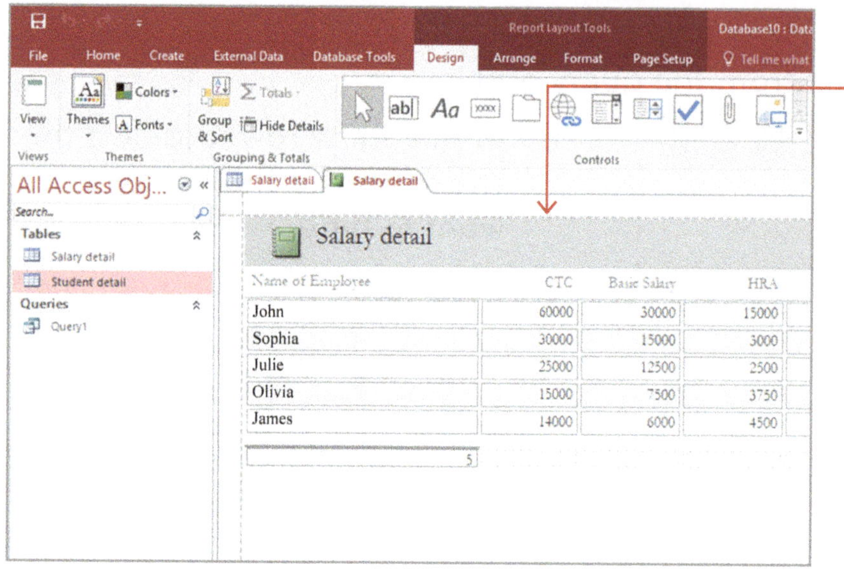

Salary detail

Name of Employee	CTC	Basic Salary	HRA
John	60000	30000	15000
Sophia	30000	15000	3000
Julie	25000	12500	2500
Olivia	15000	7500	3750
James	14000	6000	4500

Access builds the report and displays it in Layout view.

After viewing the report, you can save it and then close both the report and the underlying table that you used as a record source.

Creating a Blank Report

You can design your own reports from scratch by using either Layout view or Design view. However, Layout view is much easier to work in because it more closely resembles how the report will actually appear.

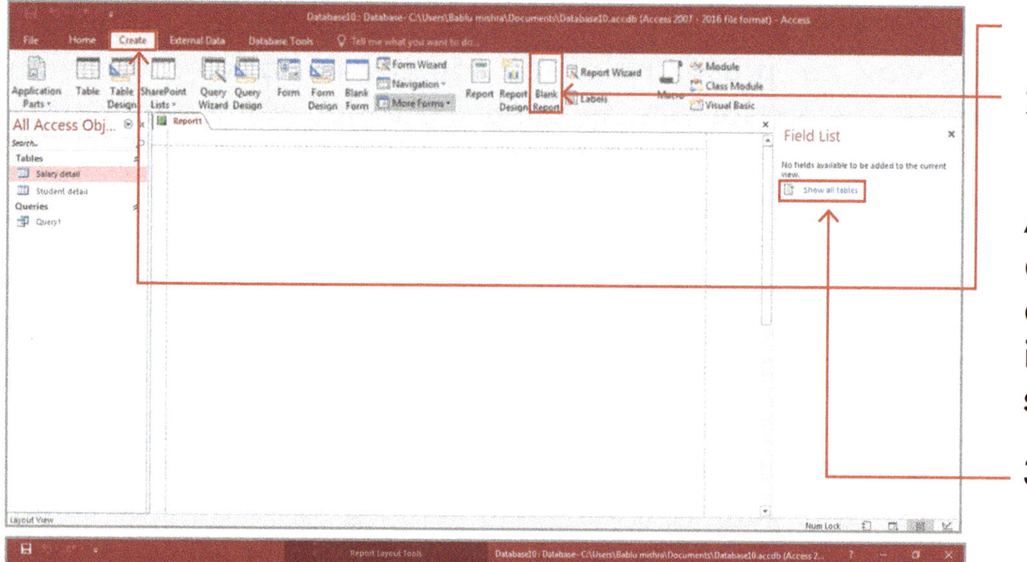

1. Click on Create tab.
2. Click on Blank Report.

A blank report is displayed in Layout view, and the Field List pane is displayed on the right side.

3. Click on Show All Tables.
4. In the Field List pane, click on the plus sign next to the table whose fields you want to see on the report.

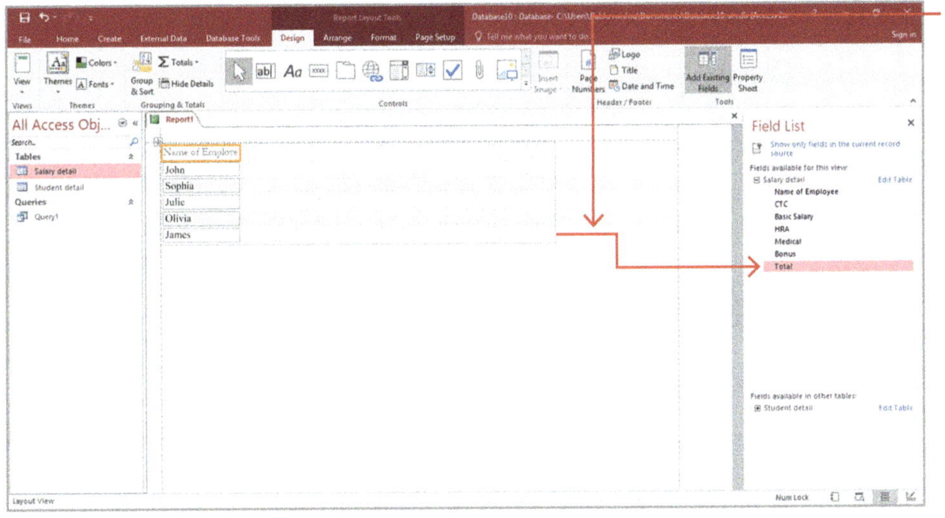

5. Drag each field onto the report one at a time, or hold down CTRL and select several fields, and then drag them onto the report at the same time.

After dragging all the fields you can use the tools in the Controls group on the Format tab to add a logo, title, page numbers or the date and time to the report.

Creating a Report with the Report Wizard

You can use the Report Wizard to create a report without having to design it manually while still having some control over its layout and formatting.

1. On the Create tab, click on Report Wizard. The Report Wizard dialog box opens.

Now, follow the instructions of dialog boxes and you will create a report manually very easily.

LET'S HAVE A LOOK

- A query is an object in Access that enables the user to retrieve information from a database.
- The most basic query type is Select query which reaches one or more database tables and locates records.
- A Design view allows to create a query from scratch.
- Sorting can arrange items in some sequence and/or in different sets.
- After creating a query, it has to be run to produce the result.
- Criteria act like filter options that filter out certain records.
- Wildcards are the symbols that represent any character or a combination of characters.
- ? and * are two special wild cards provided by Access.
- Reports are used to present information in a neat and organized format that is ready for printing.

BRAIN TEASER

1. Multiple Choice Questions

Tick (✓) the correct answer:

a. The origin of the word 'Query' comes from the Latin word:

i. Question ☐ ii. Quoerere ☐ iii. Filter ☐

b. Access provides a basic tool for retrieving information from database:
   i. Report ☐ ii. Query ☐ iii. Filter ☐

c. Shortcut key to save a query is:
   i. Ctrl+S ☐ ii. Ctrl+V ☐ iii. Alt+V ☐

d. The most common type of query:
   i. Select ☐ ii. Action ☐ iii. Crosstab ☐

e. Wild card characters provided by Access:
   i. + and ? ☐ ii. * and ? ☐ iii. * and / ☐

f. It gives you the ability to present your table and query data in a printable format:
   i. Report ☐ ii. Label ☐ iii. Form ☐

2. Fill in the blanks:

a. In a very simple term, a Query means a ____________.

b. In datadase, a ____________ is simply a question represented in a way that Access can understand.

c. Query is used to extract ____________ from the table.

d. The ____________ query is the most common type of query.

e. ____________ are symbols that represent any character or a combination of characters.

f. An ____________ query uses just one operation to makes changes to or move many records.

g. ____________ give you the ability to present your table in a printable format.

3. Write 'T' for True and 'F' for False in the boxes:

a. In a very simple term, a Query means a question. ☐

b. Action query is the most common type of query. ☐

c. + and * are two special wildcards provided by Access. ☐

d. Criteria are specifications that dictate which records will be included. ☐

e. In Access, reports are designed to be printed. ☐

f. Report view lets you fine-tune the fields and labels for adding in a report. ☐

4. Answer the following questions

(i) Answer each in a few lines:

a. What is the origin of the word 'Query'?

b. What is the meaning of quoerere?

c. What is Query?

d. On which toolbar is the Run button present?

e. Name the shortcut key to save a query.

f. Name the several types of queries in Access.

g. Name two special wild cards provided by Access.

h. What is the use of reports?

(ii) Answer each comprehensively:

a. Explain the function of Query in Access.

b. Explain the different types of queries.

c. What are wild cards?

d. What is the use of criteria in Query?

e. What is report? Explain the three views of reports.

Create a database named 'Student' and design two tables in it containing the following fields:

Table 1 : Student

Roll No.	Student Name	Address	City	Phone

Primary Key: Roll No.

Table 2 : Activities

Roll No.	Activities	Date	Fees

Primary Key: Roll No.

a. Create the two forms for the above two tables which include all the fields of both the tables. Save the forms as the table names.

b. Now enter the following records in the form.

Students:

011, Liam, 4705 Pike Street, San Diego, California, 721-039-4911

012, Jacob, 1747 Mcwhorter Road, Enumclaw, Washington, 962-513-2676

013, Charlotte, 3378 Emeral Dreams Drive, Chicago, Illinois, 815-300-8937

014, Alex, 1519 Bobcat Drive, Washington, Maryland, 888-201-3362

015, Emma, 34 Linda Street, West Brunswick Twp, Pennsylvania, 267-739-1765

Activities:

011, Cricket 01/04/2013, 3000

012, Badminton, 05/03/2022, 2500

013, Table Tennis, 01/06/2022, 2000

014, Swimming, 06/03/2022, 3500

015, Badminton, 08/08/2022, 2500

c. Close the forms and open both tables one by one to view the records entered in the table.

d. Using select Query option, design a query to extract the records of those students, which belong to Chicago.

e. Run the query to see the extracted records.

f. Save the above query as Student — Chicago.

g. Generate another query on the table Activities to extract the information of those students who have taken badminton as an activity.

h. Run the query to see the extracted records.

i. Close the database and exit from Access.

Formative Assessment - 2
(Chapters 3-5)

1. Create a table with the following fields:

Field Name	Data type	Description
Roll Number	Number	
First Name	Text	
Last Name	Text	
Class	Text	
Section	Text	
Activities	Text	
Fees	Number	

a. Add the suitable description for each Field name.

b. Now enter the 12 records in the table.

c. Save the table as 'Students Details'.

d. Close the database and Access.

2. Create a table 'Employee' in the Design View with the following fields:

Emp-ID	Name	Address	Phone	Date of Joining	Post

a. Choose appropriate data type and description for each field.

b. Save the table.

c. Open the table in Datasheet view.

d. Select 'Emp-ID' as the primary key field.

e. Now enter the 20 records in the table.

f. Add another field named 'E-mail' before the Date of Joining field and update the records accordingly.

g. Close the table.

h. Create a Report on the table 'Students'.

i. View the report in Design View and Print Preview view.

j. Close the Report window and close the database.

Summative Assessment - 1
(Chapters 1-5)

1. Fill in the blanks:

a. The basic goal of AI is to enable computers and machines to perform __________ tasks.

b. A Dual In-Line Memory Module (DIMM) has __________ pins.

c. A megabyte (MB) equals approximately __________ bytes.

d. A __________ key is a key that differentiates the records in a file.

e. A __________ warning appears while opening a database which is not trusted.

f. Query is used to extract __________ from the table.

2. Tick (✓) the correct answer:

a. An Internet-enabled phone:
i. PDA ☐ ii. Smartphone ☐ iii. Notebook ☐

b. Non-volatile memory:
i. ROM ☐ ii. RAM ☐ iii. Cache ☐

c. ROM that erases its contents by Ultraviolet light:
i. EEPROM ☐ ii. PROM ☐ iii. EPROM ☐

d. A Terabyte equals approximately __________ bytes:
i. One billion ☐ ii. One million ☐ iii. one trillion ☐

e. Access stores data in:
i. Fields ☐ ii. Table ☐ iii. File ☐

f. Each entry in the table is called:
i. Record ☐ ii. Data ☐ iii. Value ☐

g. Option for arranging the records in ascending or descending order:
i. Find ☐ ii. Data ☐ iii. Sorting ☐

3. Answer each in a few lines:

a. Define artificial intelligence.

b. Give two examples of digital assistants.

c. What do you mean by computer vision?
d. Name the temporary storage closer to the CPU's speed.
e. What is primary memory?
f. Write the full forms of DBMS and RDBMS.
g. Name any three data types of Access 2016.
h. What is the use of Find and Replace option?
i. Where is sort button present?
j. Name the different views of forms.

4. Answer each comprehensively:

a. What is technological convergence?
b. What are the benefits of using computers?
c. Explain Input, output and storage devices.
d. What is the difference between RAM and ROM?
e. Explain the purpose of cache in the computer.
f. Write a short note on database.
g. How many data types are used in Access 2016? Explain each with its functions.
h. Explain the different types of queries.
i. What is report?

5. Give the full forms of the following:

a. OMR ______________________
b. CRT ______________________
c. OCR ______________________
d. MICR ______________________
e. RAM ______________________
f. ROM ______________________
g. SRAM ______________________
h. RDRAM ______________________
i. PROM ______________________
j. MRAM ______________________

6 Graphics in HTML

In this chapter, we will learn:

⇒ HTML and Its Tags/Attributes

⇒ Images

⇒ Image Size, Alternative Text, Image Label, Alignment, Set Border, Background Image

⇒ Horizontal Rule

⇒ Creating Links

Dear friends, in your previous class, you learnt to build Web pages using HTML and its special codes known as tags. Now let's move ahead and learn to add graphics and links to a Web page. Before moving ahead, let us first review about HTML which you learnt in the previous class.

HTML

HTML stands for HyperText Markup Language which is a global programming language. It is used to create Web pages. HTML documents are made up of text content and special codes known as tags that tell Web browsers how to display the content. The Web developer uses HTML Tags to format the different parts of the Web document. The examples of tags are <B> to show bold text, <P> to indicate a new paragraph, and <HR> to display a horizontal rule across the page. You can also use HTML tags to specify headings, paragraphs, lists, tables and many more. HTML documents are identified by their .html or .htm file extensions.

HTML TAGS

HTML consists of text with special instructions known as tags. Each tag giving a specific instruction is enclosed by angle brackets < >. HTML tags tell a browser how to organize and present text, images and other Web page content.

Most tags have an opening tag and a closing tag. They are called containers that affect the text between the tags. The closing tag has a forward slash (/). However, some tags have only an opening tag. They are called empty tags.

Attributes

Some tags have attributes that offer options for the tag. Most attributes work by setting a numeric or descriptive value. Attributes always go inside the opening HTML tag, and it is a good form to enclose attribute values in quotation marks.

For example, the <FONT> tag has a COLOR attribute that allows you to change the colour of text.

```
<FONT COLOR="#0000FF">
```

IMAGES

HTML or Hyper Text Markup Language provides the facility to insert the images in the Web pages. Inserting graphic images into the Web enhances the look of the Web page. In fact, the addition of graphics in the Web page makes the document more interesting and easy-to-understand.

There are a number of image file formats available, which are supported by the Web browsers.

Some of the commonly used image file formats used widely for inserting image in the Web page are:

i. JPEG (Joint Photographic Expert Group), extension name: jpg;

ii. GIF (Graphics Interchange Format), extension name: gif;

iii. PNG (Portable Network Graphics), extension name: png;

JPEG and GIF are the two most popular types used on the Web. PNG is a newer arrival in the image file format world and is gaining popularity among Web developers. The current versions of all of today's popular Web browsers can display JPEG, GIF and PNG images.

The image you want to add to a Web page is stored in the same folder as the Web page; you can specify just the name of the image (example: cd.jpg) in order to add it to your Web page. If an image is stored in a sub-folder, you must specify the name of the sub-folder and the name of the image (example: images/cd.jpg).

ATTRIBUTES OF IMAGE

To insert, an image in a Web page, <IMG> tag which is an image element, is added to an HTML code. It is an empty element that can take attributes SRC, align, border, height, width and alt.

SRC

This is an attribute which is included in the <IMG> tag. It specifies the source or uniform resource locator of the image file. Uniform resource locator gives the path or the address of the file, which contains the image.

Syntax : <IMG SRC = "URL"> where URL specifies the address of the image file.

If the image file is in the same folder in which HTML document is there then URL contains the name of the file only.

If image file is elsewhere then complete path in src attribute needs to be specified.

Example : <IMG SRC = "C:\my pictures \toons \ mickey. jpg">

Align

Align attribute helps to position the image in the Web page. It can take any of these five values: left, right, top, bottom and middle. The align attribute is optional.

If align attribute is not used to specify the image location in the Web page then the browser will take a default value and the image will be displayed on the top-left corner of the Web page. The accompanying text on the page wraps around the image.

Syntax : <IMG SRC = "URL" align = "left/right/top/bottom/middle.">

Border

It allows to add the border around the image. The specified value decides the thickness of the border.

Syntax : <IMG SRC = "URL" border = "value" >

Height and Width

This can be specified by adding height and width attribute in the <IMG> tag. It is specified in pixels or as a percentage of the window size. If only one attribute is specified then the value of the other is automatically taken in the ratio of an original image. Image tag can be attributed with these attributes.

Syntax : <IMG SRC = "URL" height = "pixel" width = "pixels" >

INSERTING AN IMAGE

You can add images to your Web page to illustrate a topic. You can use image files from various sources like a digital camera, scanner, etc.

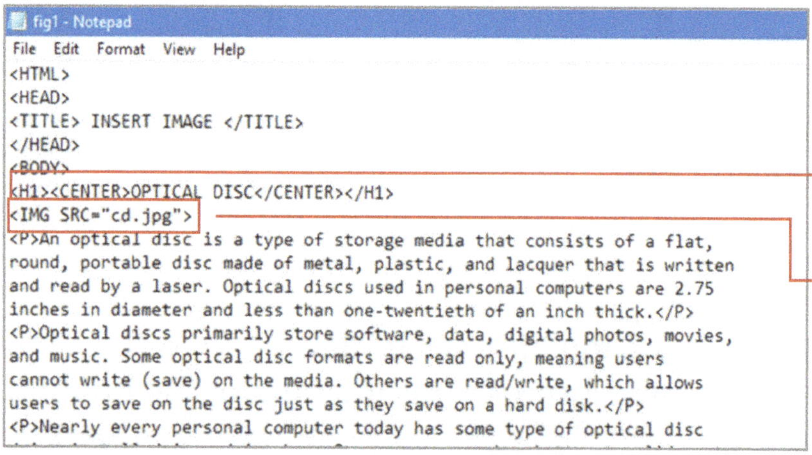

```
fig1 - Notepad
File  Edit  Format  View  Help
<HTML>
<HEAD>
<TITLE> INSERT IMAGE </TITLE>
</HEAD>
<BODY>
<H1><CENTER>OPTICAL DISC</CENTER></H1>
<IMG SRC="cd.jpg">
<P>An optical disc is a type of storage media that consists of a flat,
round, portable disc made of metal, plastic, and lacquer that is written
and read by a laser. Optical discs used in personal computers are 2.75
inches in diameter and less than one-twentieth of an inch thick.</P>
<P>Optical discs primarily store software, data, digital photos, movies,
and music. Some optical disc formats are read only, meaning users
cannot write (save) on the media. Others are read/write, which allows
users to save on the disc just as they save on a hard disk.</P>
<P>Nearly every personal computer today has some type of optical disc
```

You should store all of your Web pages and images in one folder in your computer.

1. Place the cursor where you want to insert the image.
2. Type <IMG SRC="?"> Replacing ? with the name of the image file.

Note

While typing the name of the image file in step 2, make sure that this cd.jpg file exists in the folder in which your Web page is stored. If not, then you have to specify the full path to the location of the file.

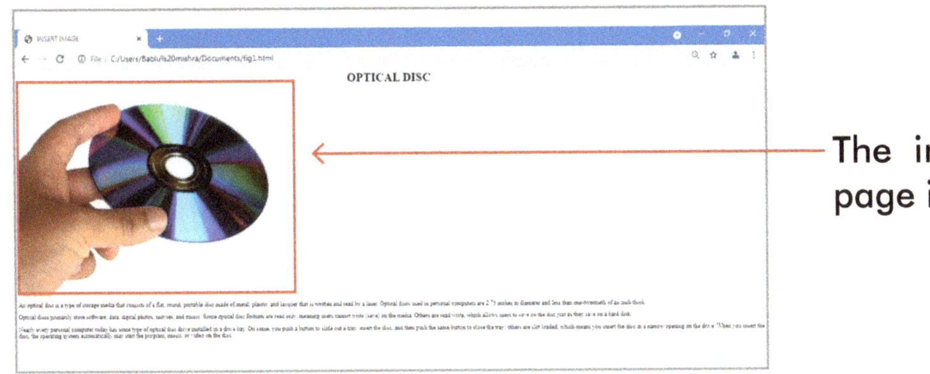

The image is inserted on the Web page in the Web browser.

Specify An Image Size

You can use Height and Width attributes in your HTML coding to change the size if your image appears too big or too small on a Web page. To maintain the image quality, one should always maintain the height and width ratio.

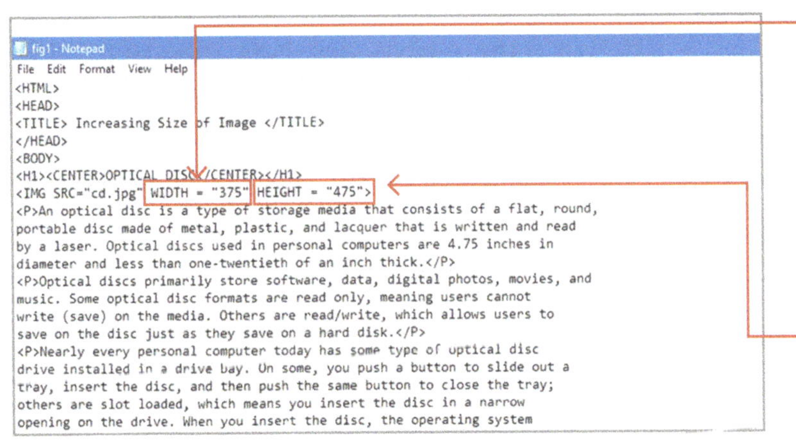

1. Click inside the <IMG> tag and type WIDTH="?", replacing ? with the width measurement you want to set.
2. Insert a space by pressing the Spacebar key.
3. Type HEIGHT="?", replacing ? with the height measurement you want to set.

You can also set the attribute value as a percentage. This tells the browser to display the image as a percentage of the browser window size. While giving a percentage value, be sure to follow it with a per cent sign (%).

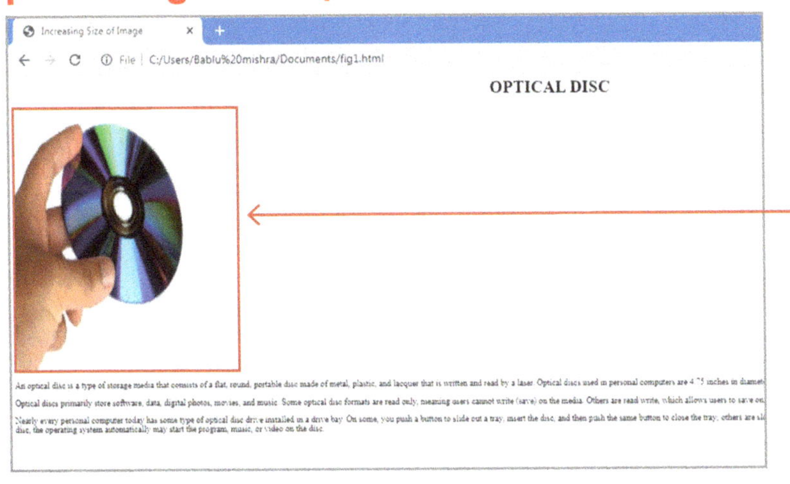

The image with the new size appears in the Web browser.

Alternative Text

Many a time, to load the files faster, viewer uses text only browser or may have turned off the images. So, the image will not appear in the browser window. The text written in alt attribute will appear as pop-up text in a browser.

Alt attribute can be added to have an alternative text which would appear in the page if the image doesn't appear. Attribute text should give a description of the image, which you have inserted.

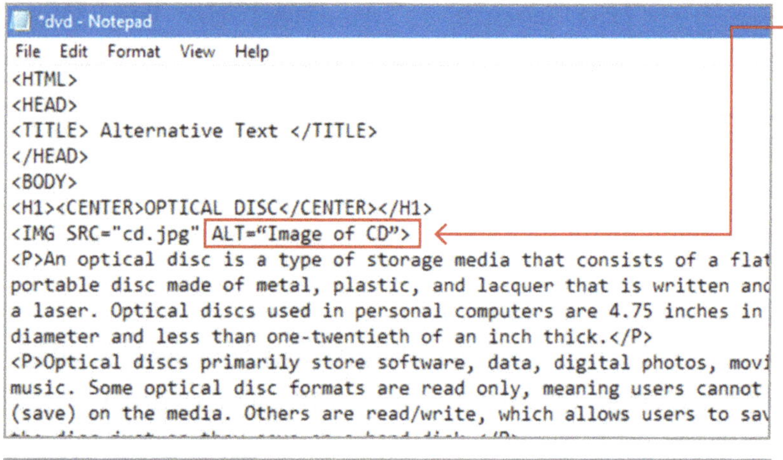

1. Click inside the <IMG> tag and type ALT="? ", replacing ? with alternative text describing the image.

For example, if you want to display the 'image of CD' as alternative text for image, type:

<IMG SRC = "cd.jpg" ALT="Image of CD">

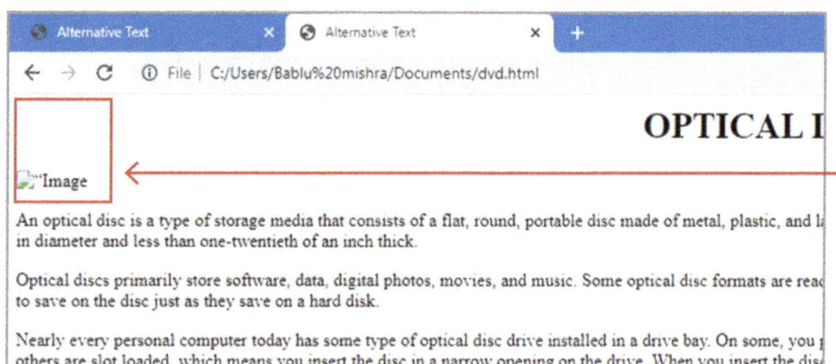

If the user's browser has images turned off, or if the image can't be found on the Web server, the browser displays the alternative text in place of the image.

Creating an Image Label

You can add an image label on a Web page. This image label will appear whenever the user moves the mouse pointer over a particular image. These labels offer detailed information about the image.

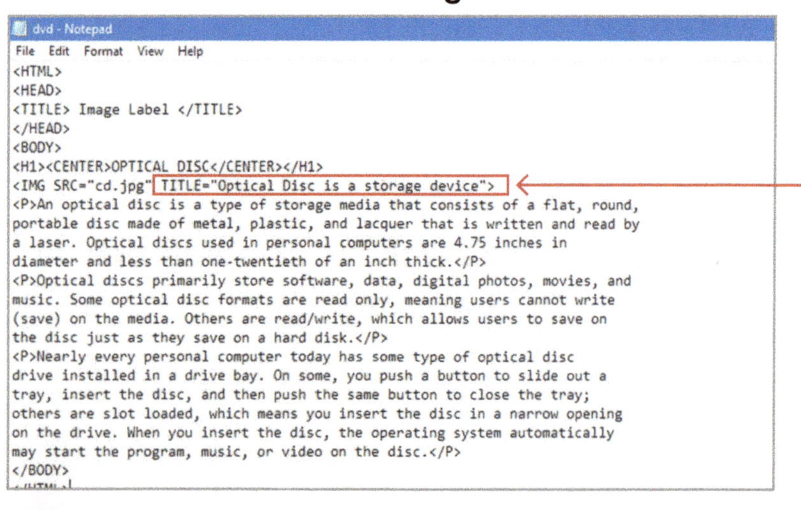

1. Click inside the <IMG> tag and type TITLE=" ? ", replacing ? with the image label you want to appear.

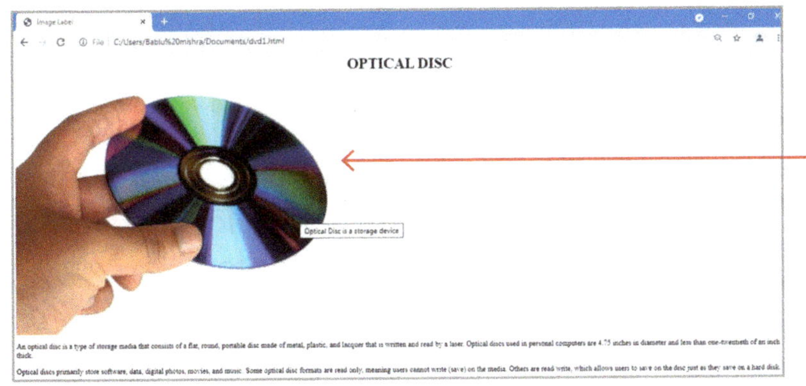

The label appears when you move the mouse pointer over the image in the browser window.

Working of Labels and alternative text is different. When images are turned off, alternative text appears on the page itself. When the user moves the mouse over the image, a label appears in a pop-up box.

Align an Image Horizontally

You can use the align attribute to control the horizontal positioning of an image on a page. These attributes also control how text wraps around the image.

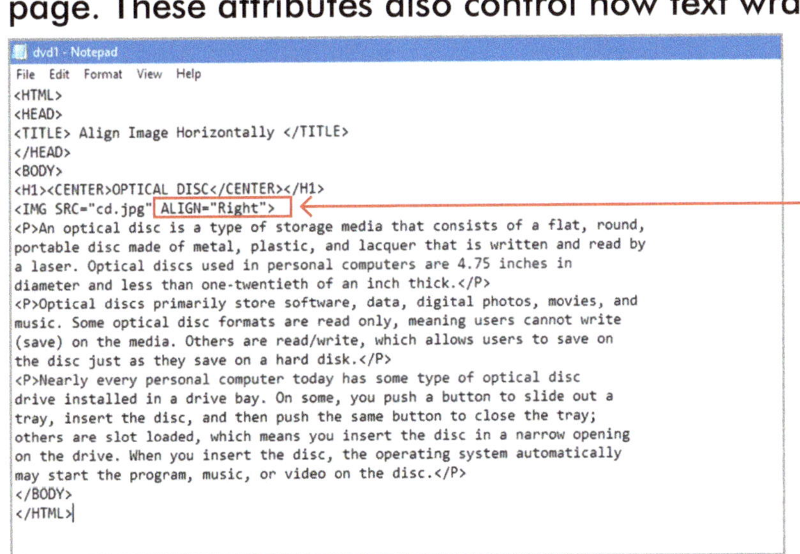

```
dvd1 - Notepad
File  Edit  Format  View  Help
<HTML>
<HEAD>
<TITLE> Align Image Horizontally </TITLE>
</HEAD>
<BODY>
<H1><CENTER>OPTICAL DISC</CENTER></H1>
<IMG SRC="cd.jpg" ALIGN="Right">
<P>An optical disc is a type of storage media that consists of a flat, round,
portable disc made of metal, plastic, and lacquer that is written and read by
a laser. Optical discs used in personal computers are 4.75 inches in
diameter and less than one-twentieth of an inch thick.</P>
<P>Optical discs primarily store software, data, digital photos, movies, and
music. Some optical disc formats are read only, meaning users cannot write
(save) on the media. Others are read/write, which allows users to save on
the disc just as they save on a hard disk.</P>
<P>Nearly every personal computer today has some type of optical disc
drive installed in a drive bay. On some, you push a button to slide out a
tray, insert the disc, and then push the same button to close the tray;
others are slot loaded, which means you insert the disc in a narrow opening
on the drive. When you insert the disc, the operating system automatically
may start the program, music, or video on the disc.</P>
</BODY>
</HTML>
```

1. Click inside the <IMG> tag and type ALIGN="?", replacing ? with the alignment you want to apply, either left or right.

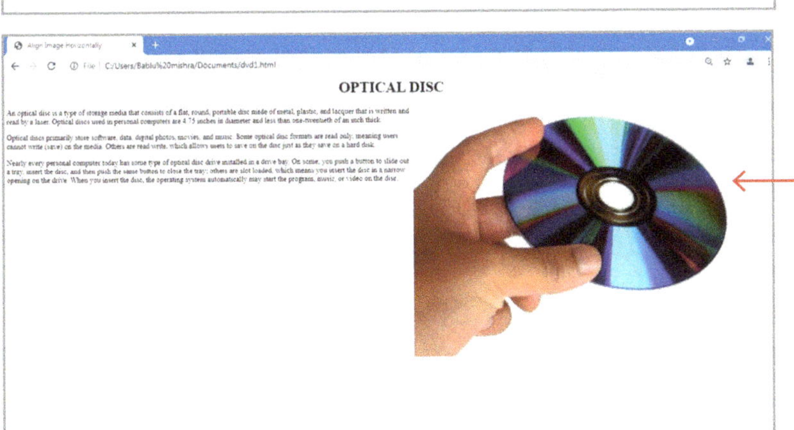

The Web browser aligns the image as specified.

In this example, the image is aligned to the right.

Align an Image Vertically

You can use the align attribute to control the vertical positioning of an image on a page. These alignment attributes are top, middle and bottom.

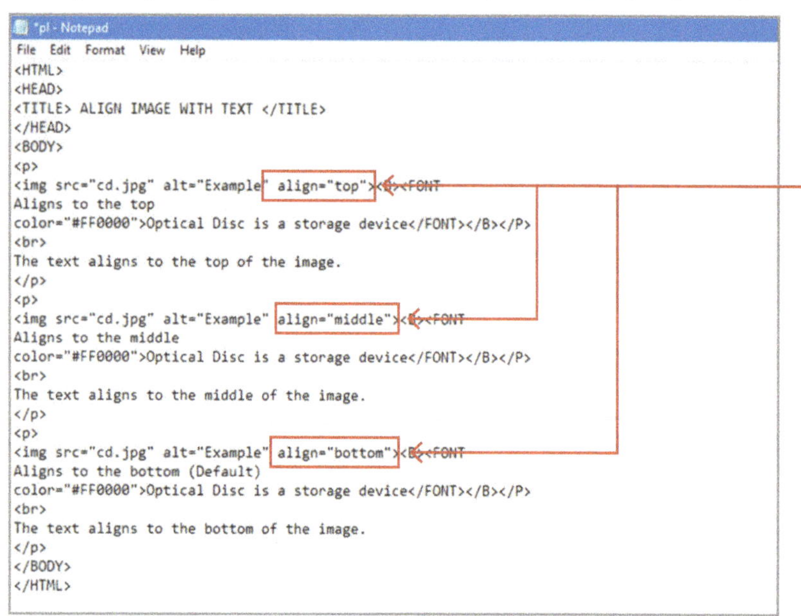

```
<HTML>
<HEAD>
<TITLE> ALIGN IMAGE WITH TEXT </TITLE>
</HEAD>
<BODY>
<p>
<img src="cd.jpg" alt="Example" align="top"><B><FONT
Aligns to the top
color="#FF0000">Optical Disc is a storage device</FONT></B></P>
<br>
The text aligns to the top of the image.
</p>
<p>
<img src="cd.jpg" alt="Example" align="middle"><B><FONT
Aligns to the middle
color="#FF0000">Optical Disc is a storage device</FONT></B></P>
<br>
The text aligns to the middle of the image.
</p>
<p>
<img src="cd.jpg" alt="Example" align="bottom"><B><FONT
Aligns to the bottom (Default)
color="#FF0000">Optical Disc is a storage device</FONT></B></P>
<br>
The text aligns to the bottom of the image.
</p>
</BODY>
</HTML>
```

1. Click inside the <IMG> tag and type ALIGN="?", replacing ? with the alignment you want to apply, either middle, top, or bottom (bottom is the default).

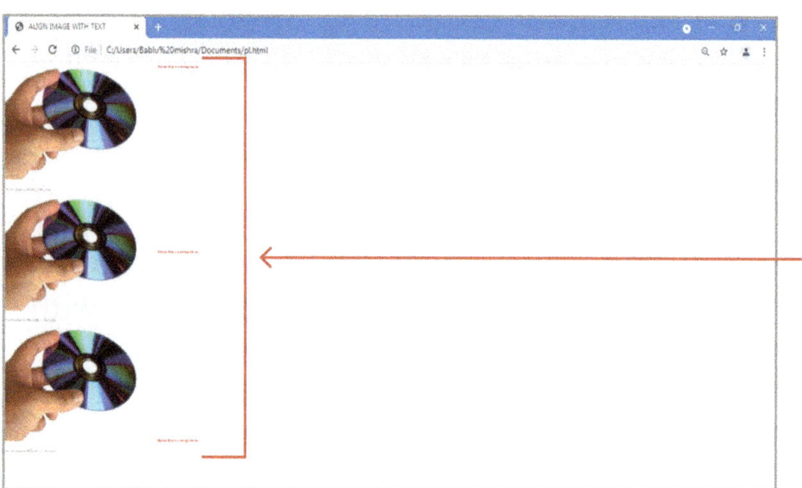

The image with added space around the left and right sides of the image appears in the Web browser.

Centring an Image Horizontally

You can centre your image on the page.

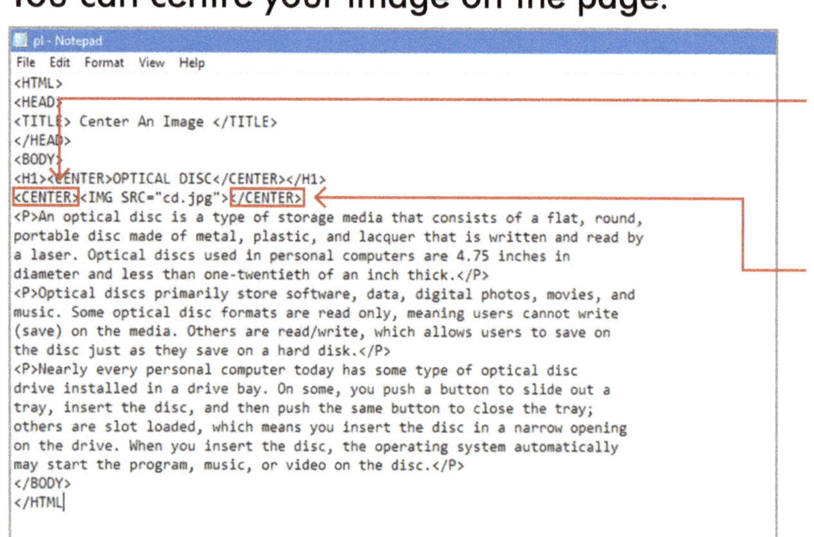

```
<HTML>
<HEAD>
<TITLE> Center An Image </TITLE>
</HEAD>
<BODY>
<H1><CENTER>OPTICAL DISC</CENTER></H1>
<CENTER><IMG SRC="cd.jpg"></CENTER>
<P>An optical disc is a type of storage media that consists of a flat, round,
portable disc made of metal, plastic, and lacquer that is written and read by
a laser. Optical discs used in personal computers are 4.75 inches in
diameter and less than one-twentieth of an inch thick.</P>
<P>Optical discs primarily store software, data, digital photos, movies, and
music. Some optical disc formats are read only, meaning users cannot write
(save) on the media. Others are read/write, which allows users to save on
the disc just as they save on a hard disk.</P>
<P>Nearly every personal computer today has some type of optical disc
drive installed in a drive bay. On some, you push a button to slide out a
tray, insert the disc, and then push the same button to close the tray;
others are slot loaded, which means you insert the disc in a narrow opening
on the drive. When you insert the disc, the operating system automatically
may start the program, music, or video on the disc.</P>
</BODY>
</HTML>
```

1. Type <CENTER> in front of the image you want to align in centre.
2. Type </CENTER> after the image you want to align in centre.

A centre-aligned image appears in the Web browser.

Wrapping Text between Two Images

To change the layout of your Web page, you can wrap text between two images.

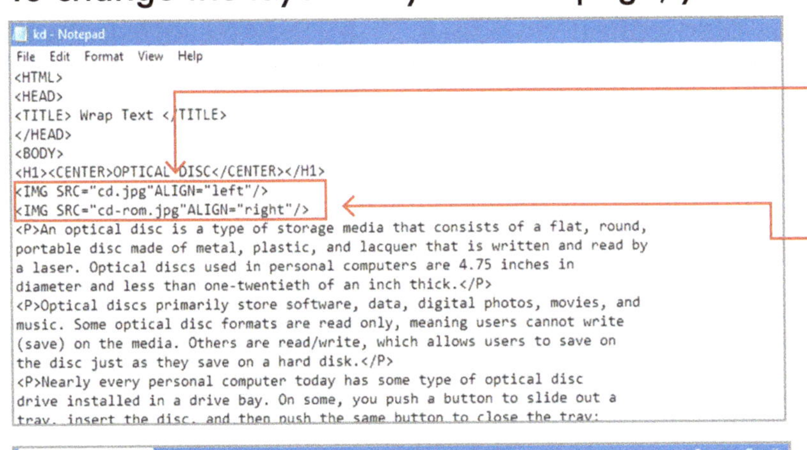

```
<HTML>
<HEAD>
<TITLE> Wrap Text </TITLE>
</HEAD>
<BODY>
<H1><CENTER>OPTICAL DISC</CENTER></H1>
<IMG SRC="cd.jpg"ALIGN="left"/>
<IMG SRC="cd-rom.jpg"ALIGN="right"/>
<P>An optical disc is a type of storage media that consists of a flat, round,
portable disc made of metal, plastic, and lacquer that is written and read by
a laser. Optical discs used in personal computers are 4.75 inches in
diameter and less than one-twentieth of an inch thick.</P>
<P>Optical discs primarily store software, data, digital photos, movies, and
music. Some optical disc formats are read only, meaning users cannot write
(save) on the media. Others are read/write, which allows users to save on
the disc just as they save on a hard disk.</P>
<P>Nearly every personal computer today has some type of optical disc
drive installed in a drive bay. On some, you push a button to slide out a
tray, insert the disc, and then push the same button to close the tray;
```

1. In the <IMG> tag for the image you want to appear on the left side of text, type ALIGN=left.
2. In the <IMG> tag for the image you want to appear on the right side of text, type ALIGN=right.

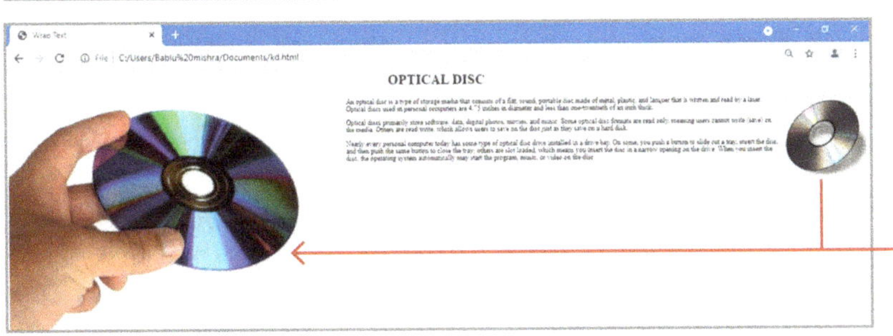

The text wrapped around the two images appears in the Web browser.

Set an Image Border

A border can be added to an image to make it look more attractive on the page. The thickness of the border can be defined in pixels.

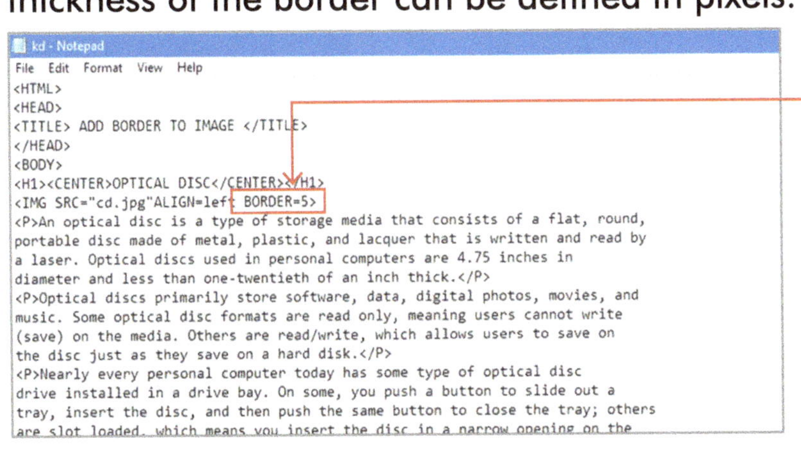

```
<HTML>
<HEAD>
<TITLE> ADD BORDER TO IMAGE </TITLE>
</HEAD>
<BODY>
<H1><CENTER>OPTICAL DISC</CENTER></H1>
<IMG SRC="cd.jpg"ALIGN=left BORDER=5>
<P>An optical disc is a type of storage media that consists of a flat, round,
portable disc made of metal, plastic, and lacquer that is written and read by
a laser. Optical discs used in personal computers are 4.75 inches in
diameter and less than one-twentieth of an inch thick.</P>
<P>Optical discs primarily store software, data, digital photos, movies, and
music. Some optical disc formats are read only, meaning users cannot write
(save) on the media. Others are read/write, which allows users to save on
the disc just as they save on a hard disk.</P>
<P>Nearly every personal computer today has some type of optical disc
drive installed in a drive bay. On some, you push a button to slide out a
tray, insert the disc, and then push the same button to close the tray; others
are slot loaded, which means you insert the disc in a narrow opening on the
```

1. Click inside the <IMG> tag and type BORDER= ?, replacing ? with the thickness of the border you want to use in pixels like 1, 2, 3...

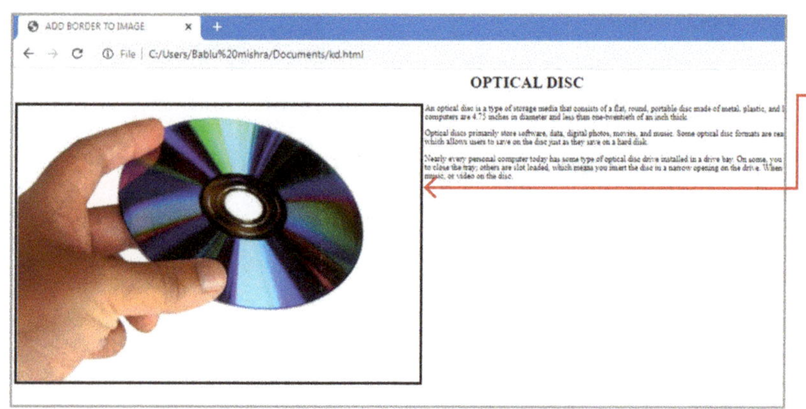

The Web browser displays the image with a border around it on your Web page.

To remove an existing border, specify the width with number 0. For example, <IMG SRC = "cd.jpg" BORDER = 0>

Adding Space around the Image

You can add space between images and text to make the page more visually appealing and easier to read. This amount of space is also called padding. The HSPACE attribute is used to control padding on the left and right sides of an image. The VSPACE attribute is used to control the padding above and below an image.

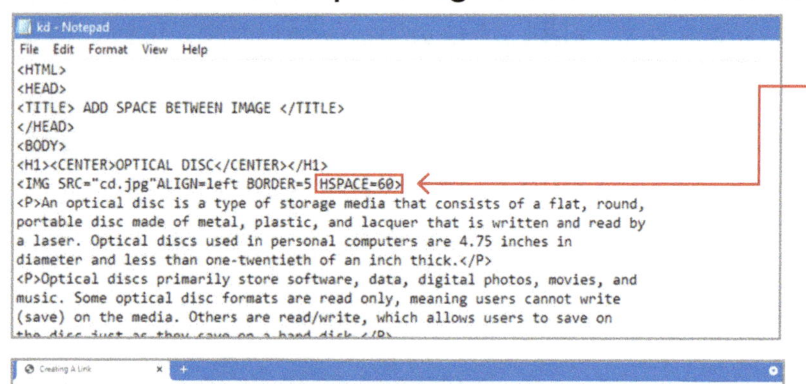

```
kd - Notepad
File  Edit  Format  View  Help
<HTML>
<HEAD>
<TITLE> ADD SPACE BETWEEN IMAGE </TITLE>
</HEAD>
<BODY>
<H1><CENTER>OPTICAL DISC</CENTER></H1>
<IMG SRC="cd.jpg"ALIGN=left BORDER=5 HSPACE=60>
<P>An optical disc is a type of storage media that consists of a flat, round,
portable disc made of metal, plastic, and lacquer that is written and read by
a laser. Optical discs used in personal computers are 4.75 inches in
diameter and less than one-twentieth of an inch thick.</P>
<P>Optical discs primarily store software, data, digital photos, movies, and
music. Some optical disc formats are read only, meaning users cannot write
(save) on the media. Others are read/write, which allows users to save on
```

1. Click inside the <IMG> tag and type HSPACE = ?, replacing ? with the amount of space you want to add to both the left and right sides of the image in pixels.

The image with the specified margin around it appears in the Web browser.

Adding a Background Image

A background image can be added to improve the layout of the entire page by setting an attribute in the <BODY> tag.

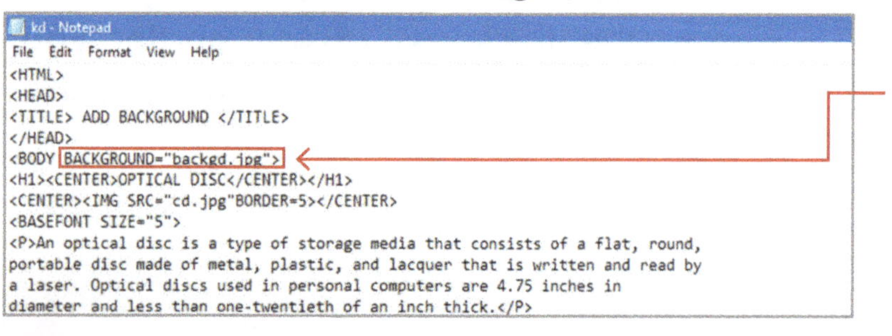

```
kd - Notepad
File  Edit  Format  View  Help
<HTML>
<HEAD>
<TITLE> ADD BACKGROUND </TITLE>
</HEAD>
<BODY BACKGROUND="backgd.jpg">
<H1><CENTER>OPTICAL DISC</CENTER></H1>
<CENTER><IMG SRC="cd.jpg"BORDER=5></CENTER>
<BASEFONT SIZE="5">
<P>An optical disc is a type of storage media that consists of a flat, round,
portable disc made of metal, plastic, and lacquer that is written and read by
a laser. Optical discs used in personal computers are 4.75 inches in
diameter and less than one-twentieth of an inch thick.</P>
```

1. Click inside the <BODY> tag and type BACKGROUND="?", replacing ? with the location and name of the background file on your computer.

The Web page with a background image is displayed by the Web browser.

NOTE: Adding background images increases the loading time of a Web page.

HORIZONTAL RULE

You can add a solid line or horizontal rule across your page to separate the blocks of information. Horizontal rules must occupy a line by themselves and cannot appear within a paragraph. The <HR> tag specifies that a horizontal rule be drawn across the page. The attributes of Horizontal Rule are:

ELEMENTS	USES
ALIGN	It aligns the horizontal rule. The default alignment is the left.
NOSHADE	It removes the 3-D effect to horizontal rule.
SIZE	It defines the thickness of rule. The default size is 1.
WIDTH	It defines the width of horizontal rule in pixels or in per cent relative to the page width.

Syntax :

<HR ALIGN = "LEFT" NOSHADE SIZE = "X" WIDTH = "Y">

<HR ALIGN = "RIGHT" NOSHADE SIZE= "X" WIDTH = "Y">

<HR ALIGN = "CENTER" NOSHADE SIZE = "X" WIDTH = "Y">

(**Note :** 'X' is the thickness and 'y' is the width in pixels.)

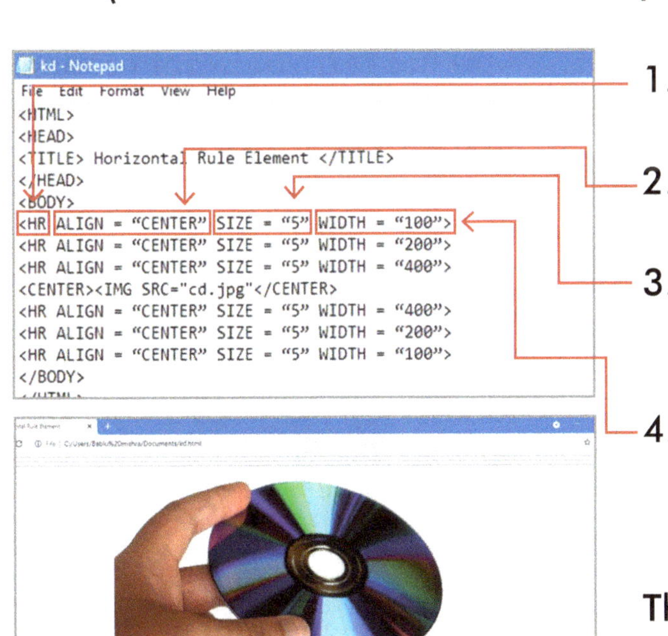

1. Type <HR> where you want to insert a horizontal rule on your Web page.
2. Type ALIGN = "?" in the <HR> tag, replacing ? with the left, centre or right alignment.
3. Type SIZE = "?" in the <HR> tag, replacing ? with the thickness you want to use for the horizontal rule.
4. Type WIDTH = "?" in the <HR> tag, replacing ? with the percentage of the page you want the rule to extend across.

The Web browser displays the result of horizontal rule.

CREATING LINKS

Hyperlinks or simply links are all those underlined words or images that you see in the Web page. It will take you from one Web page to another Web page when you click on them. Making links in HTML is really very simple. So, let's make a link to the Moserbaer Web site. Moserbaer is a big company which makes optical discs.

To start, you need a pair of anchor tags, <a> and </a>, which tell the browser that "Hey, here is the beginning and the end of a link". Between the anchor tags, you want to put the text that will be your link. In this example, we have used the words "Optical Disc":

<a> Optical Disc </a>

But wait, that's not all. The Web browser doesn't know what Web page you want to link to. So, in order to tell the Web browser what page you want to link to, you need to use a hypertext reference attribute, HREF, as well as a URL for the value. The URL, which stands for Uniformed Resource Locator, is nothing more than the Web address that is displayed in the location bar of the Web browser.

<a	HREF=	"URL goes here">	write some text to identify the link	</a>
↑	↑	↑	↑	↑
start tag	attribute	value	this will be your link	end tag

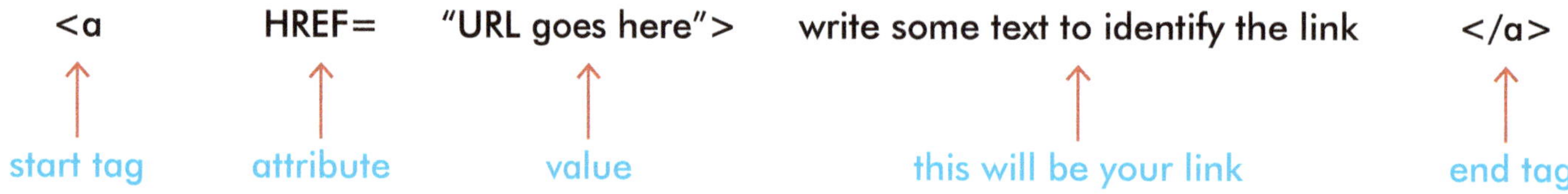

Here is the HTML for making a link to the Moserbaer Web site.

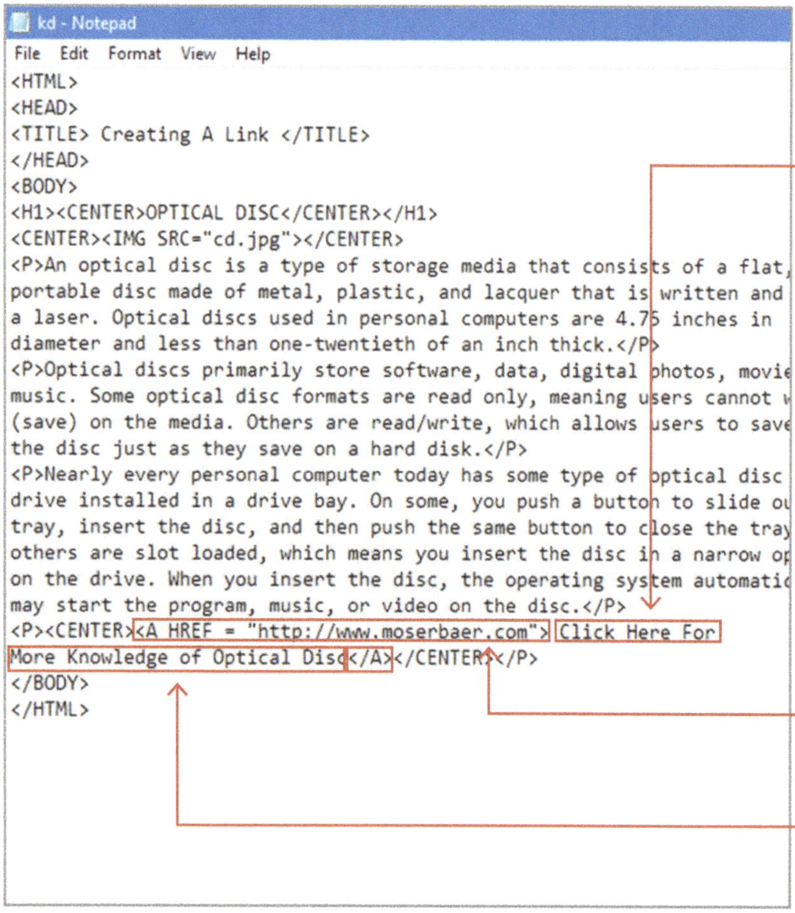
```
kd - Notepad
File  Edit  Format  View  Help
<HTML>
<HEAD>
<TITLE> Creating A Link </TITLE>
</HEAD>
<BODY>
<H1><CENTER>OPTICAL DISC</CENTER></H1>
<CENTER><IMG SRC="cd.jpg"></CENTER>
<P>An optical disc is a type of storage media that consists of a flat,
portable disc made of metal, plastic, and lacquer that is written and
a laser. Optical discs used in personal computers are 4.75 inches in
diameter and less than one-twentieth of an inch thick.</P>
<P>Optical discs primarily store software, data, digital photos, movie
music. Some optical disc formats are read only, meaning users cannot w
(save) on the media. Others are read/write, which allows users to save
the disc just as they save on a hard disk.</P>
<P>Nearly every personal computer today has some type of optical disc
drive installed in a drive bay. On some, you push a button to slide ou
tray, insert the disc, and then push the same button to close the tray
others are slot loaded, which means you insert the disc in a narrow op
on the drive. When you insert the disc, the operating system automatic
may start the program, music, or video on the disc.</P>
<P><CENTER><A HREF = "http://www.moserbaer.com"> Click Here For
More Knowledge of Optical Disc</A></CENTER></P>
</BODY>
</HTML>
```

1. Type the text you want readers to select in order to display another Web page.
2. Type <A HREF= "?"> in front of the text, replacing ? with the address of the Web page you want to display.
3. Type </A> after the text.

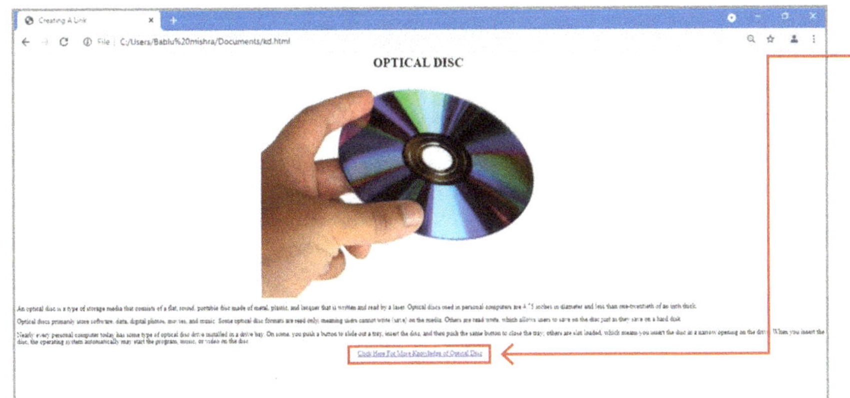

The text link displays and appears coloured and underlined in the Web browser.

When you place the mouse pointer on the image, the linked Web address displays in the status bar.

To display the Web site, click on the link.

When the visitors select or click on the link, the Website you specified appears.

LET'S HAVE A LOOK

- HTML stands for HyperText Markup Language.
- HTML documents are made up of text content and special codes known as tag.
- Most tags have an opening tag and a closing tag.
- Attributes always go inside the opening HTML tag, and it is good form to enclose attribute values in quotation marks.
- HTML provides the facility to insert the images in the Web pages.
- JPEG and GIF are the two most popular types used on the Web.
- PNG is a newer arrival in the image file format world and is gaining popularity among Web developers.
- IMG stands for 'Image Element'.
- SRC stands for 'source'. It is an attribute, a command inside a command.
- Large-size images can take a long time to display, especially if the Internet connection speed is slow.
- You should store all of your Web pages and images in one folder in your computer.
- Alt attribute can be added to have an alternative text which would appear in the page if the image doesn't appear.
- Hyperlinks or simply links are all those underlined words or images that you see in the Web page. It will take you from one Web page to another Web page when you click on them.

Acronyms

HTML	:	HyperText Markup Language
JPEG	:	Joint Photographic Experts Group
GIF	:	Graphics Interchange Format
IMG	:	Image
SRC	:	Source
PNG	:	Portable Network Graphics

1. Multiple Choice Questions

Tick (✓) the correct answer:

a. Each tag in HTML is enclosed by:
   i. < > ☐ ii. ' ' ☐ iii. [ ] ☐

b. A tag for horizontal line:
   i. <TR> ☐ ii. <UL> ☐ iii. <HR> ☐

c. File name extension used by Joint Photographic Expert Group file:
   i. .doc ☐ ii. .png ☐ iii. .jpg ☐

d. A tag that specifies the source or uniform resource locator of the image file:
   i. <IMG> ☐ ii. <SRC> ☐ iii. <TR> ☐

e. A tag that created an ordered list:
   i. <HR> ☐ ii.
 ☐ iii. <OL> ☐

f. Which of these is the attribute for IMG tag?
   i. ALT ☐ ii. <OL> ☐ iii. <TT> ☐

g. Which attribute is used to control padding on the left and right sides of an image?
   i. VSPACE ☐ ii. Border ☐ iii. HSPACE ☐

h. A tag that tells the browser about the beginning and the end of a link:
   i. <HR> ☐ ii. <A> ☐ iii. <OL> ☐

2. Fill in the blanks:

a. ______________ stands for HyperText Markup Language.

b. HTML consists of text with special instructions known as ______________.

c. Some tags have ______________ that offer options for the tag.

d. ______________ specifies the source or uniform resource locator of the image file.

e. ______________ and ______________ are the two most popular file formats used on the Web.

f. File extension for JPEG is ______________.

3. Answer the following questions

(i) Answer each in a few lines:

a. What do IMG and SRC stand for?

b. What do JPEG and PNG stand for?

c. What are IMG and SRC?

d. What are anchors?

(ii) Answer each comprehensively:

a. What do you mean by HTML tags and its attributes?

b. What is the use of IMG and SRC?

c. Differentiate between alternative text and image label.

d. What is the use of horizontal line?

e. What are the advantages of links in the Web page?

f. Write the tags used for:

i. To add an image

ii. Alternative text

iii. Centre an image

iv. Add Horizontal rule

Type the following HTML code using Notepad and save it as an HTML file. View the output in your Web browser.

```
<HTML>
<HEAD>
<TITLE>VIDEO JUNCTION</TITLE>
<BODY BGCOLOR = "YELLOW" TEXT = "BLUE">
<BASEFONT FACE = "ARIAL" SIZE = "5">
<FONT FACE = "HELVETICA" SIZE = "7" COLOR = "RED">
<CENTER> MOVIES GALLERY </CENTER></FONT>
```

```
<CENTER> Latest Movies and Songs </CENTER>
<HR SIZE = "10" NOSHADE>
<FONT FACE = "IMPACT" SIZE = "7" COLOR = "GREEN"><U><I>
LATEST MOVIES : </I></U></FONT><BR>
1. Avengers <BR>
2. Spiderman <BR>
3. Joker <BR>
4. Batman <BR>
<HR>
<FONT FACE = "IMPACT" SIZE = "7" COLOR = "GREEN"><U><I>
NEW SONGS : </I></U></FONT><BR>
1. Closer <BR>
2. Shape of You <BR>
3. Devil Doesn't Bargain <BR>
4. Just the Way You Are <BR>
<HR>
Contact: videojunction@gmail.com
</BODY>
<HTML>
```

- Add an image of your favourite actor or actress above the first horizontal line and it should be centre-aligned.
- Write your own name in the last line "This Web page is designed by ....."
- In the last, give a text link to the Hollywood Web site. For this, write the text "Click here to know more about the latest movies". The Web site address is "www.hollywood.com".
- Save the Web page as 'Video Junction'.

7 Visual Basic - Visual Studio 2017

In this chapter, we will learn:

⇒ What is Visual Basic?
⇒ Event-driven Programming
⇒ Starting VS Express
⇒ Components of the VB window
⇒ Various Controls in VB
⇒ Opening and Existing a VB program in VS Express

VISUAL BASIC

The language BASIC provides text-only environment. Visual Basic is an extended version of the language. Some of the features of Visual Basic are stated below.

- Unlike BASIC, it is a visual and event-driven programming language.
- It is simple and easy to learn.
- It provides a visual and graphical environment for programming and developing Graphical User Interface (GUI) applications.

The first ever version of Visual Basic was released by Microsoft Corporation in 1991 with the help of Alan Cooper. Since then, there have been total six different versions of Visual Basic released–1.0, 1.0 for MS-DOS, 2.0, 3.0, 4.0, 5.0 and 6.0. The latest version was released in 1998, after which Microsoft moved Visual Basic to the .NET Framework which included total seven versions–Visual Basic. NET, Visual Basic .NET 2003, Visual Basic 2005, Visual Basic 2008, Visual Basic 2010, Visual Basic 2012 and Visual Basic 2017.

Before we discuss and try to understand the working of this language, you must know the meaning of the term event-driven programming.

EVENT-DRIVEN PROGRAMMING

Whenever some action is performed on a graphical component, an event is generated. For example, while filling a form, you provide various kinds of details including your personal and professional details, and to do so, you perform various actions, such as key press, mouse-click, etc. To every such action, the application on which you are working, responds accordingly. Now, in the application, you may click on a certain object randomly.

So, in order to respond to these random actions, each object has to be programmed independently. These responses that the application gives on the actions you perform are known as events and the programming executed to respond to these events independently is known as event-driven programming.

Visual Basic is one such programming language which contains many subprograms, each having its own programming codes and each able to be executed independently. These programs are executed at the same time and can be linked together in one way or the other.

Alan Cooper known as the "Father of Visual Basic"

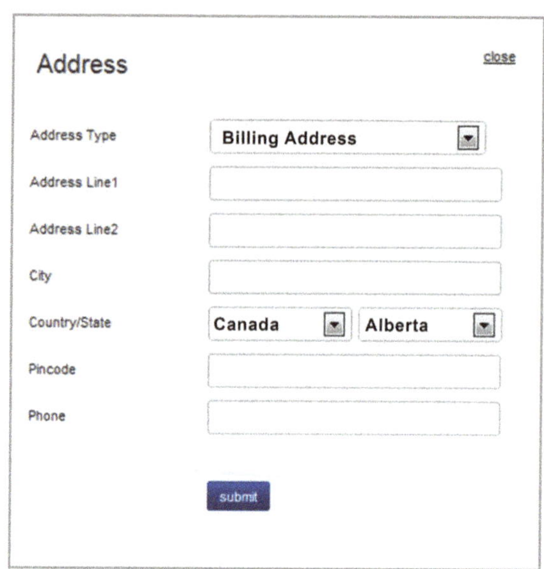

A basic address form

VISUAL STUDIO 2017 EXPRESS FOR WINDOWS DESKTOP

To create a Visual Basic program, you will have to download an integrated development environment (IDE) named Visual Studio. It is like a text editor for Visual Basic programs as well as other corresponding languages, such as Visual C#, Visual C++ and SQL Server.

You can download and run the VS Express application program easily from the following link.

https://visual-basic-express.soft32.com/free-download/?dm=0

STARTING VS EXPRESS

To open the VS Express application, follow the steps given below.

Step 1 : Open the Start menu and scroll down to the letter V.

Step 2 : Select the VS Express for Windows Desktop option form the list. The Start Page in the Microsoft Visual Studio Express 2017 Windows Desktop window appears.

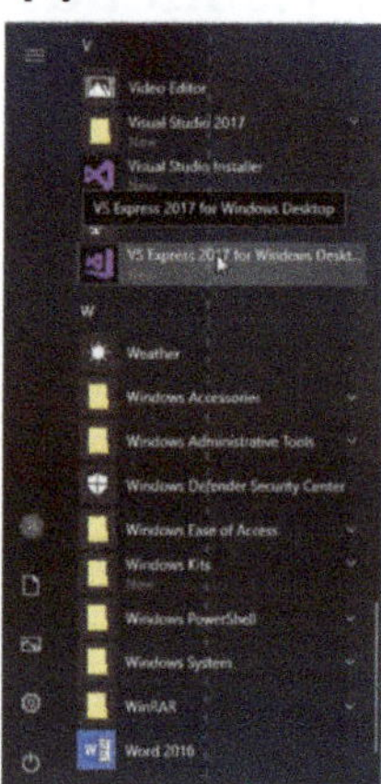

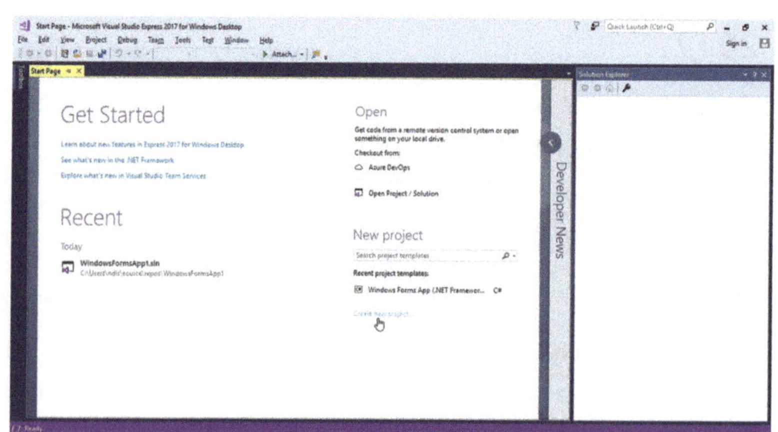

Opening Visual Studio

Step 3 : Click Create new project option in the New project section. The New Project dialog box appears.

Step 4 : Select the Visual basic option from the Installed drop-down list on the left side of the dialog box.

Step 5 : Select the Windows Form App (.NET Framework) option in the middle section.

Step 6 : Type a name for the file in the Name text box and set the location of the file.

Creating a new Visual Basic project

Step 7 : Click OK. The Windows Forms App window appears with the project in the sub window.

COMPONENTS OF THE WINDOW

Given below in the image are displayed the components of the Windows Forms App window.

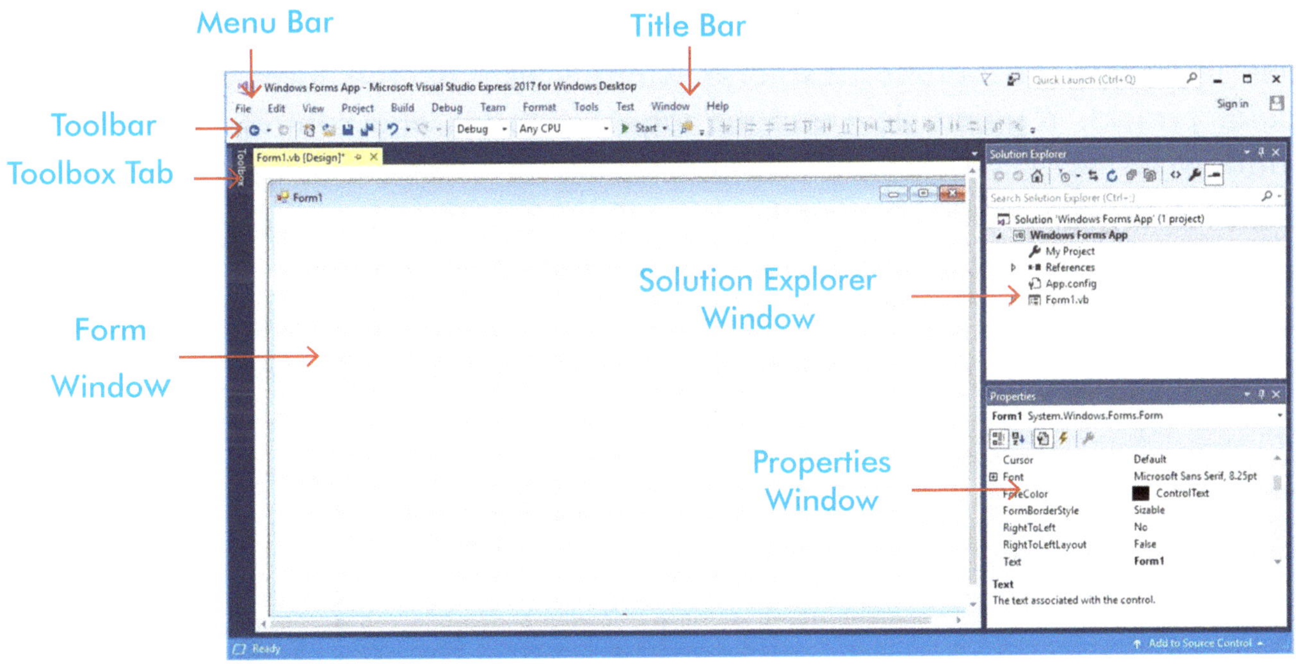

Components of the window

Read below to know about all the components.

Title Bar : The title bar, present at the top of the window, displays the name of the project along with the application name. It also contains the Quick Launch search text box and Control buttons.

Menu Bar : The menu bar, placed just below the title bar, contains various menus, including File, Edit, View, Project, Build, Debug, Team, Format, Tools, Test, Window and Help menus. Each menu provides various options that allow you to perform different operations.

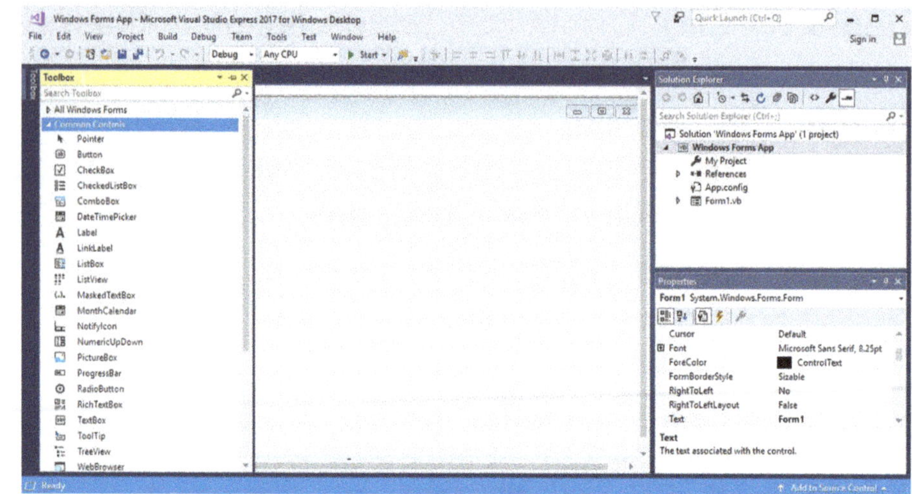

Toolbox containing the Common Controls

Tool Bar : The toolbar, present below the menu bar, contains the frequently used task options such as Navigate backwards, New Project, Open File, Save, Save All and so on.

Toolbox Tab : The Toolbox tab contains the Toolbox which contains controls available in Visual Basic such as Pointer, Button, Label, ListView, TextBox, etc., you can close it by clicking the Close (×) button.

Form Window : A form is the basic component of a Visual Basic program which allows you to interact with the application. The Form window provides you with a blank form on which you can place various controls to create an application and the forms and controls together form the GUI of a Visual Basic application.

Solution Explorer Window : A solution is an arrangement for putting the Visual Basic projects in order. The Solution Explorer window lists all the forms and controls of a particular project. You can view and manage the forms and controls in a project using this window.

Code Editor Window : The Code Editor window is used to write and edit the Visual Basic code. To open this window, simply double-click the Form window.

Properties Window : The Properties of a form describes the characteristics of any control inserted in the form, such as its colour, size, name, font and caption.

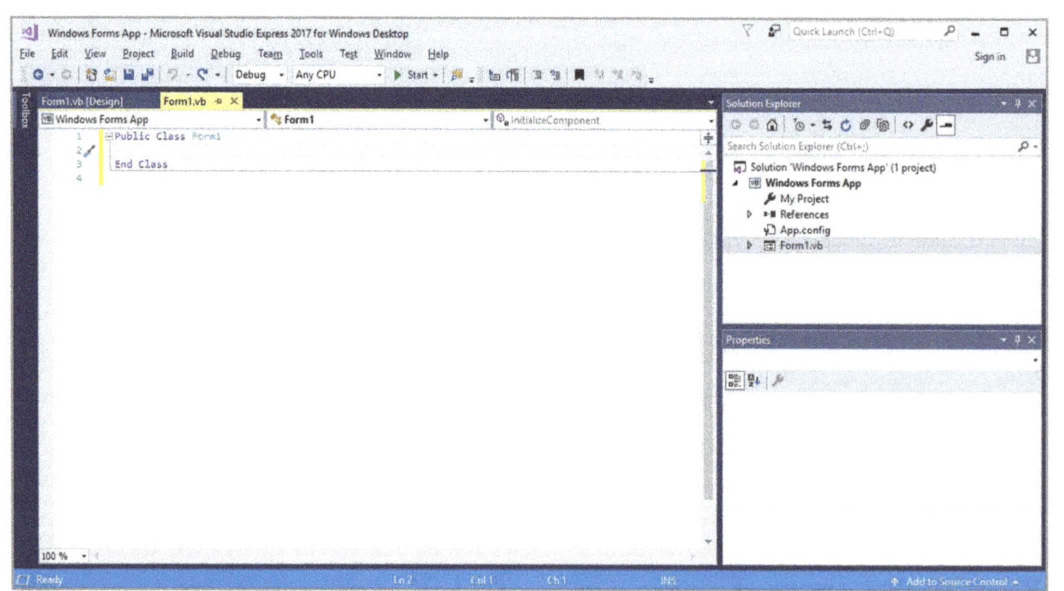

Code Editor Window

A project is a collection of forms, controls and modules.

MODES OF THE WINDOW

There are three different modes of the VS Express application window–design mode, in which an application is designed; run mode, in which an application is executed and break/suspended mode, which appears when the execution of an application is halted due to some errors.

PROPERTIES, METHODS AND EVENT

Every control that you insert in a program code contains a set of properties, methods and events. The properties define the characteristics of a control; the methods define the actions that can be performed on the control and the events define the occurrence of actions performed by the user on the control.

VARIOUS CONTROLS IN VB

The objects which are placed or inserted in a form to receive input and display output are known as the controls. Let us learn about some of the most commonly used controls in VB.

Properties	Methods	Events
Name: to rename the form using the Name property **Text:** to specify the title of the form **ForeColor:** to set the colour of the text and graphics to be displayed on the form **BackColor:** to set the background colour of the form	**Show:** to make the form visible on the screen **Hide:** to make the form invisible from the screen **Activate:** to activate the form **Close:** to close the form	**Load:** occurs when the form is loaded into the memory and displayed on the screen at run time **Disposed:** occurs when the form is closed

Label Control

The Label control is used to display some information on the interface which cannot be altered during the execution of the program.

Some of the properties, methods and events associated with the Label control are explained below.

Properties	Methods	Events
Name: to give a name to the label which is used for refer to the label while writing the program	**Show:** to make the label visible on the screen	**Click:** occurs when you click on the label

Text: to specify the text to be displayed on the label **Font:** to set the font attributes of the text to be displayed in the label **ForeColor:** to set the colour of the text to be displayed in the label **BackColor:** to set the background colour of the label	**Hide:** to make the label invisible from the screen **Focus:** sets input focus to the label	**DoubleClick:** occurs when you doubleclick on the label

Text Box Control

The Text Box control is used to receive input as well as display output to the user.

Some of the properties, methods and events associated with the TextBox control are explained below.

Properties	Methods	Events
Name: to give a name to the text box **MaxLength:** to specify the maximum length of the text that can be entered in the text box **Font:** to set the font attributes of the text to be displayed in the text box **Password Char**: to hide the text with special characters (like*) usually for a password or any other code	**Clear:** clears all the text from the text box **Copy:** copies the selected text in the text box and stores it in the Clipboard **Focus:** sets input focus to the text box **Show:** to make the text box visible on the screen **Hide:** to make the text box invisible on the screen	**Text Changed:** occurs when you change the text of the text box **Click:** occurs when you click on the text box **DoubleClick:** occurs when you doubleclick on the text box

Button Control

The Button control is used to give commands to the program. When the button is clicked, an event occurs and the program is executed accordingly.

Some of the properties, methods and events associated with the Button control are explained here.

Properties	Methods	Events
Name: to give a name to the button **Text:** to specify the text to be displayed on the button **Font:** to set the font attributes of the text to be displayed in the button	**Select:** to activate the button control **Show:** to make the button control visible on the screen **Hide:** to hide the button control from the screen	**Text Changed:** occurs when you change the text appearing in the button control **Click:** occurs when you click on the button **Double Click:** occurs when you double-click on the button

WORKING WITH THE CONTROLS

Let us now learn to work with the controls. You can insert a control and change its properties in the form as well as in the run mode.

Inserting Controls in the Form

To add a control in the form, follow the steps given below:

Step 1 : Click the Toolbox tab. The Toolbox appears with various tools on it.

Note that, in this image the Toolbox is pinned to the screen by clicking the ( ) button.

Step 2 : Click on the desired tool from the list. For example, we select the option Text Box.

Step 3 : Click and drag the mouse in the form to insert the selected control.

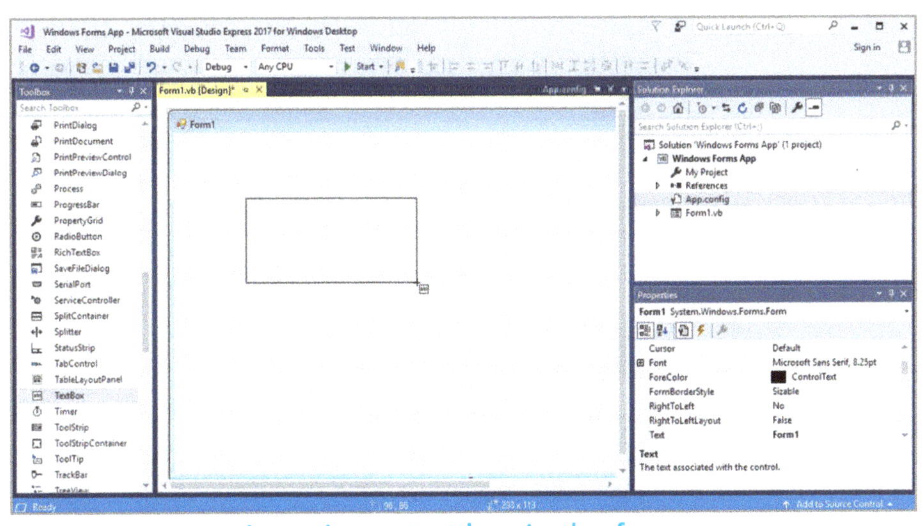

Inserting a text box in the form

Do you know 

To insert a control in the form, you can also double-click on the icon of the desired control in the Toolbox. The control will be placed on the top left corner of the form.

Now, you can resize the control, relocate the control and define the properties of the control in the form.

To move a control, place the cursor on it and when the cursor turns into ( ), click and drag the control to the desired position.

- To resize the control, place the cursor on the edge and when the cursor changes into (⟺), click and drag the pointers horizontally, vertically or diagonally.

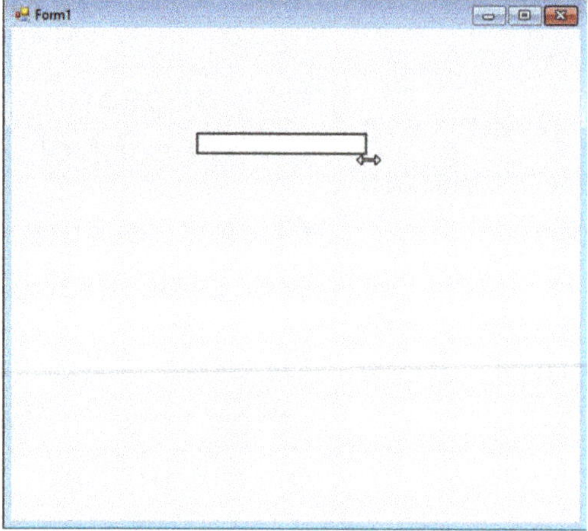

Resizing a control

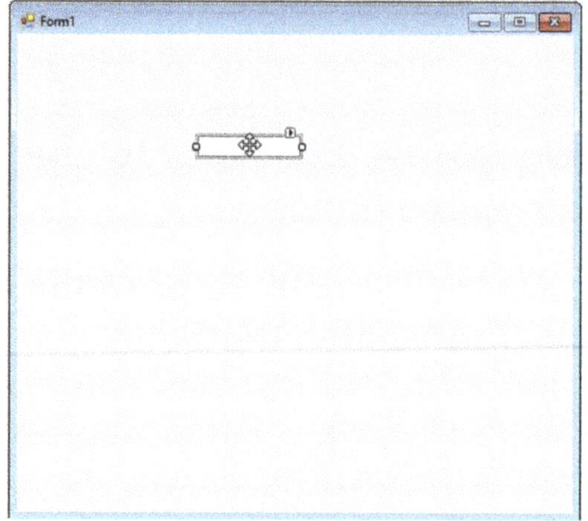

Moving a control

Changing the Properties of a Control

To change the properties of the controls in design mode, follow the steps given below:

Step 1 : Select the control whose property you want to change.

Step 2 : Locate and set/change the desired property inside the Properties window. For example, we change the Font, Text and Max Length properties of the text box we inserted previously.

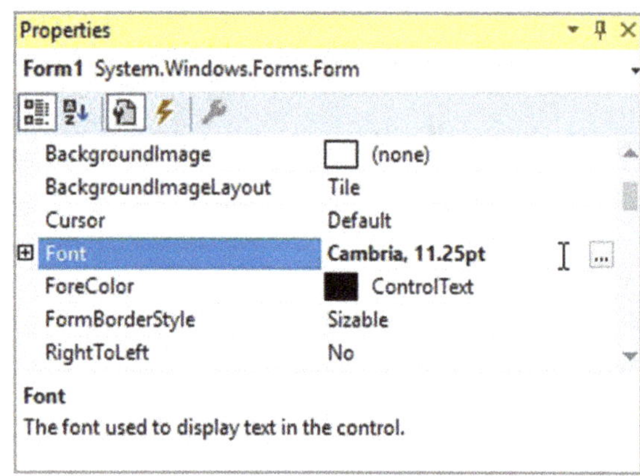

Font property

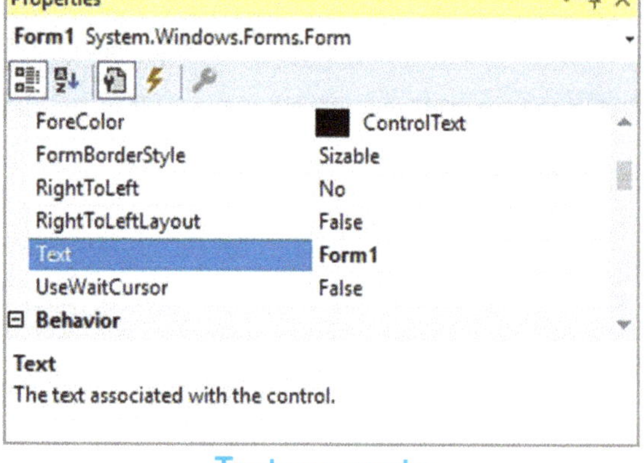

Text property

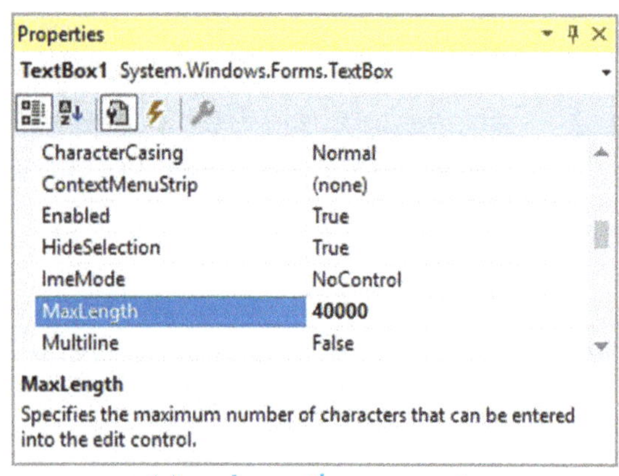

Max Length property

If you want to set the font attributes of the text in the text box, you can click the () button next to the Font text box in the Properties window and select the desired font settings in the Font dialog box.

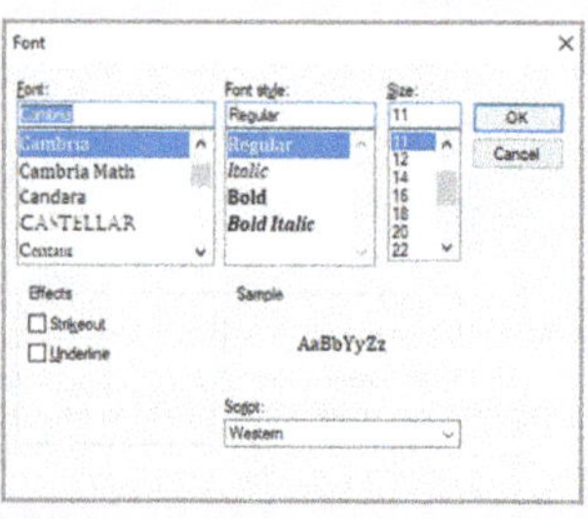

When you complete setting the properties, the text box in the form will appear like in the image given below.

To change the properties of the controls in run mode, follow the steps given below:

Step 1 : Double-click on the control. The Code Edit or window appears.

Step 2 : Write the code to change the desired property by using the syntax given below.

<Name of the control><Property>=<Value>

Given below is a program to change the colour of the text in the text box.

```
PublicClassForm1
Private Sub TextBox1_TextChanged(sender As Object, e As Event Args) Handles TextBox1.
TextChanged
TextBox1.ForeColor = Color. Coral
End Sub
EndClass
```

Step 3 : Press the F5 key on the keyboard to run the program. Another window opens up with the name of the form.

You can stop the execution of the program by clicking the Cross (×) button on the form window.

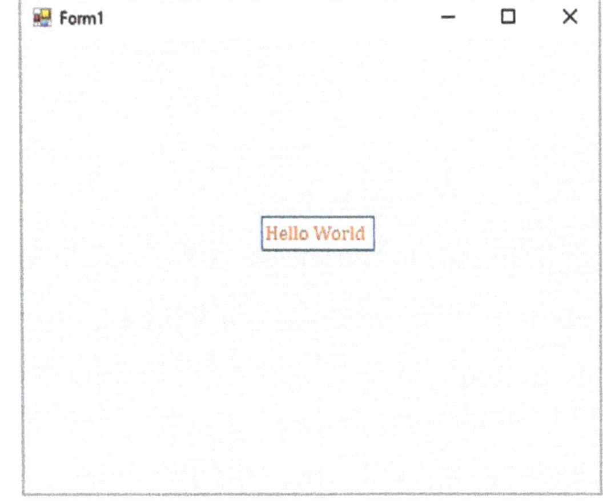

Output of the program setting desired properties of the text box

SOME COMMONLY USED FUNCTIONS IN VISUAL BASIC

Functions are built-in block of codes in a program which performs operations in a specific order using some values called arguments. Given below are the some of the most commonly used functions in Visual Basic.

MsgBox() Function

The Msg Box() function is used to display messages to the user in the form of a message box.

Syntax : Value = Msg Box(Message, Style_value, Title)where,

Style_value	Buttons displayed
0	OK
1	OK, Cancel
2	OK, Abort, Retry, Ignore
3	Yes, No, Cancel
4	Yes , No
5	Retry, Cancel

- Value is the variable which stores the value returned by the MsgBox ( ) function.
- Message refers to the message that is displayed in the message box. The maximum length of the message is 1024 characters.

- Style_value specifies the type of command button that is displayed in the message box.
- Title refers to the text that is displayed in the title bar of the message box.

The parameter Style_value can take various values, some of which are listed in the following table.

Input Box () Function

The Input Box () function is used to accept value from the user.

Syntax: Value=InputBox(Message, Title, Default_text)where,

Value : It is the variable which stores the value entered by the user.

Message : It refers to the text which is displayed in the input box. This argument is mandatory.

Title : It refers to the text that is displayed in the title bar of the input box.

Default_text : It specifies the string that appears in the text box of the input box, when it appears on the screen. The user can overwrite this text by typing the new text. It is an optional argument.

SAVING A VISUAL BASIC APPLICATION

When you create a Visual Basic program in VS Express application, you mention the name and location of the file as well as the project. After working on the program to save the changes, simply click the File menu and select the Save or Save All option. The VB program will be saved with the extension .vb and the project will be saved with the extension .sln. You can also press the keyboard key combination Ctrl + S to use the Save option and Ctrl + Shift + S to use the Save All option.

OPENING AN EXISTING VB PROJECT

To open an existing Visual Basic program in VS Express application program, follow the steps given below:

Step 1 : Click the File menu and then click Open Projector press the keyboard key combination Ctrl + O. The Open Project dialog box appears.

Step 2 : Locate the desired file and click the Open button.

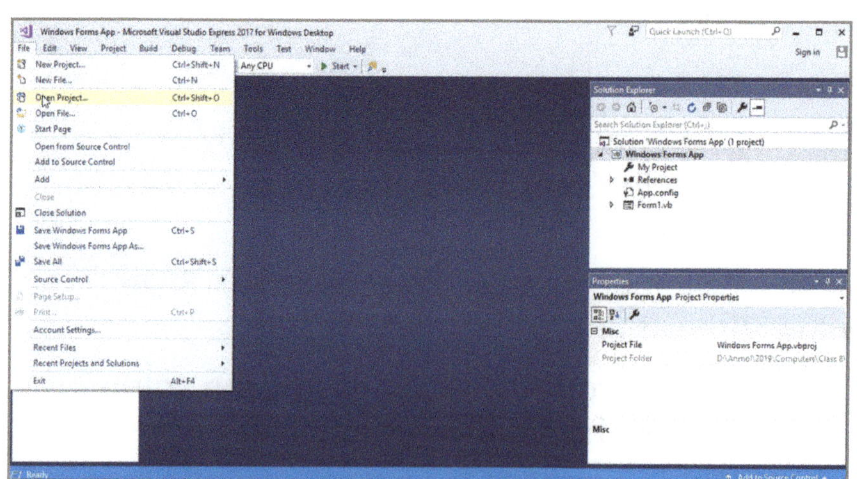

Opening an existing VB project

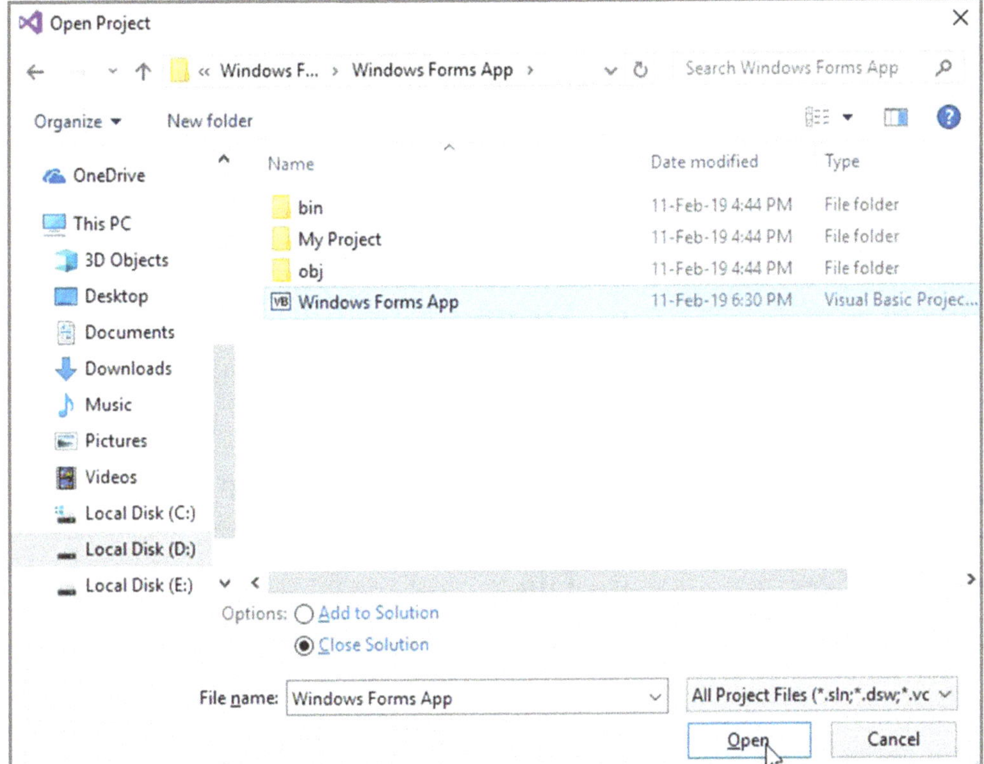

Open Project dialog box

LET'S HAVE A LOOK

- The language BASIC provides a text-only environment. Visual Basic is an extended version of the language.
- The response to any action performed on a control in a programming language is known as an event and the programming executed to respond to these events independently is known as event-driven programming.
- To create a Visual Basic program, you will have to download an integrated development environment (IDE) named Visual Studio.
- There are three different modes of the VS Express application window–design mode, in which an application is designed; run mode — in which an application is executed and break/suspended mode — which appears when the execution of an application is halted due to some errors.
- Every control that you insert in a program code contains a set of properties, methods and events.
- The properties define the characteristics of a control; the methods define the actions that can be performed on the control and the events define the occurrence of actions performed by the user on the control.
- The objects which are placed or inserted in a form to receive input and display output are known as the controls.
- Some of the commonly used controls in VB are Form, Label, TextBox and Button.
- You can insert a control and change its properties in the form as well as in the run mode.

BRAIN TEASER

1. Multiple Choice Questions

Tick (✓) the correct answer:

a. Visual Basic provides a ________ interface to work in.
   i. Graphical ☐ ii. Visual ☐ iii. Both (i) and (ii) ☐

b. Which of the following language is not included in the Visual Studio?
   i. QBasic ☐ ii. Visual C++ ☐ iii. SQL Server ☐

c. The ________ tab is present on the Menu bar in the Windows Forms App window.
   i. Home ☐ ii. File ☐ iii. Design ☐

d. A collection of forms, controls and modules is known as a
   i. Program ☐ ii. Application ☐ iii. Project ☐

e. Which key is pressed to run a program in Visual Basic?
   i. F2 ☐ ii. F4 ☐ iii. F5 ☐

f. Which of the following arguments is mandatory in the Input Box () function?
   i. Value ☐ ii. Message ☐ iii. Title ☐

2. Fill in the blanks with the suitable words.

a. The full form of IDE is ____________.

b. Visual Basic is an extended version of ____________.

c. The TextBox control is used to receive ____________ and give ____________.

d. The ____________ method is used to activate the button control.

e. The cursor changes into (⟺) when you want to ____________ the control.

f. The ____________ function is used to accept value from the user.

3. Write 'T' for true statements and 'F' for false ones.

a. Whenever some action is performed on a graphical component, a control is created. ☐

b. In VB, programs cannot be linked together. ☐

c. The default name of a form is Form1. ☐

d. Putting zero value in the Max Length text box property makes the length of the text zero. ☐

e. You can change the properties of a control in run mode. ☐

4. Answer the following questions.

a. State the features of the language Visual Basic.

b. What do you mean by event-driven programming? Explain with an example.

c. Define Visual Studio. How do you open the VS Express application?

d. What are the steps to open an existing project in VS Express application program?

e. What is the difference between the Solution Explorer window and the Code Editor window?

5. Define the following terms.

a. Properties – ____________________

b. Form – ____________________

c. Control – ____________________

d. Solution – ____________________

e. Project – ____________________

6. Match the following:

a.	IDE	a.	Activates the button control
b.	Father of Visual Basic	b.	Cannot be altered
c.	Label Box Ctrl	c.	Stores the value
d.	Text Box Ctrl	d.	Alan Cooper
e.	Button Ctrl	e.	Save All Option
f.	Value Function	f.	Gives name to the text box
g.	Ctrl + Shift + S	g.	Integrated Development Environment

8 Photoshop

In this chapter, we will learn:

- ⇒ Introduction to Photoshop
- ⇒ Getting Images for Work
- ⇒ Starting Photoshop, Photoshop Workplace
- ⇒ Photoshop Tools
- ⇒ Working with Images
- ⇒ Opening Image or Creating Image Window
- ⇒ Photoshop 7
- ⇒ Saving file in Photoshop

PHOTOSHOP

Adobe Photoshop is a graphics editor software, developed and published by Adobe Systems, that allows you to create, modify, combine and optimize digital images. You can then save the images to print, share via e-mail, publish online, or view on a handheld device, such as an iPod.

You can use Photoshop's Paintbrush, Airbrush and Pencil tools to apply colours or patterns to your images after selecting their pixels.

You can brighten, darken and change the hue (shade) of colours in parts of your image with Photoshop Dodge, Burn, and similar tools. Photoshop effects let you easily add Drop shadows, 3D shading, and other styles to your images.

After you have edited your work, you can use your images in a variety of ways. Photoshop lets you print your images, save them in a format suitable for use on a Web page. Photoshop is so popular that when we notice that an image has been altered, we say it has been Photoshopped. Even when we go to some photo studio to have a passport- size photograph, the photographer shoots the photo and gives effects to the photo in Photoshop.

Photoshop Tools

Photoshop tools let you move, colour, stylize and add text to elements of your image.

Understanding Pixels : Digital images in Photoshop are made up of tiny, solid colour squares called pixels.

Selecting Pixels : To edit specific pixels in your image, you first have to select them by selection tools.

Painting Image : You can apply colour to pixels after selecting them by Paintbrush and Airbrush.

Adjusting Color : You can brighten, darken and change the hue of colours in the parts of your image with Photoshop Dodge, Burn, and similar tools.

Applying Effects : You can easily add drop shadows, frame border, 3D shading, etc. to your images.

Apply Filters : Photoshop filters can make your image look like an impressionist painting, sharpen or blur your image or distort your image in various ways.

Add Text : Photoshop tools make it easy to apply titles and labels to your images.

FIND IMAGES FOR YOUR WORK

You can get raw material for using Photoshop from a variety of sources.

Start From Scratch

You can create your Photoshop image from scratch by opening a blank canvas in the image window. Then you can apply colour and patterns with Photoshop painting tools.

Scanned Photos and Art

You can use a scanner to convert existing paper-based content into digital form. You can scan photos and art into your computer, retouch and stylize them in Photoshop and then output them to a colour printer.

Clip Art

You can use clipart collection if you want a wide variety of image content to work with. Such collections usually include illustrations, photos and decorative icons that you can use in imaging projects.

Digital Photo

Digital cameras are a great way to get digital images onto your computer. Most digital cameras save their images in JPEG or TIFF format, both of which can be opened and edited in Photoshop.

Download Photo

There are many Web sites that feature images that are in the public domain or are available for non-commercial use.

STARTING PHOTOSHOP

You can start Photoshop on your computer and begin creating and editing digital images.

1. Click on Start button.
2. Click on Adobe Design Premium CC 2021.

3. Select Adobe Photoshop CC 2021.

Adobe Photoshop **CC 2021 window** appears.

The Photoshop Workspace

You can use a combination of tools, menu commands and palette-based features to open and edit your digital images in Photoshop.

Application Bar : Displays menus that contain most of Photoshop commands and functions. Special icon-based menus allow you to change the layout of the program.

Option bar : Displays controls that let you customize the selected tool in the toolbox.

Toolbox : Displays a variety of icons, each one representing an image-editing tool. It also displays the current foreground and background colours.

Image window : You can open an image in the Image Window in Photoshop.

Title tab : Displays the name, magnification, and colour mode of an open image. You can switch between images by clicking their respective tabs.

Status Bar : Displays the magnification of the current image and the amount of computer memory that the image is using.

Panel : Small windows that give you access to common commands and resources.

The Photoshop Toolbox

The Toolbox contains many separate tools. You can simply click on the Tool to select it for working on your image. If you leave your mouse cursor over the tool, Adobe Photoshop will indicate the name of the tool and the keyboard shortcut to access the tool. Some of the tools are stacked in groups of tools. A small black arrow in the bottom right corner of the toolbox indicates that additional tools are stacked behind. To access any of the tools in this stack, click and hold down the mouse button on the uppermost tool for a second.

Adobe Photoshop Tools

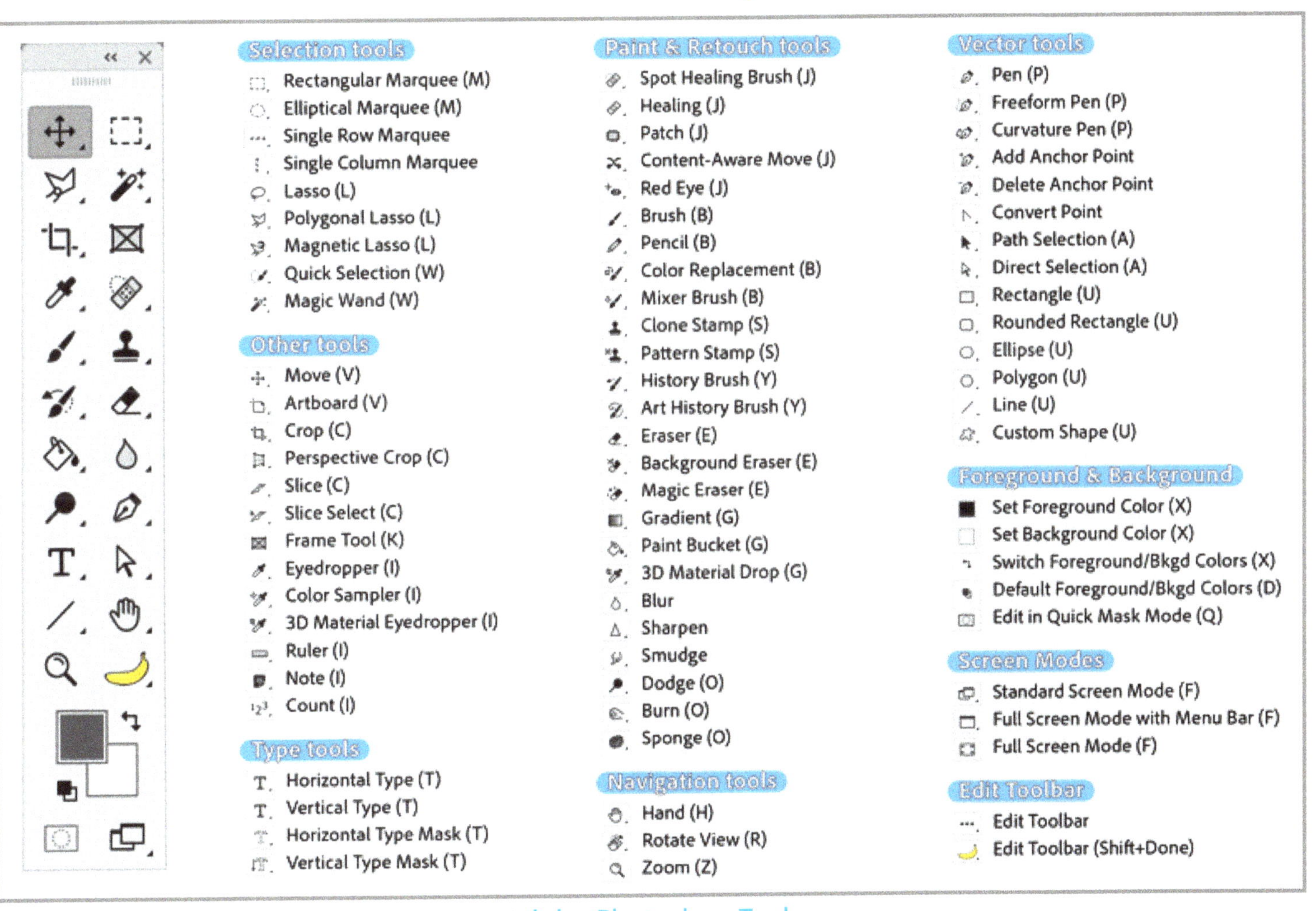

Adobe Photoshop Tools

Opening an Image

You can open an existing image file in Photoshop as follows:

1. Click on File on the menu bar. The file menu will open.
2. Click on Open. The Open dialog box appears.

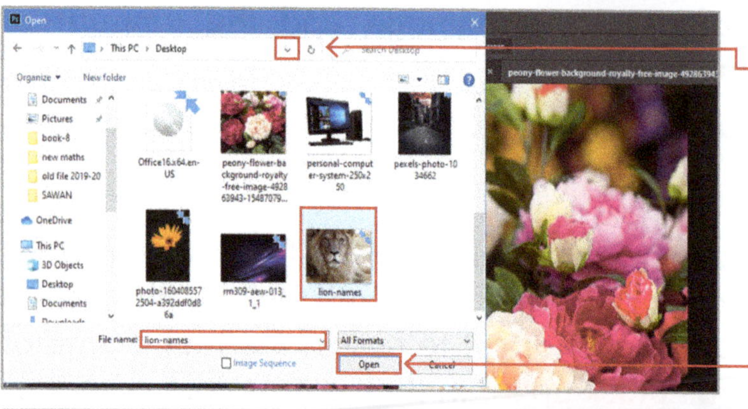

3. Click on the down arrow to navigate the folder that contains the image you want.
4. Click on the file name to open.

A preview of the desired image is displayed.

5. Click on Open.

The image appears in a new window of Photoshop.

The name of the file appears in the **title tab** of the image.

Changing On-screen Size of Image

You can change the size of an image on the computer monitor in order to view the entire image at one time.

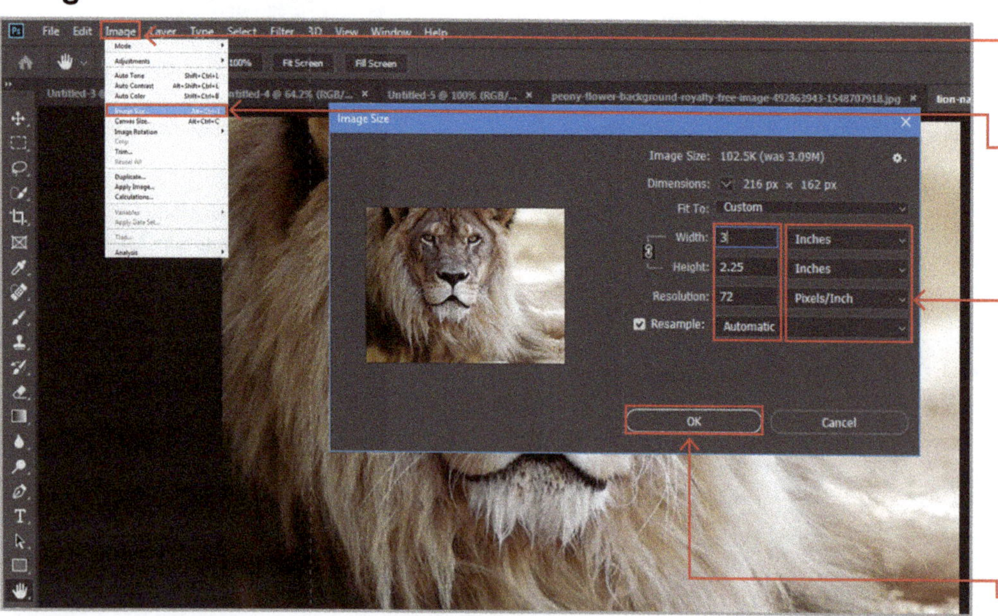

1. Click on Image in the menu bar.
2. Click on Image Size.

The Image Size dialog box appears.

3. Type a new size for the dimension in this area.
4. Make sure that Resample Image is selected.
5. Click on OK.

Photoshop resizes the image. You should start this with an image that is too big than one that is too small as you lose less detail when you increase it.

Changing the Print Size of an Image

You can change the print size of an image by the following steps.

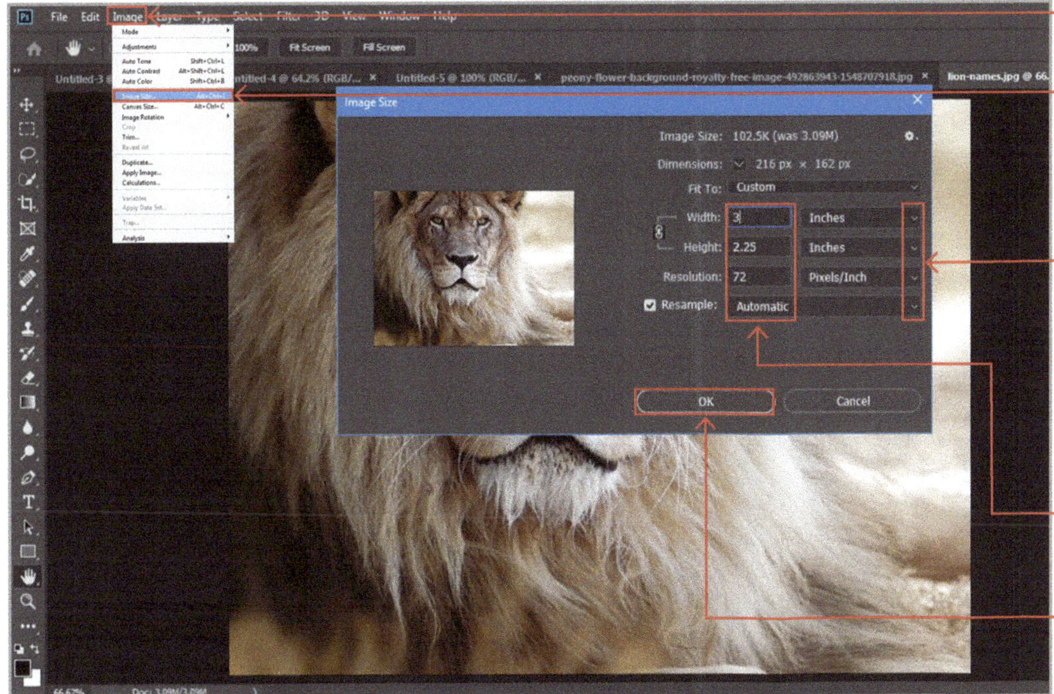

1. Click on Image in the menu bar.
2. Click on Image Size.

The Image Size dialog box appears.

3. Click on the down arrow to change the unit of measurement.
4. Type a new size for the dimension.
5. Click on OK.

Photoshop resizes the image.

Changing the Canvas Size of an Image

You can change the canvas size of an image to add blank space to its sides.

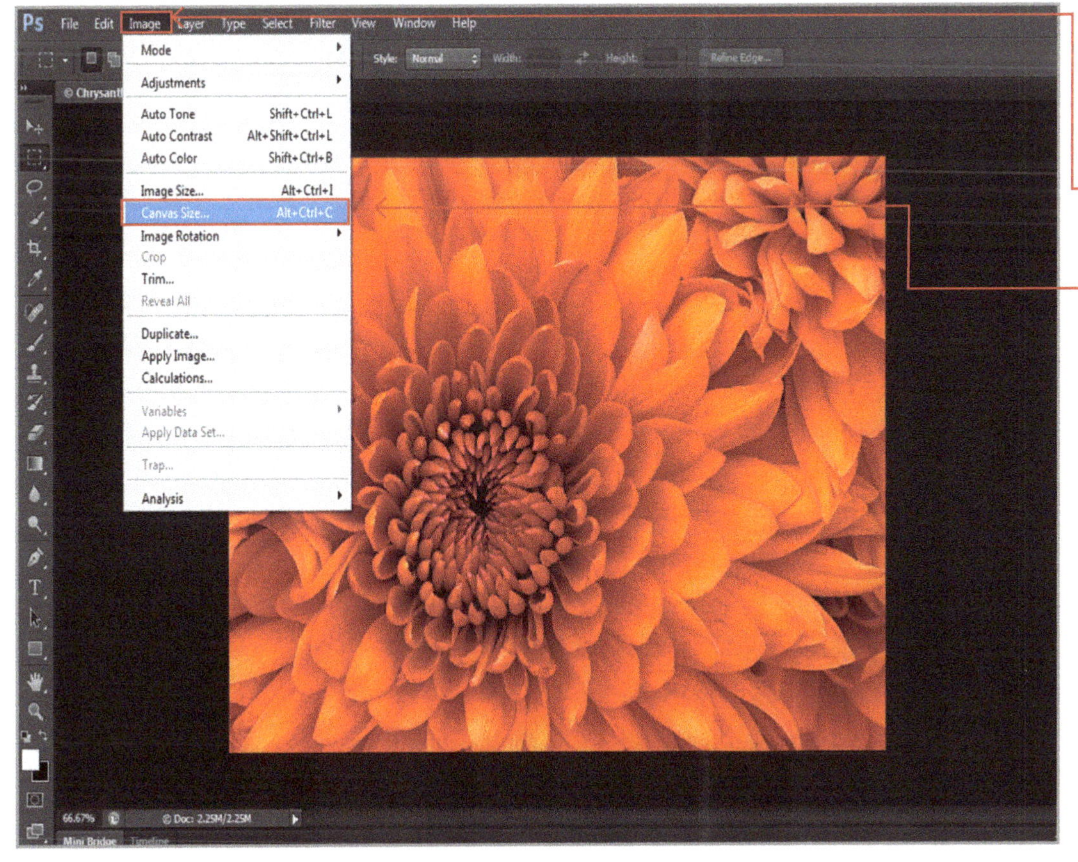

1. Click on Image in the menu bar.
2. Click on Canvas Size.

The Canvas Size dialog box appears.

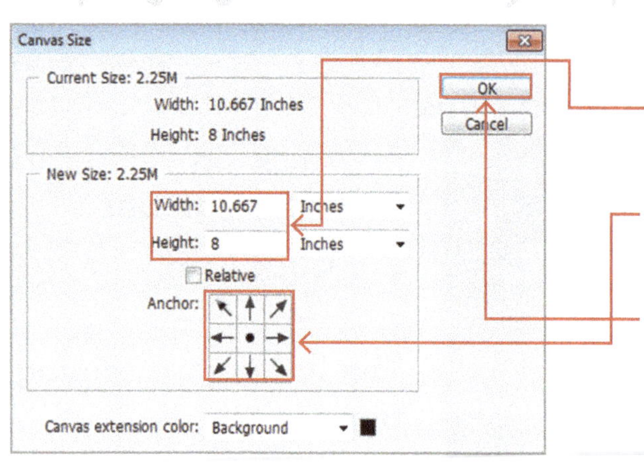

3. Type the dimensions for the new canvas.
4. Click an anchor point (such as the middle one).
5. Click on OK.

Photoshop changes the canvas size of the image.

The canvas changes equally on opposite sides because you have selected the middle anchor point.

Cropping the Image

Crop tool can be used to change the size of an image.

1. Click on the Crop tool (⌗).
2. Click and drag to select the area of the image you want to keep.

3. You can click and drag the sides and corner handles to adjust the size of the cropping boundary.
4. Click on the right button or press the Enter key on the keyboard.

Press Esc button on the keyboard to exit from the cropping process.

Photoshop crops the image, deleting the pixels outside the cropping boundary.

Zoom Tool

With the help of the Zoom tool, you can change the magnification of an image.

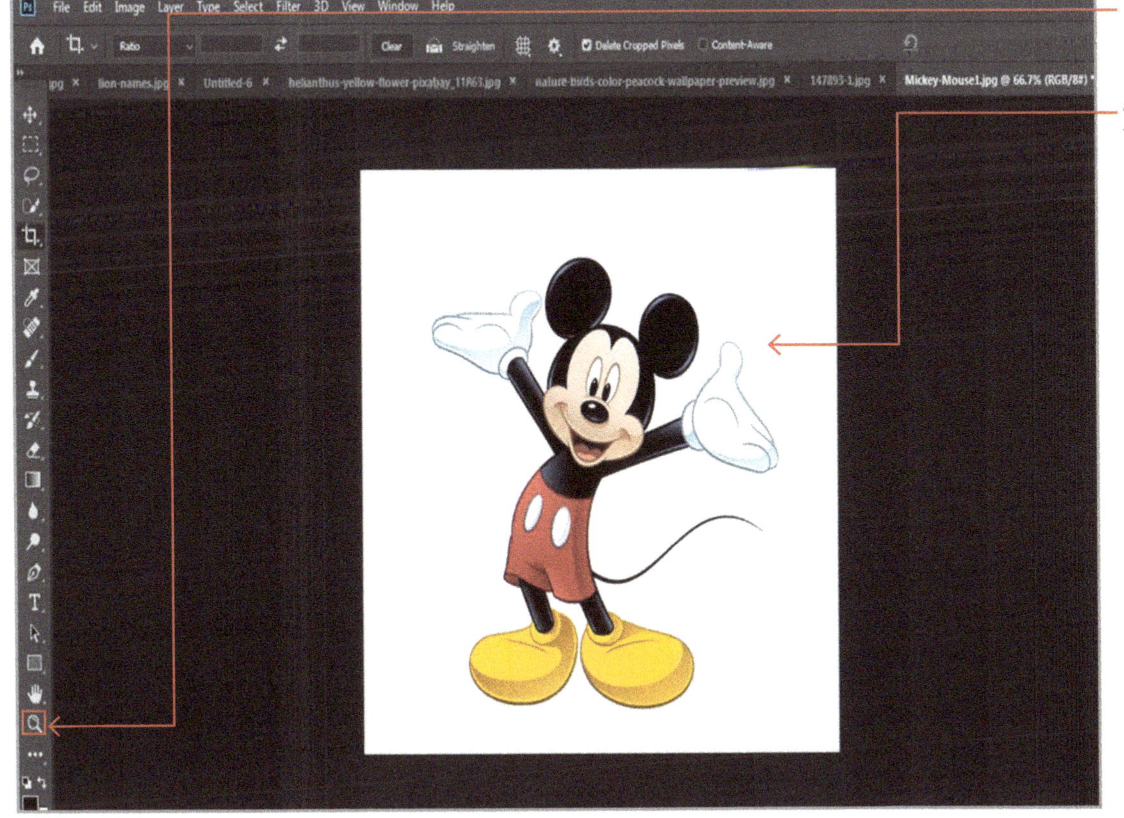

1. Click on the Zoom tool (🔍).
2. Click on the image that you want to magnify.

Photoshop increases the magnification of the image.

After clicking on the Zoom tool ( ), press and hold the Alt key on the keyboard and click on the image to decrease the magnification.

Changing Screen Modes

You can switch the screen mode to change the look of your workspace on the screen.

In standard screen mode, you can see multiple images at once.

1. Click on Screen Mode arrow.
2. Click on the Full Screen Mode with Menu Bar button ( ).

Photoshop puts the current image window in the centre of a blank, full-screen canvas with the menu options at the top of the screen.

Switch to Full Screen

1. Click on Screen Mode arrow.
2. Click on the Full Screen Mode ( ) button.

The image appears in full screen without the menu options.

Close Toolbox and Palette

1. Press the Tab button on the keyboard.

Photoshop closes all the toolboxes and palettes.

2. Now press the Tab button again on the keyboard to view the toolbox and palettes.

Selecting with Marquee Tools

Marquee tools are used to select a rectangular or an elliptical area of your image. You can move, delete or stylize the selected area using other Photoshop commands.

Rectangular Marquee Tool

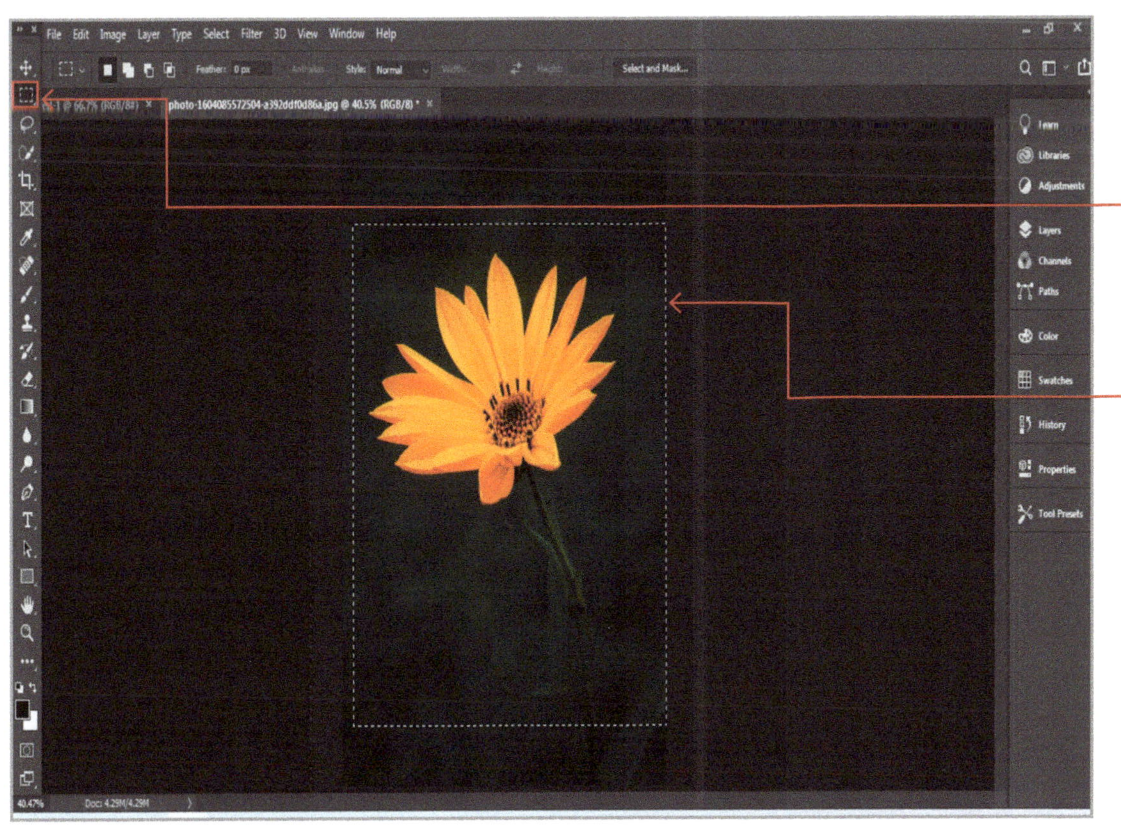

1. Click on the Rectangular Marquee Tool ( ).
2. Click and drag diagonally inside the image window.

Elliptical Marquee Tool

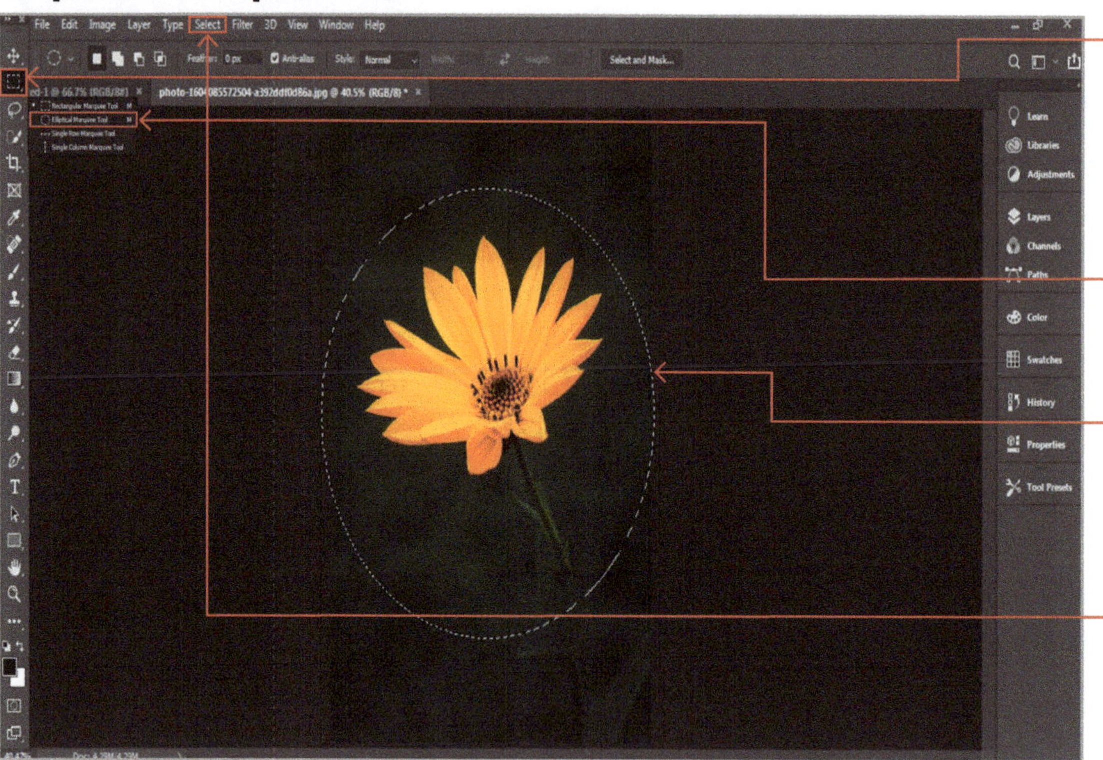

1. Click and hold Rectangular Marquee Tool. A box will appear.
2. In the box, select Elliptical Marquee Tool.
3. Click and drag diagonally inside the image window.

You can deselect a selection by clicking on Select in the menu bar and then click on Deselect.

Selecting with Lasso Tool

You can create oddly shaped selections with Lasso tool. Then you can move, delete or stylize the selected area using other Photoshop commands.

Regular Lasso Tool

1. Click on the Lasso tool.
2. Click and drag with your cursor to make a selection.
3. Drag to the beginning point and release the mouse button to complete the selection.

Polygonal Lasso Tool

1. Click and hold Lasso Tool.

A box will appear.

2. In the box, select Polygonal Lasso Tool.
3. Click multiple times along the border of the area you would like to select.
4. To complete the selection, click on the starting point.

Magnetic Lasso Tool

Magnetic Lasso Tool is used to select the elements of your image that have well-defined edges.

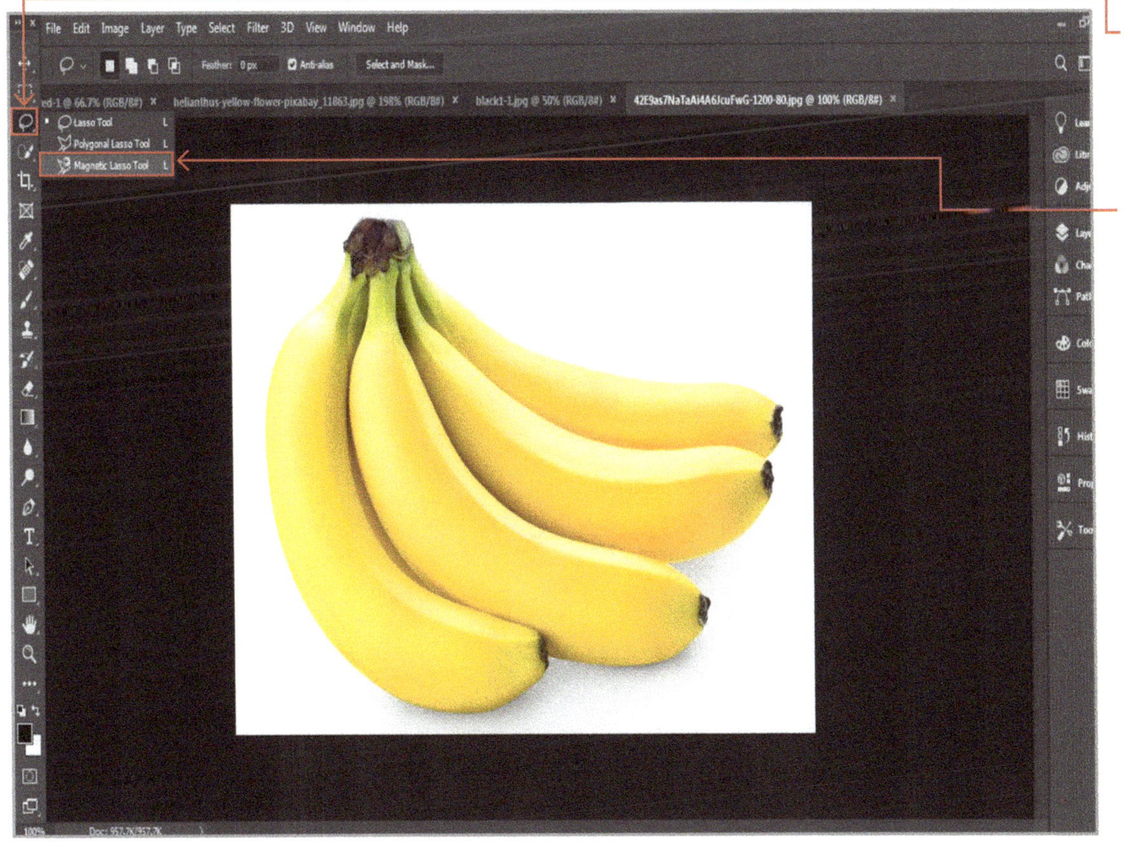

1. Click and hold Lasso Tool.

A box will appear.

2. In the box, select Magnetic Lasso Tool.
3. Click on the edge of the element you want to select, to create the beginning anchor point.

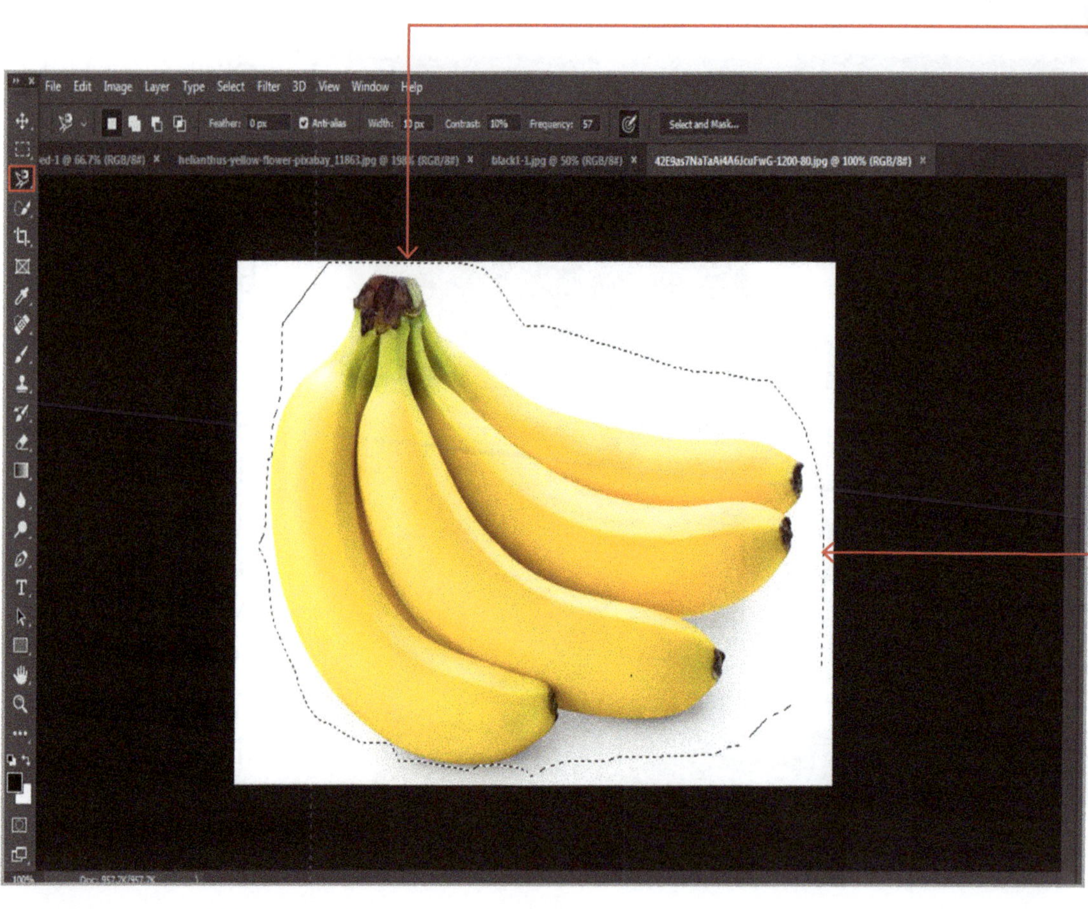

4. Drag your cursor along the edge of the element.

Magnetic Lasso snaps on to the edge of the element as you drag.

You can click to add anchor points as you go along, to guide the lasso.

5. Click on the beginning anchor point to finish your selection.

Selecting with Magic Wand Tool

Groups of similarly coloured pixels can be selected with the use of Magic Wand tool.

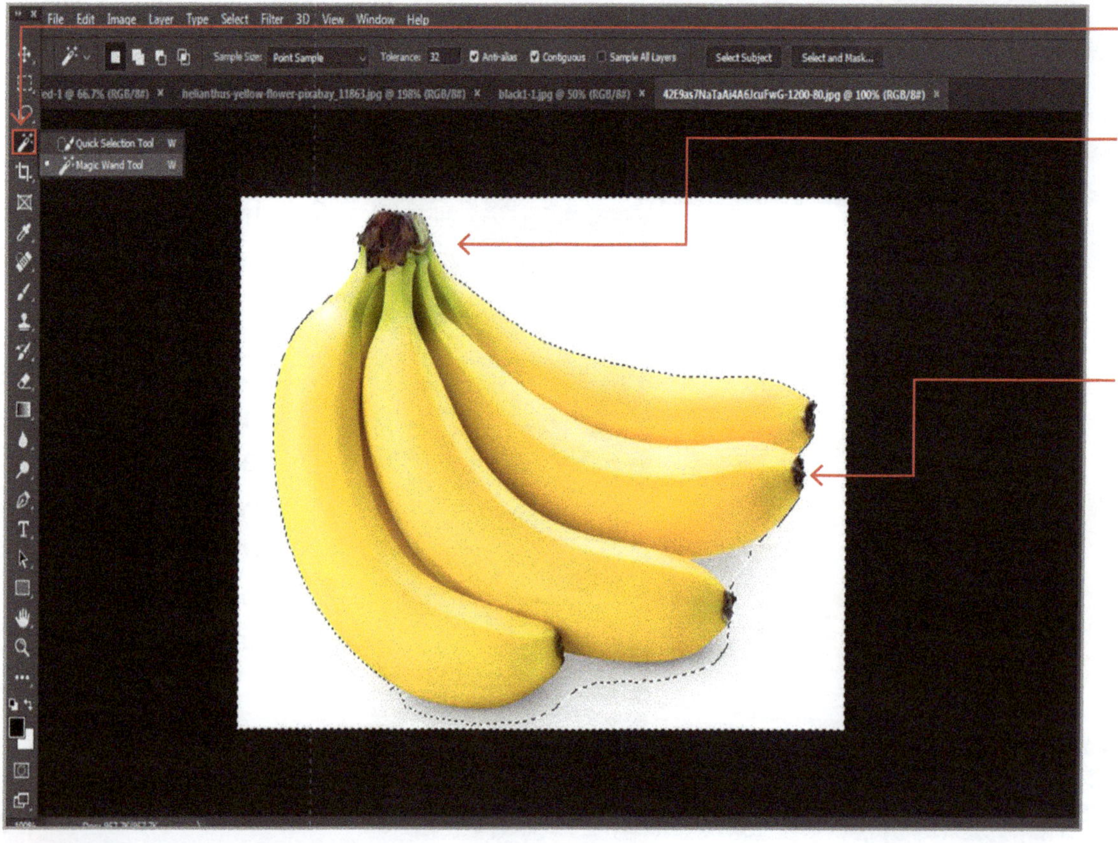

1. Click on Magic Wand Tool ( ).

2. Click on the area (pixels) you want to select inside the image.

Photoshop selects the pixel you clicked, and any similarly coloured pixels near it.

Delete Selected Pixels

1. Select the area you want to delete with the Magic Wand tool.

   Press the Delete key on the keyboard to delete the selected pixels.

   The pixels are replaced with the background colour (in this case, white).

Moving the Selection

With the help of Move Tool, you can move a selection which lets you rearrange the elements of your image.

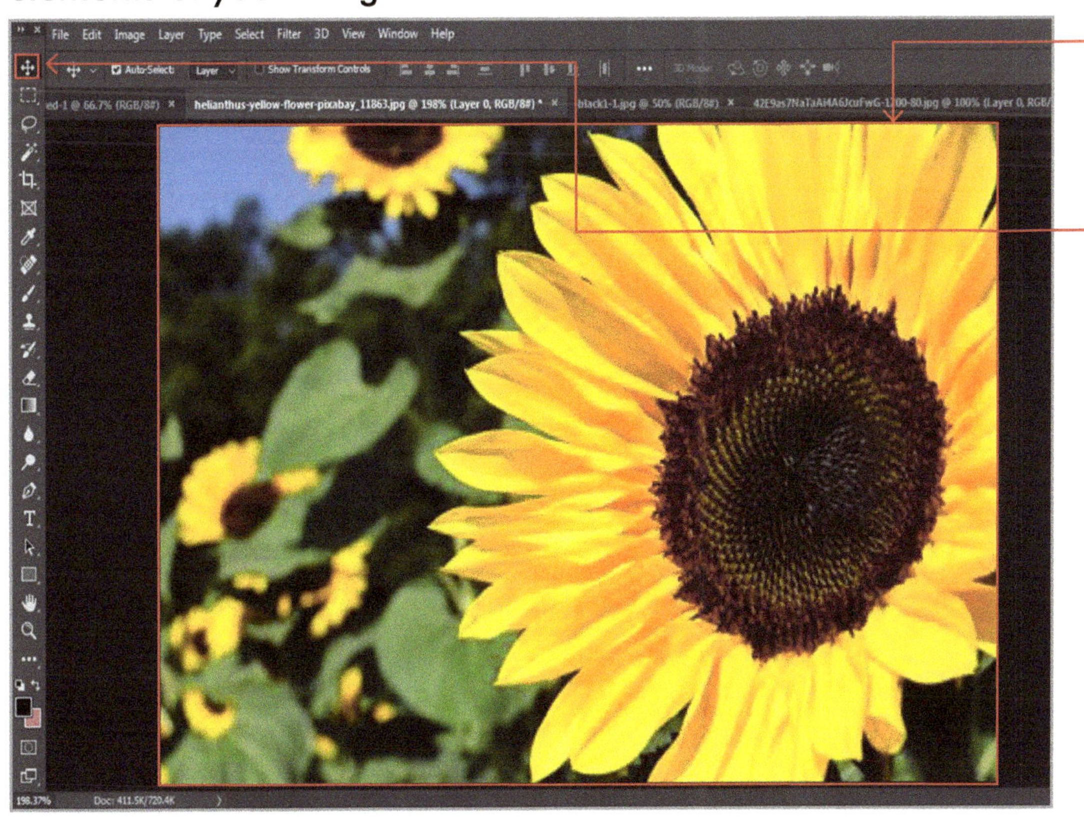

1. Make a selection with any of the selection tools.
2. Click on Move Tool (✥).

3. Click inside the selection and drag.

The area appears where the selection used to be filled with the current background colour.

White is the default background colour.

Selecting All Image

You can select all the pixels in a image by using a single command. This lets you perform a subsequent command on the entire image, such as copying it to a different image window.

1. Position your mouse pointer on Select menu and click. Select menu will appear.
2. Click on All.

The entire image window is selected.

With the entire image window selected, you can easily delete your image by pressing the delete key or copy and paste it into another window.

Clone Stamp Tool

You can copy exact detail and colour from one part of an image to another area with the help of Clone Stamp Tool.

1. Click on the Clone Stamp in the tool bar.
2. Click on the down arrow of Brush.
3. Select the brush size and type.
4. Press the Alt key on the keyboard.
5. Click on the area of the image where you want to copy from.

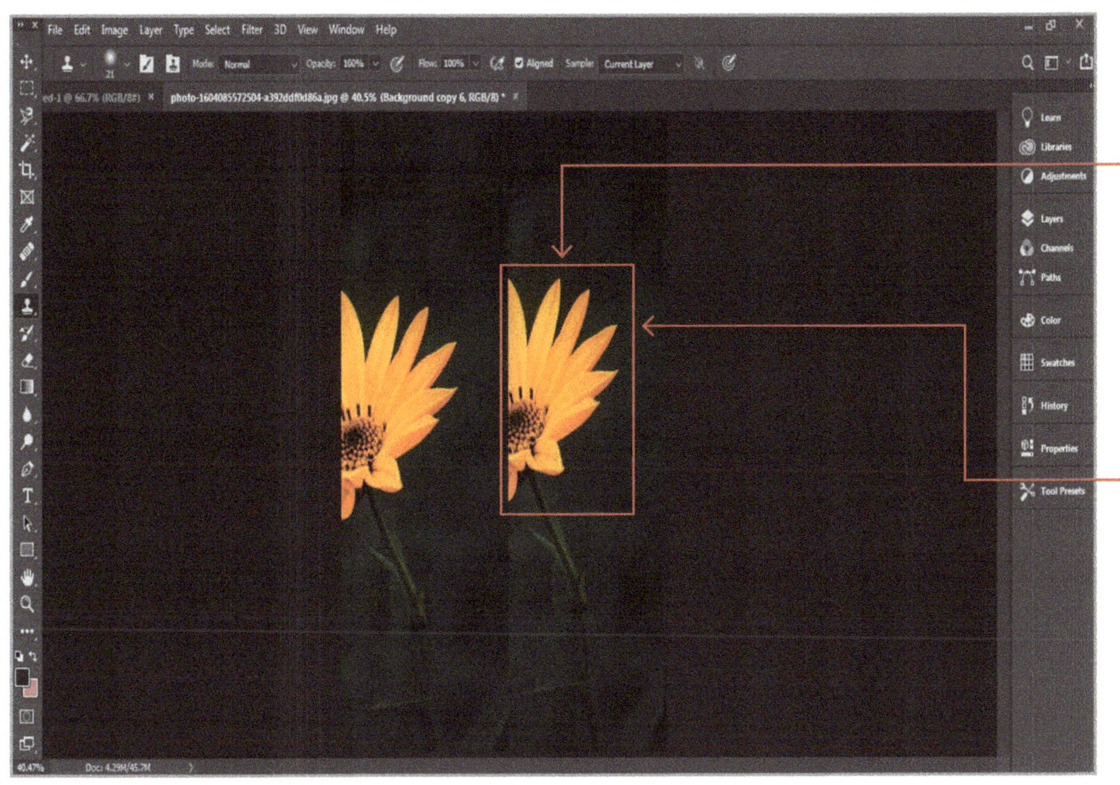

6. Click and drag to apply the clone stamp.

The area is copied to where you click and drag.

7. Click and drag repeatedly over the area to achieve the desired effect.

Color Modes

You can change the colour modes in the picture.

RGB Mode

RGB is the most common mode for working with colour images in Photoshop.

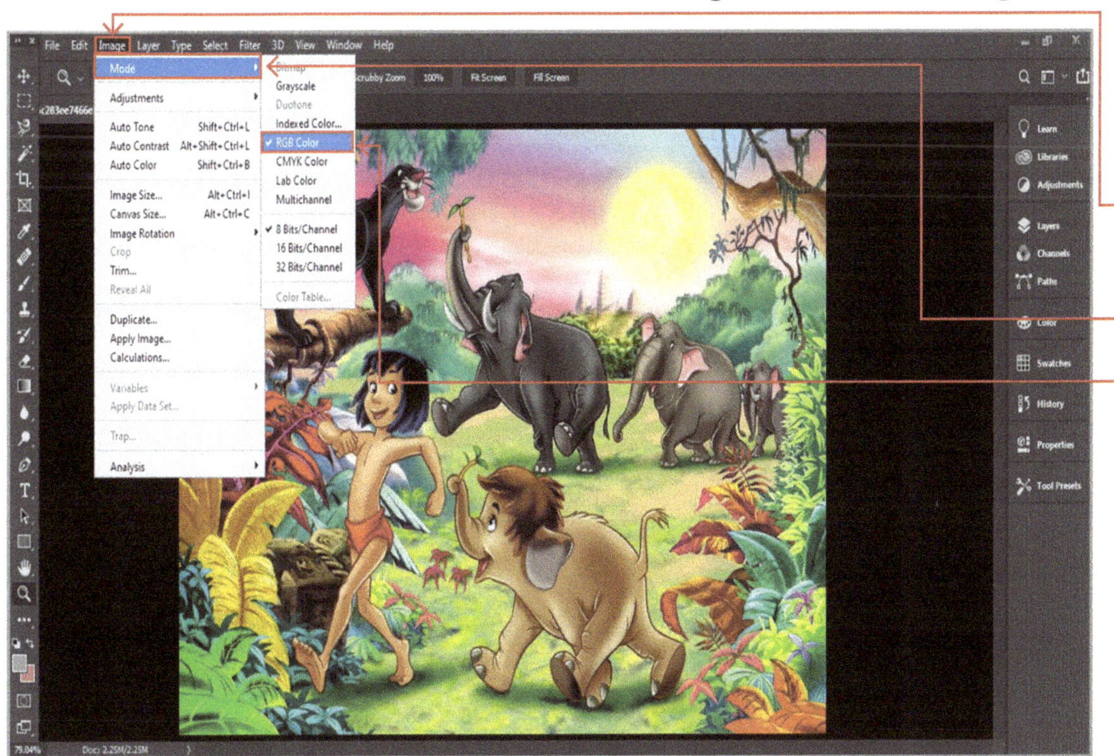

1. Click on Image in the menu bar.
2. Click on Mode.
3. Click on RGB Color.

RGB is displayed in the title bar of the image.

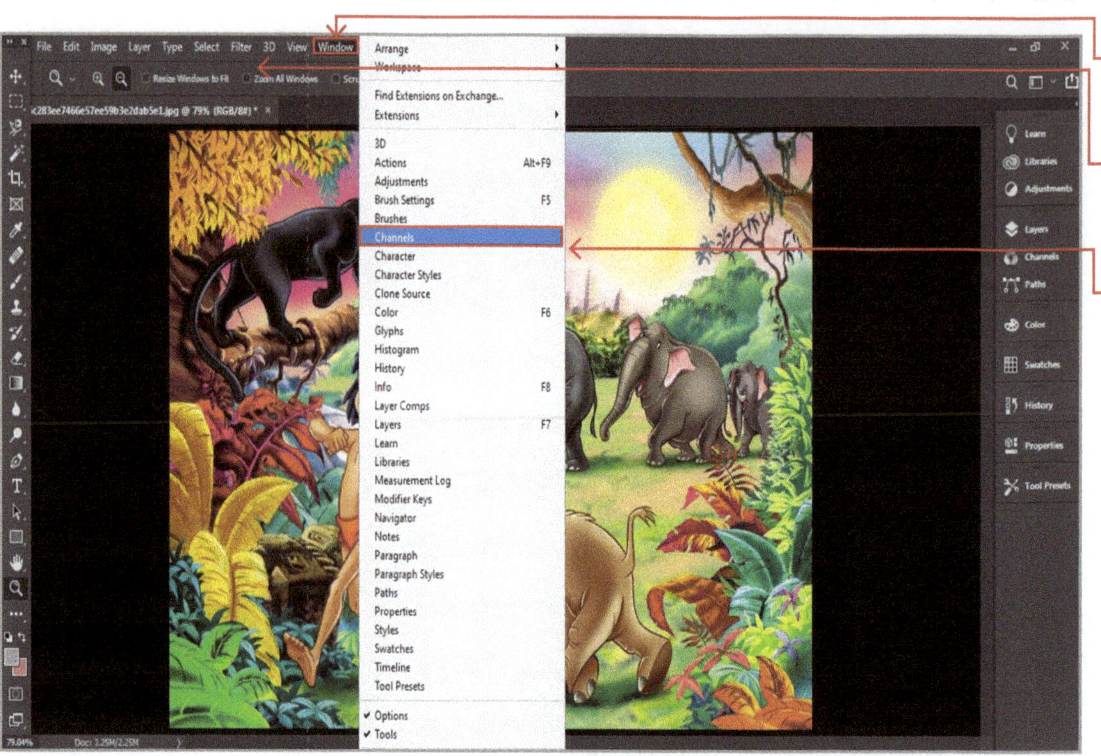

4. Click on Window to view the different colour components of an RGB image.
5. Click on Channels.
6. Click on any channel (Red, Green or Blue).

A greyscale version of the image displays the amount of channels the image contains.

For example, when you choose the red channel, the lighter areas show a lot of red; the darker areas show very little red.

Converting Colour Images to Greyscale

You can convert a colour image into greyscale mode to remove the colour from the image.

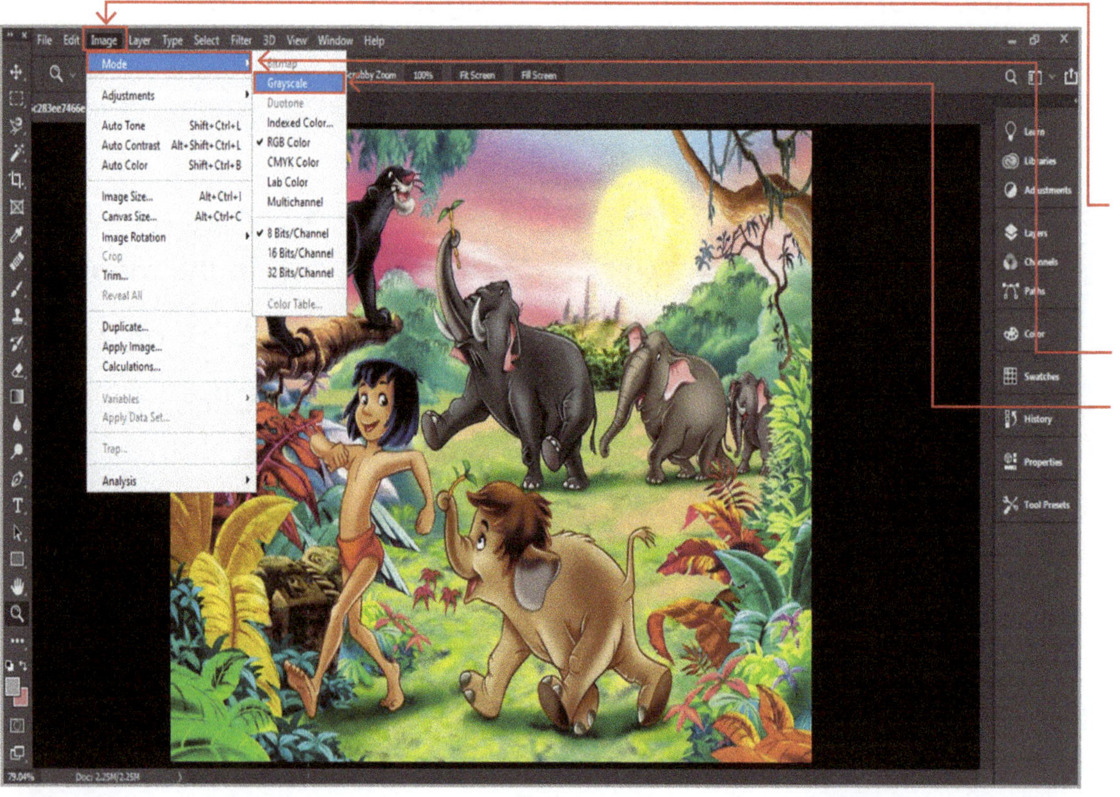

1. Click on Image in the menu bar.
2. Click on Mode.
3. Click on Greyscale. Photoshop displays an alert box.
4. Click on Discard.

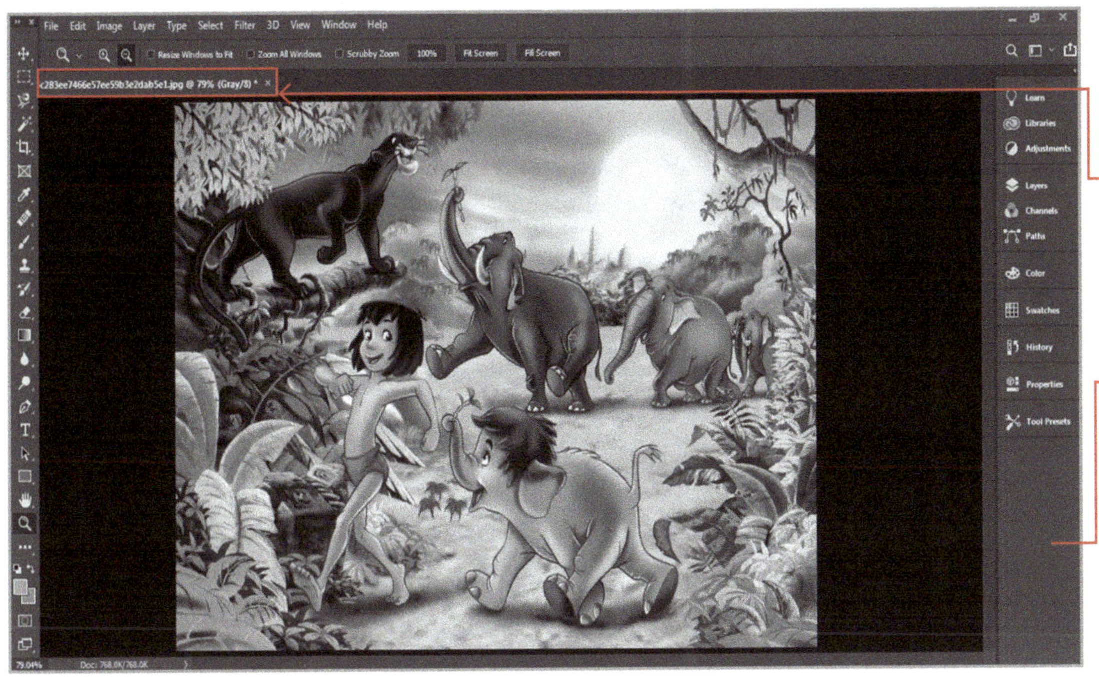

Grey is displayed in the image title bar.

Greyscale images have a single channel, that is why greyscale image files take up less space than RGB images.

Foreground and Background Colours

You can select two colours to work with at a time in Photoshop: a foreground colour and a background colour. Painting tools, such as the Brush tool, apply the foreground colour. You apply the background colour when you use the Eraser tool on the Background layer, enlarge the image canvas or cut pieces out of your image.

Foreground Colour

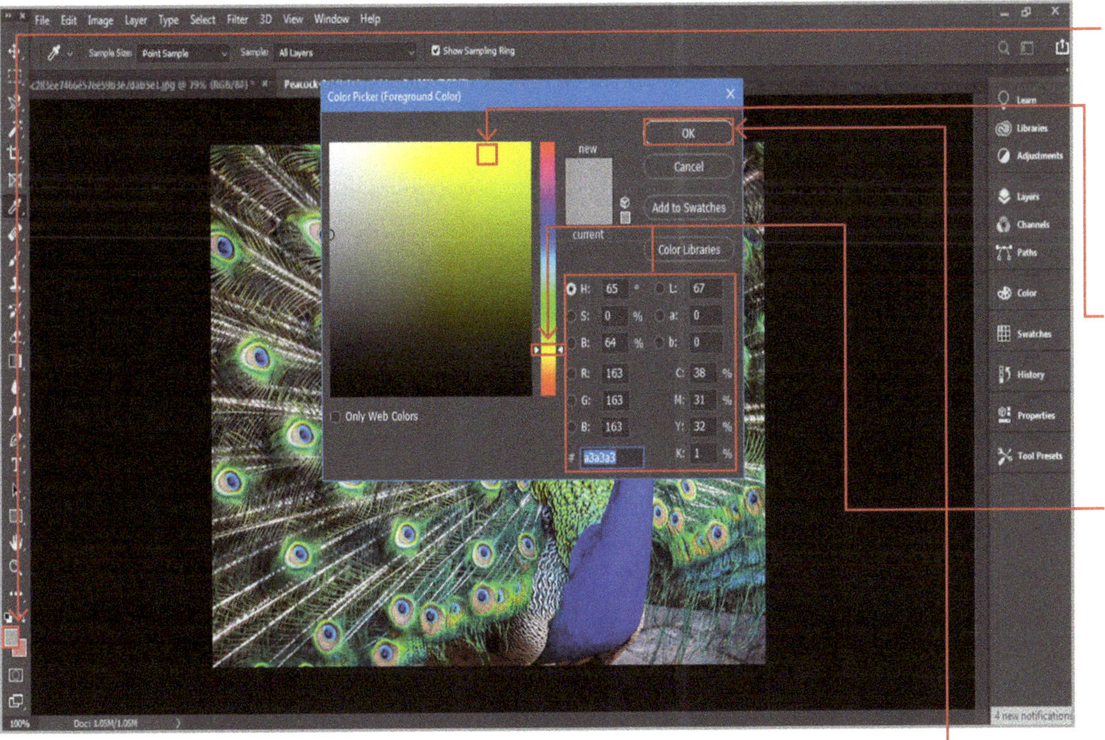

1. Click on the Foreground Color icon.

The Color Picker dialog box will appear.

2. Click in the colour window to select a colour.
3. Drag the slider or enter the value in the boxes to change the range of colour in the window.
4. Click on OK.

Background Color

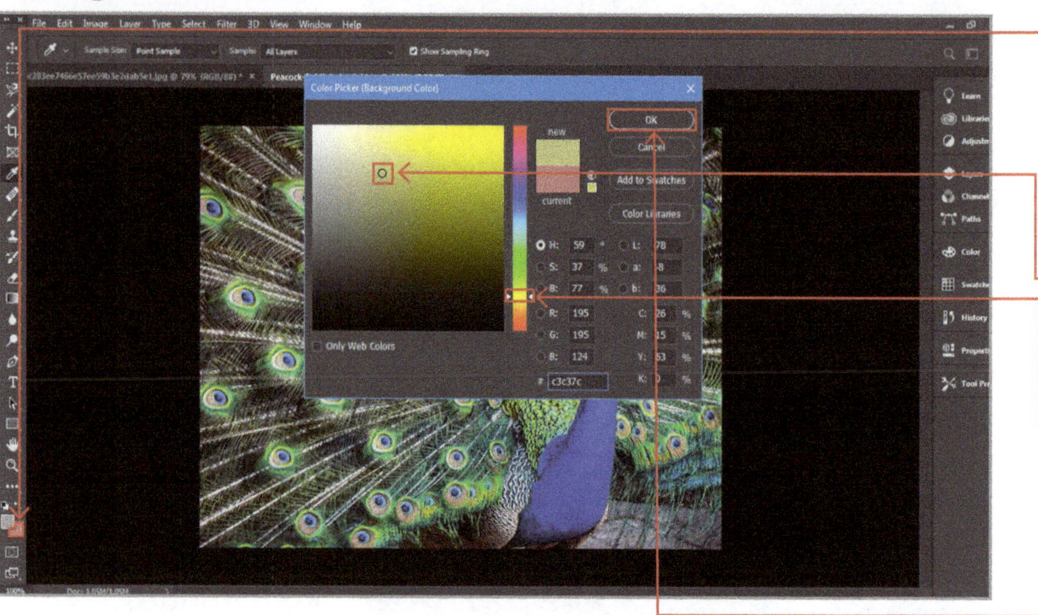

1. Click on the Background Color icon.

The Color Picker dialog box will open.

2. Click in the colour window to select a colour.
3. Drag the slider to change the range of colour in the window.
4. Click on OK.

Selecting Colour using Eyedropper Tool

You can select a colour from an open image with the Eyedropper tool. This tool enables you to paint using a colour already present in your image.

1. Click on the Eyedropper tool ( ).
2. Place the Eyedropper tool over an open image and click to select the colour under Eyedropper tool's tip.

The colour becomes the new foreground colour.

To select the new background colour, perform the step 2 while pressing the Alt key on the keyboard.

Using Paintbrush Tool

You can use the Paintbrush Tool to add colours to your image.

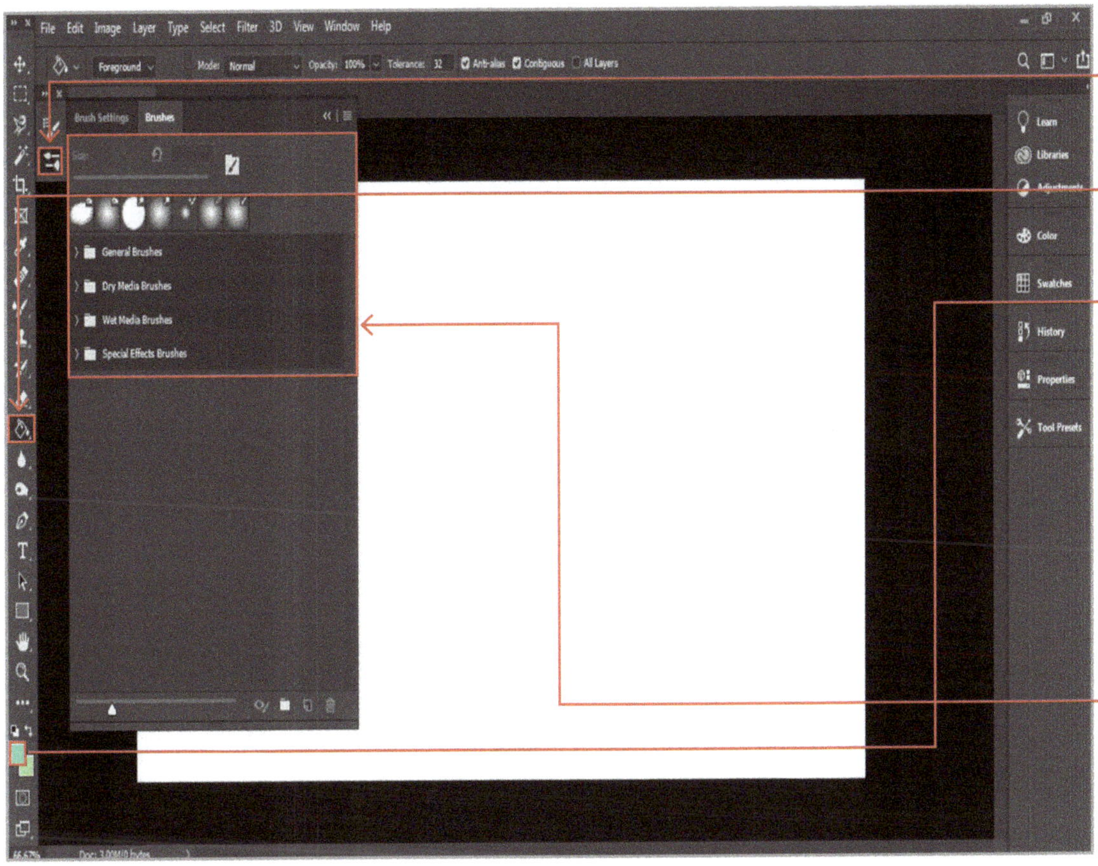

1. Click on the Paintbrush Tool.
2. Click the Foreground Colour icon to select a colour to paint with.
3. Click on the down arrow of Paintbrush.
4. Select a brush size and type.

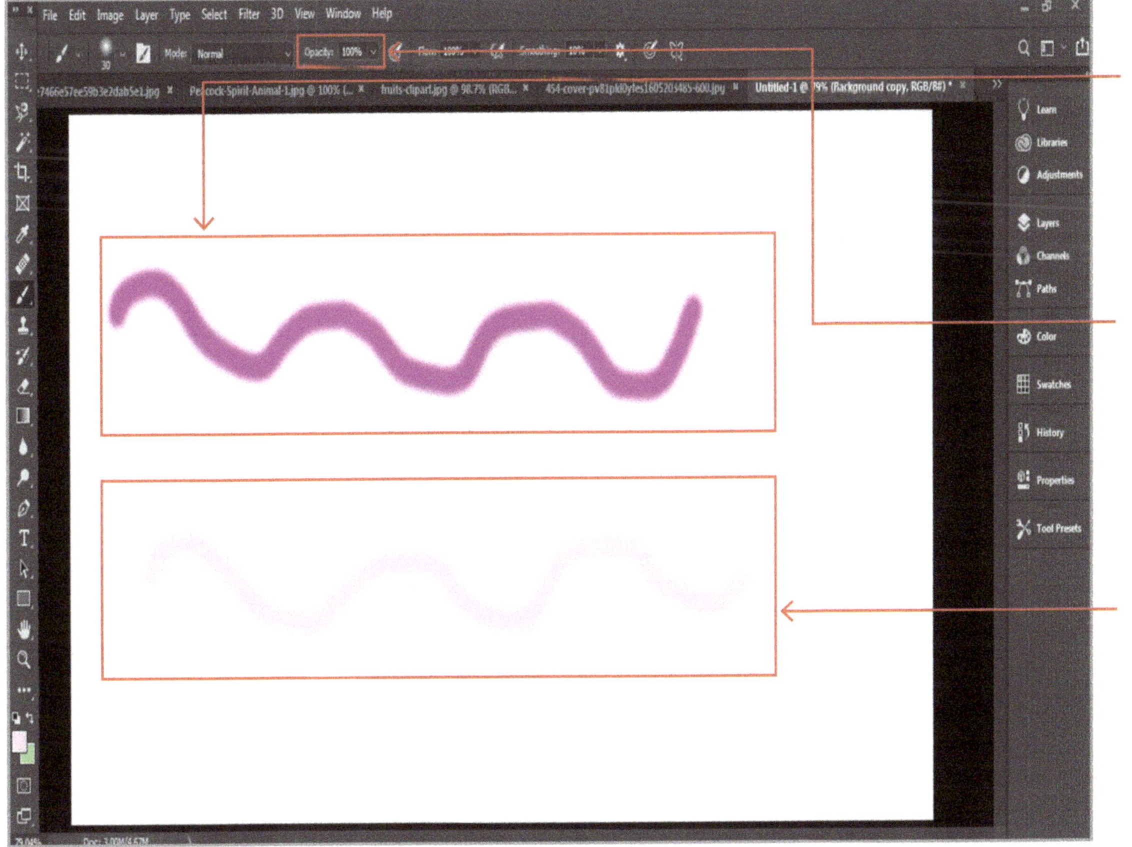

5. Click and drag to apply the foreground colour to the image.
6. Type the percentage value to change the opacity of the brush strokes.
7. Click and drag to apply the semi-transparent paintbrush.

Using Pencil Tool

Pencil Tool is used to draw the straight lines of colour in Photoshop.

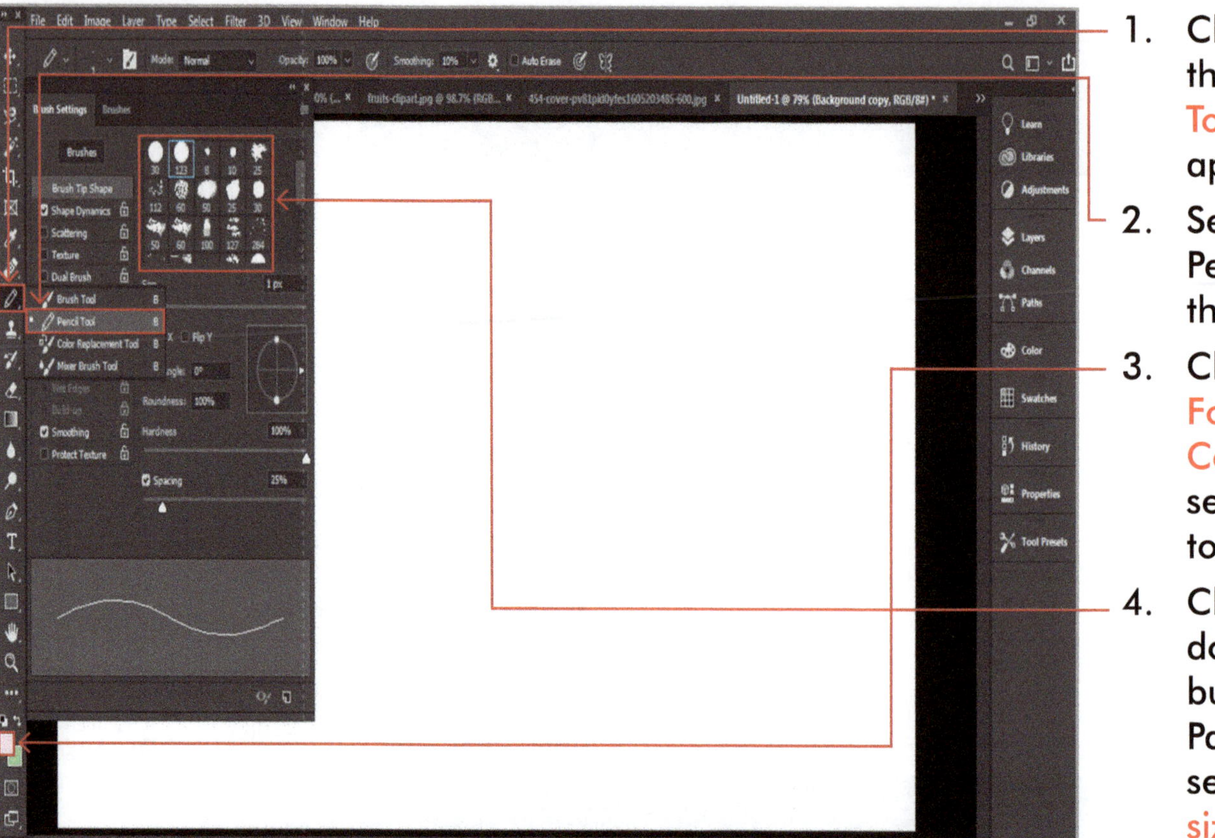

1. Click and hold the Paintbrush Tool. A box appears.
2. Select the Pencil Tool from the box.
3. Click on the Foreground Color icon to select a colour to draw with.
4. Click on the down arrow button of Paintbrush and select a brush size and type.

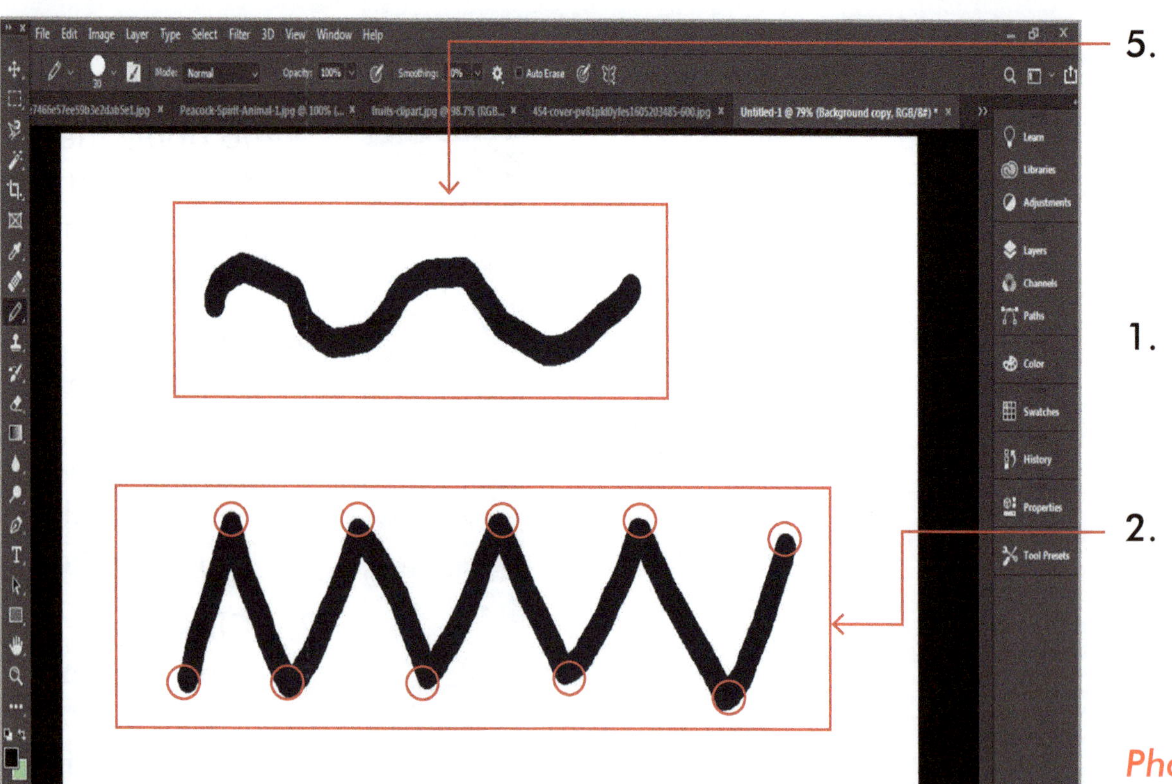

5. Click and drag to apply the foreground colour to the image.

1. Press and hold the Shift key from the keyboard.
2. Click on several places inside your image, without dragging.

Photoshop draws straight lines.

Using Paint Bucket Tool

An area can be filled in your image with solid colour using the Paint Bucket Tool.

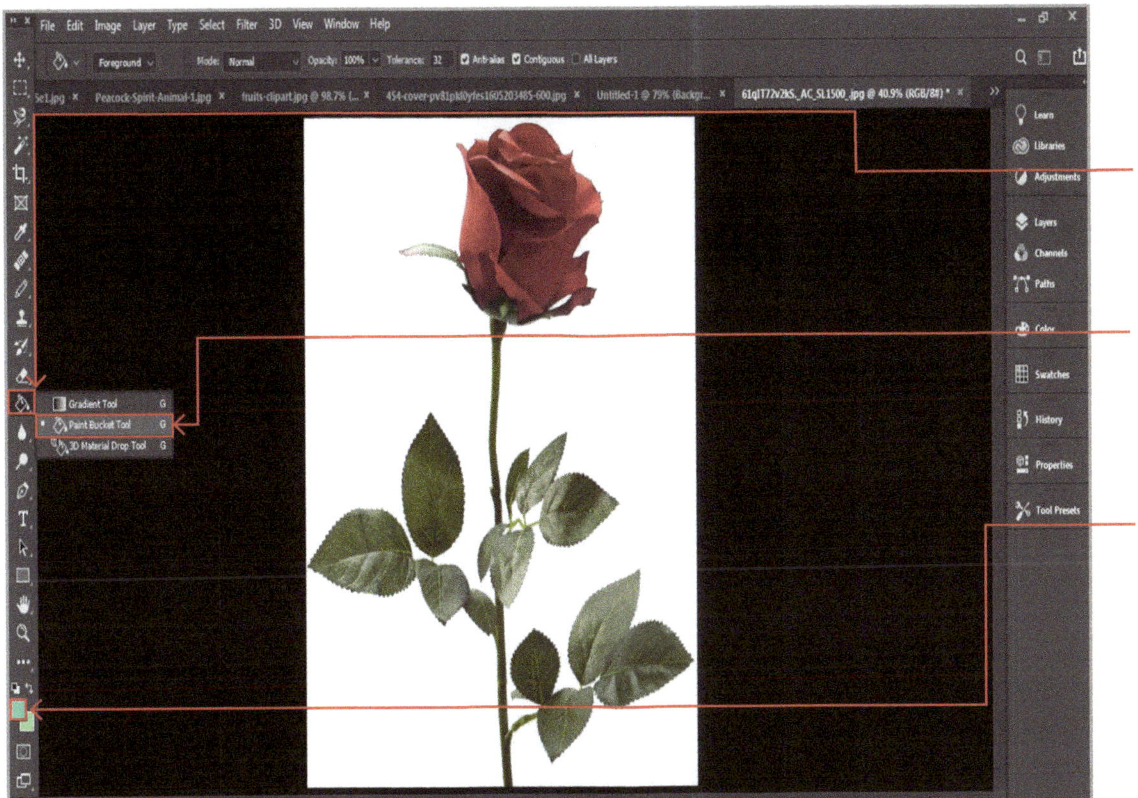

1. Click and hold the Gradient Tool.
2. Click the Paint Bucket Tool ( ) in the window that appears.
3. Click on the Foreground Color icon to select a colour for painting.

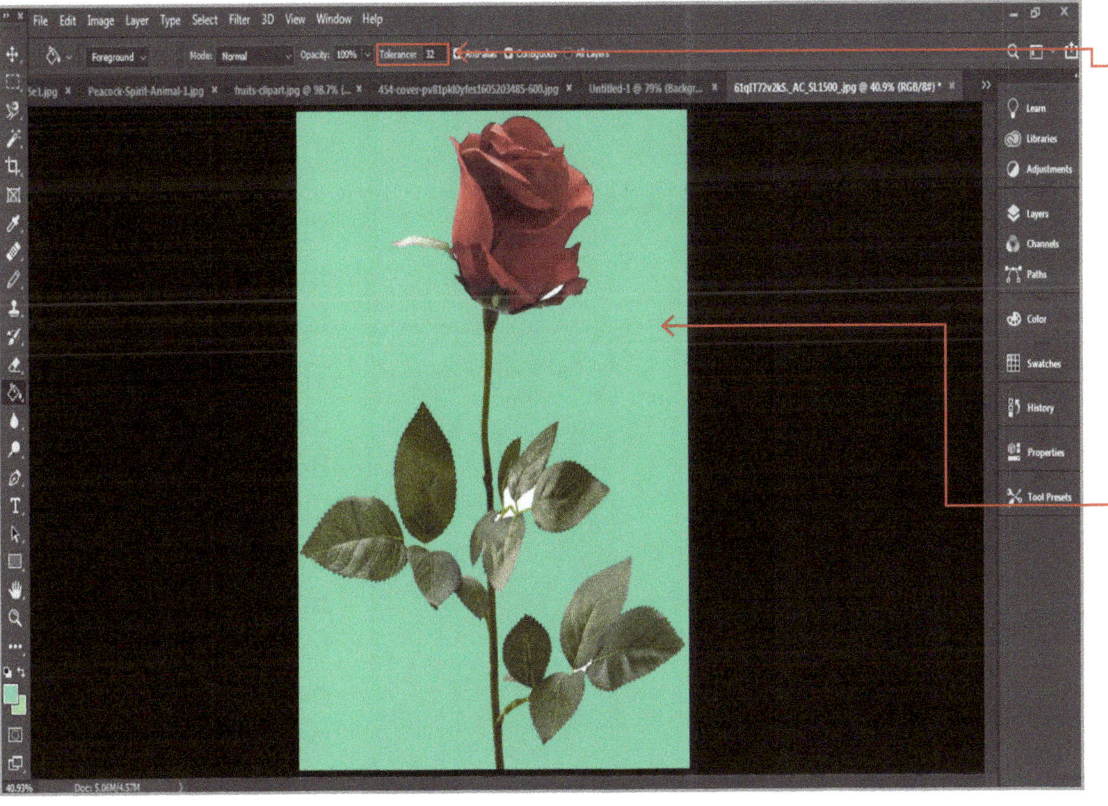

4. Type a Tolerance value from 0 to 255.

The Tolerance value determines what range of colours the paint bucket affects in the image when applied.

5. Click inside the image.

Photoshop fills an area of image with the foreground colour.

The Paint Bucket Tool affects adjacent pixels in the image.

Fill in the Selection

Fill command is used to fill a selection. It is an alternative to the Paint Bucket Tool.

1. Make a selection using any selection tools in an image.
2. Click on Edit in the menu bar.
3. Click on Fill. The Fill dialog box will appear.
4. Click on the down arrow button and choose the option.
5. Click on OK.

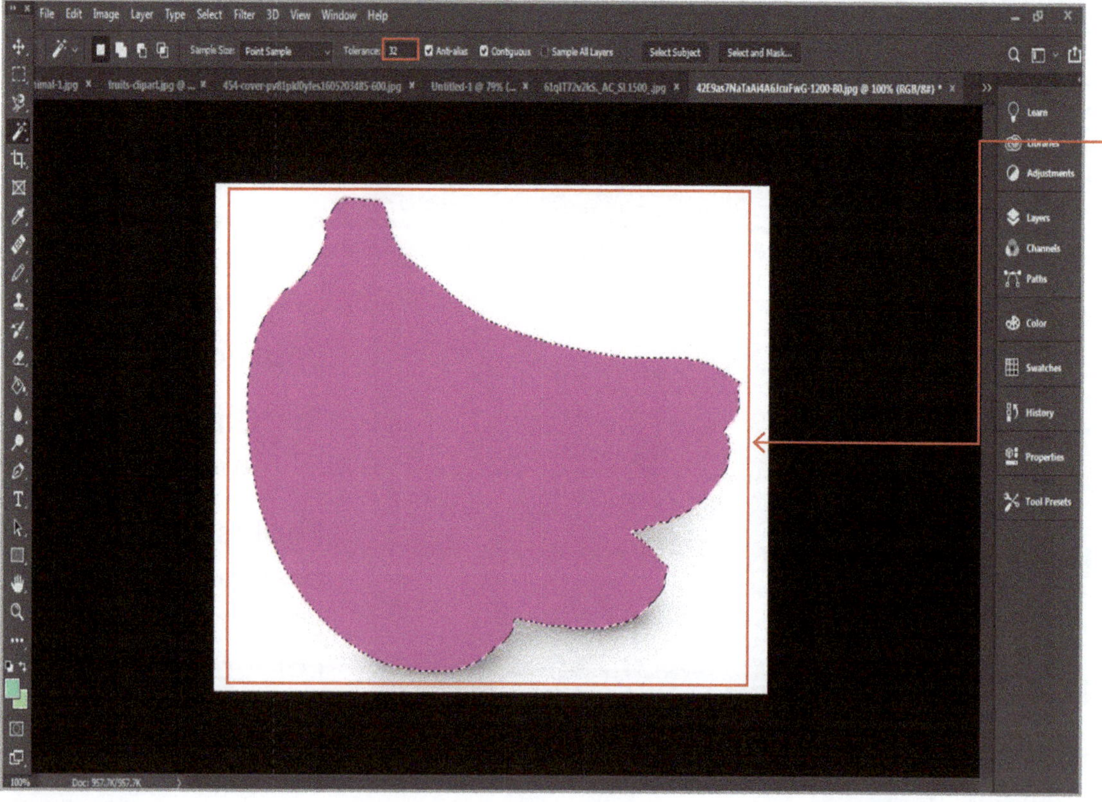

Photoshop fills the area with the foreground colour.

The main difference between Paint Bucket Tool is that Fill command fills the entire selected area with the foreground colour, not just adjacent pixels based on the tolerance value.

Brightness and Contrast

You can adjust the brightness and contrast of your image.

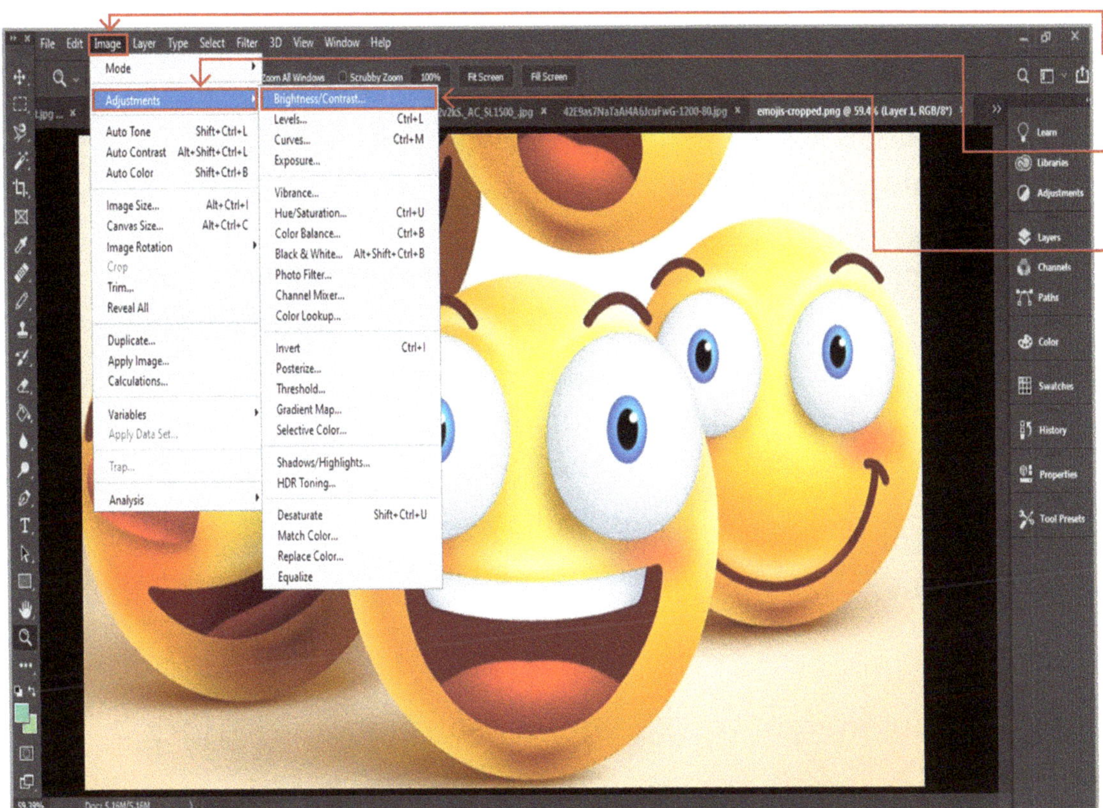

1. Click on Image in the menu bar.
2. Click on Adjustments.
3. Click on Brightness/ Contrast.

A dialog box appears.

4. To lighten the image, click and drag the Brightness: slider to the right, or darken the image by dragging it to the left.

5. To increase the contrast, click and drag the Contrast slider to the right, or to decrease contrast, drag it to the left.
6. Click on OK.

Colour Balance

To change the amount of specific colours in your image, you can use the Color Balance command.

1. Click on Image in the menu bar.
2. Click on Adjustments.
3. Click on Color Balance. A dialog box appears.

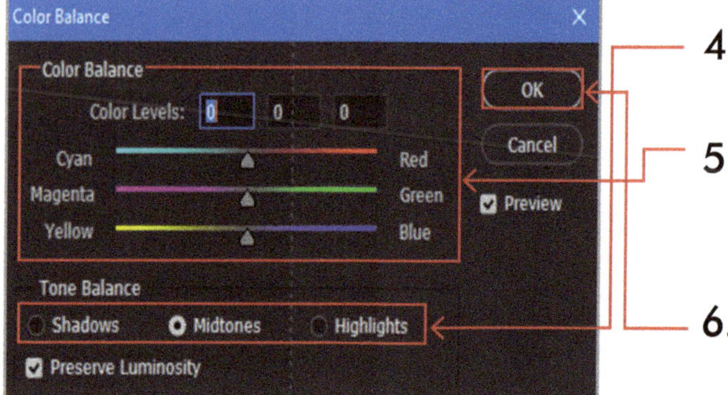

4. Select the radio button of Tone Balance in the image that you want to affect.
5. Click and drag the color sliders to adjust the colour or type a number from 1 to 100 in the Colour Levels field.
6. Click on OK.

HDR Toning

To make colour adjustments in your image, you can get a user-friendly interface by HDR Toning command.

1. Click on Image in the menu bar.
2. Click on Adjustments.
3. Click on HDR Toning.

The HDR Toning window will appear.

4. Click on the Advanced to select the different tones in image.
5. Move the slider left to make Fine (small) adjustments or right to make Coarse (large) adjustments.

6. Click on OK.

Photoshop makes colour adjustments to the image.

Using Dodge Effect

You can use the Dodge tool to lighten a specific area of an image. Dodge is a photographic term that describes the diffusing of light while developing a film negative.

1. Click on the Dodge tool.
2. Click on the down arrow button of Brush menu and choose the brush size and type that you would like to use.
3. You can also select the range of colours you want to affect.
4. Click and drag over the area that you want to lighten.

Using Burn Effect

You can use the Burn Tool to darken a specific area of an image. Burn is a photographic term that describes the focusing of light while developing a film negative.

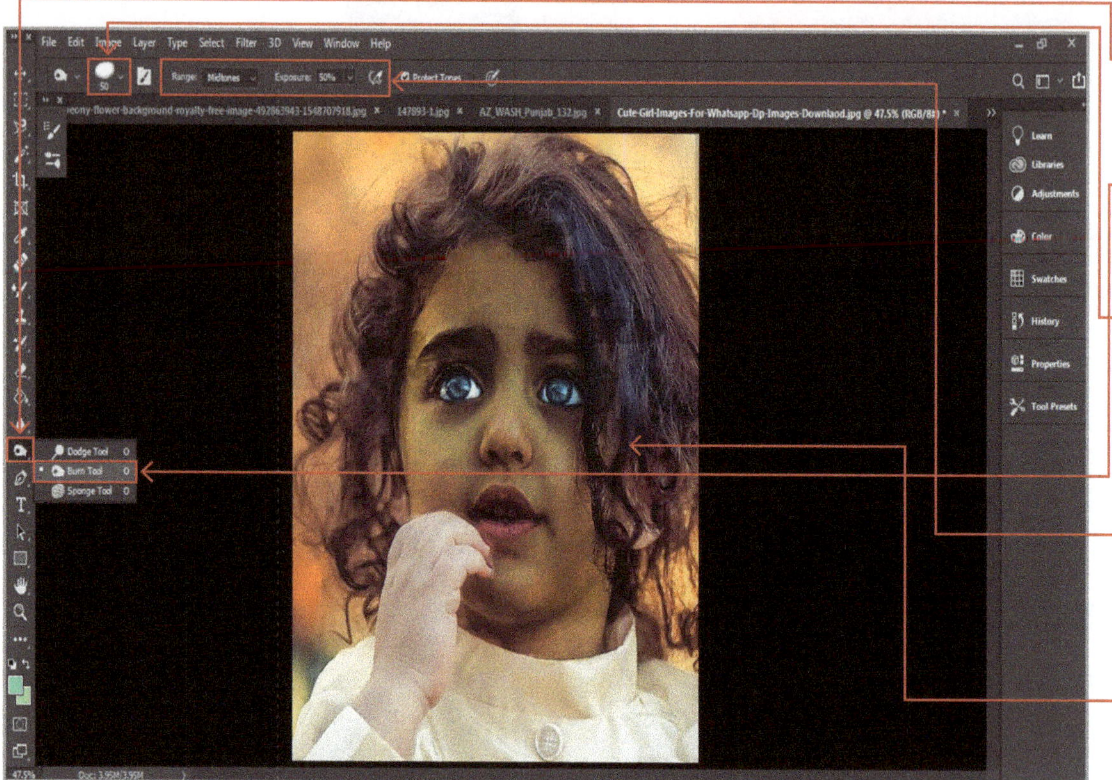

1. Click and hold the Dodge Tool. A box appears.
2. Click the Burn Tool in the box that appears.
3. Click on the down arrow button of Brush: menu and choose the brush size and type.
4. You can also select the range of colours you want to affect.
5. Click and drag over the area that you want to darken.

Saving A Photoshop Image

You can save your image in Photoshop native image format. This format enables you to retain multiple layers in your image.

1. Click on File. The File menu will appear.
2. Click on Save. If the file has yet to be named and saved, the Save as dialog box appears.

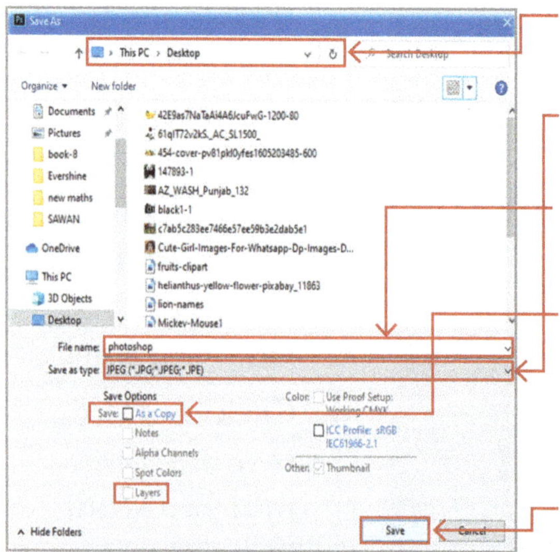

3. Click the down arrow button and choose a folder in which to save the image file.
4. Click the down arrow button and select the Photoshop file format.
5. Name the image file.

Photoshop automatically assigns .psd extension.

If you would like to save a copy of the file and keep the existing file open, click the checkbox of As a Copy.

If you would like to merge the multiple layers of your image into one layer, click Layer check box.

6. Click on Save.

Photoshop saves the image file.

Saving An Image For Use In Another Application

You can save your image in a format that can be opened and used in other imaging or page layout application. TIFF (Tagged Image File Format) and EPS (Encapsulated PostScript) are standard printing formats that are supported by many application on both Windows and Macintosh platform. BMP (bitmap) is a popular Windows image format, and PICT is a popular Macintosh image format.

LET'S HAVE A LOOK

- Adobe Photoshop is a graphics editor software developed and published by Adobe Systems.
- Photoshop tools let you move, colour, stylize and add text to the elements of your image.
- A foreground colour helps to paint, fill and strike selection.
- A background colour helps to make gradient fills in the erased areas of an image.
- You can select a rectangular or an elliptical area of your image by using the Marquee tools.
- Eyedropper tool enables you to paint using a colour already present in your image by selecting a colour from it.
- You can adjust the highlights and shadows of your image by Brightness and Contrast command.
- You can change the amounts of specific colours in your image by the Color balance command.
- Burn Tool is used to darken a specific area of an image.
- The Toolbox contains many separate tools. You can simply click on the tool to select it for working on your image.
- Magnetic Lasso Tool is used to select the elements of your image that have well-defined edges.

BRAIN TEASER

1. Multiple Choice Questions

Tick (✓) the correct answer:

a. It displays control that customizes the selected tool in the toolbar:

i. Toolbox ☐ ii. Option bar ☐ iii. Panel ☐

b. Small windows that give you access to common commands and resources:

i. Panel ☐ ii. Option bar ☐ iii. Toolbox ☐

c. It can be used to change the size of an image:

i. Crop tool ☐ ii. Lasso tool ☐ iii. Marquee tool ☐

e. To darken a specific area of an image:

i. Burn Effect ☐ ii. Brush Strokes ☐ iii. Dodge Effect ☐

d. It can be used to copy information from one area of an image to another:

   i. Magic Wand tool ☐ ii. Lasso tool ☐

   iii. Clone Stamp tool ☐

2. Fill in the blanks:

a. A small black arrow in the __________ corner of the toolbox indicates additional tools.

b. Panel is a small window that can access common __________ & __________.

c. When an image has been altered, it is usually known as __________.

d. Marquee tool can select __________ or __________ area of an image.

e. __________ tool can select the groups of similarly coloured pixels.

3. Write 'T' for True and 'F' for False in the boxes:

a. Adobe Photoshop is a presentation software. ☐

b. The default background colour is black. ☐

c. Lasso Tool is also used to create curved or jagged selection. ☐

d. Dodge tool is used to lighten a specific area of an image. ☐

e. Photoshop toolbox contains many separate tools. ☐

f. Burn tool is used to lighten a specific area of an image. ☐

4. Answer the following questions

(i) Answer each in a few lines:

a. What is Photoshop?

b. Which tool is used to darken the specific area of an image?

c. Which lasso tool can easily create a selection composed of straight lines?

d. What is the purpose of Eyedropper tool?

e. What is the default background colour of Photoshop?

(ii) Answer each comprehensively:

a. Explain Photoshop tools.

b. What is the importance of using brightness and contrast on an image?

c. What do you mean by the term Photoshop?

d. Write the procedure to:

i. Select an image using any of the selection tools.
ii. Lighten a specific area of an image.

LAB ACTIVITY

1. Each of the students will insert a picture from the photo gallery.

1. Change the background colour.
2. Change the size of the image by using crop tool.
3. Make the canvas size bigger than the original image.
4. Change the brightness and colour balance of the picture.
5. Save the image by your name on the desktop.

2. Match the tools name with their uses:

a. Crop Tool	a. Fill Image with Solid Colour
b. Zoom Tool	b. Encopsulated Portscript
c. Full Screen	c. Add Colour to Images
d. Marquee Tool	d. Copy Information
e. Move Tool	e. Move, delete or stylize images
f. Clone Stamp Tool	f. Make Rectangular Selection
g. Paintbrush Tool	g. Changes Screen Modes
h. Paint Bucket Tool	h. Cropping the Image
i. EPS	i. To Magnity the Image

Formative Assessment - 3
(Chapters 6-8)

1. Fill in the blanks:

a. ____________ stands for HyperText Markup Language.

b. HTML consists of text with special instructions known as ____________ .

c. Some tags have ____________ that offer options for the tag

d. The full form of IDE is ____________ .

e. All the other controls are placed on the ____________ control.

f. Marquee tool can select ____________ or ____________ area of an image.

g. The ____________ tool can select the groups of similarly coloured pixels.

2. Answer the following questions:

a. What is Photoshop?

b. Which tool is used to darken the specific area of an image?

c. State the features of the language Visual Basic.

d. What do you mean by event-driven programming? Explain with an example.

e. Define Visual Studio. How do you open the VS Express application?

f. What do you mean by HTML tags and its attributes?

g. What is the use of IMG and SRC?

h. Differentiate between alternative text and image label.

i. What are hyperlinks in HTML?

j. What are the three different modes of the Visual Studio Express?

3. Define the following terms of Visual Studio 2017:

a. Properties – ____________

b. Form – ____________

c. Control – ____________

d. Solution – ____________

e. Project – ______________________________

f. GUI – ______________________________

g. CONTROLS – ______________________________

4. Write the full form of given Acronyms:

a. HTML : ______________________________

b. IMG : ______________________________

c. JPEG : ______________________________

d. SRC : ______________________________

e. GIF : ______________________________

f. PNG : ______________________________

5. Lable the different components of Windows Form App window:

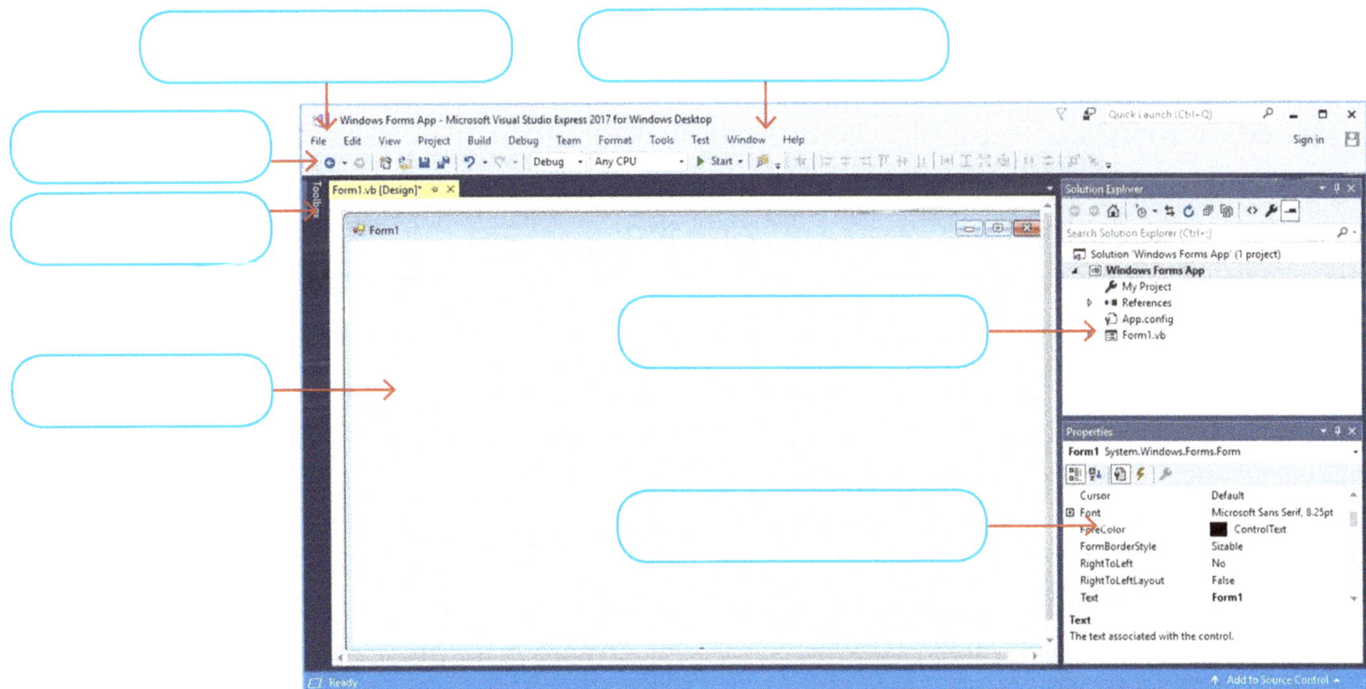

9 Network Topology

In this chapter, we will learn:

⇒ Computer Network and Its Kinds
⇒ Components of Computer Network
⇒ Network Topologies
⇒ Communication Channels of Computer System

Hello friends, in your previous class you learnt about network. In this chapter you will learn to design a computer network which is called network topology. Let us first review what we learnt in the previous class.

NETWORK

A network is a collection of interconnected computers. Networks can be divided into three kinds on the basis of number of computers attached and the area in which they are spread out.

A network consists of multiple computers connected using some type of interface, each having one or more interface devices, such as a Network Interface Card (NIC). Each computer is supported by network software that provides the server or client functionality. The hardware used to transmit data across the network is called the media. It may include copper cable, fibre optic or wireless transmission.

A network may vary from another network. Three kinds of network are:

LAN : In Local Area Network (LAN), computers are connected by wires, cables, etc. It is generally installed by small organisations, like offices, hospitals, etc.

MAN : Metropolitan Area Network (MAN) covers a larger area as compared to 'LAN'. This kind of network is spread over a city or a town. For example, cable TV network.

WAN : In Wide Area Network (WAN) kind of network, computers are separated by large distances in different cities, states and countries. For example, the network spreads throughout the world, like the Internet.

Computer Network

Components of Computer Network

The basic components of computer network can be divided into two types. These are:

1. Hardware components
2. Software components

Hardware components in a network include:

⇒ Computer systems, which are called servers or clients.

⇒ Shared resources like printers, scanners, etc.

⇒ Physical media that connects them.

Software Components

These components are required to run the computer network.

Protocols: The protocols help to specify rules and procedures for communication and transfer of data in the computer network. For instance, TCP or Transmission Control Protocol and IP or Internet Protocol.

Network Software: Network Software is a software that performs various network- related functions. For example, data routing, error detection, etc.

NETWORK TOPOLOGY

On the basis of the computer components, the network can be classified into two categories:

Client-Server Network: Servers are the computers that receive requests from clients and make the resources available to them. Different computers that access shared resources on the network are clients. Client-server networks are the networks which have a dedicated server. This dedicated server works only as a server and is not used as a work station. So, all the communication from the clients is routed through the server which makes the shared resources available to the clients.

Peer-to-peer Network: Peer-to-peer networks do not have any dedicated server. Each computer serves the purpose of a client as well as a server. These are easy to maintain as a server. Basically, they are suitable for small organisations. Many networks are a combination of peer-to-peer and server-based networks. The network operating system uses a network data protocol to communicate on the network to other computers. The network operating system supports the applications on that computer; it includes Windows NT, Linux, Unix and others. Peer-to-peer networks are also known as work groups.

The term 'topology' refers to the layout structure of connected devices on a network. Network topology states how a network is designed. A network topology has two levels, *i.e.* physical and logical.

The physical level is composed as the parts of a network that physically exist, such as computers, cables and connectors. This level specifies where the computers on a network are located and how all the parts of the network are connected. Cables are the most popular transmission media to transfer information on network.

The logical level traces the path on which the information takes to reach its destination on a network. The logical level of a network depends on many factors, such as the applications used and the volume of information transferred over the network. Computers share information by exchanging electrical signals.

Signals are sent via the transmission medium that connects computers.

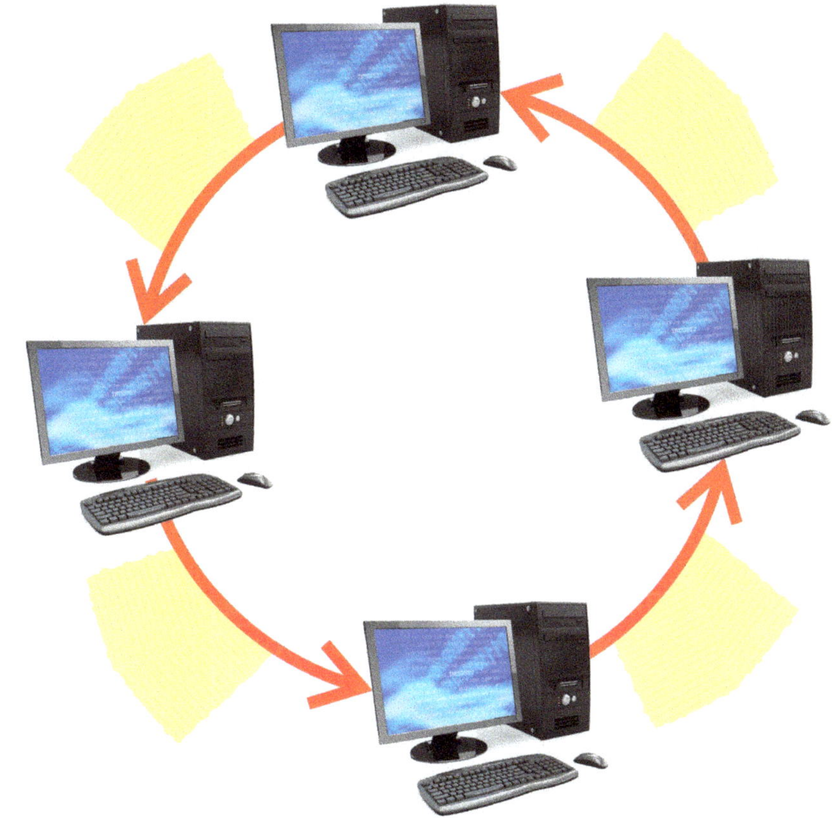

Physical

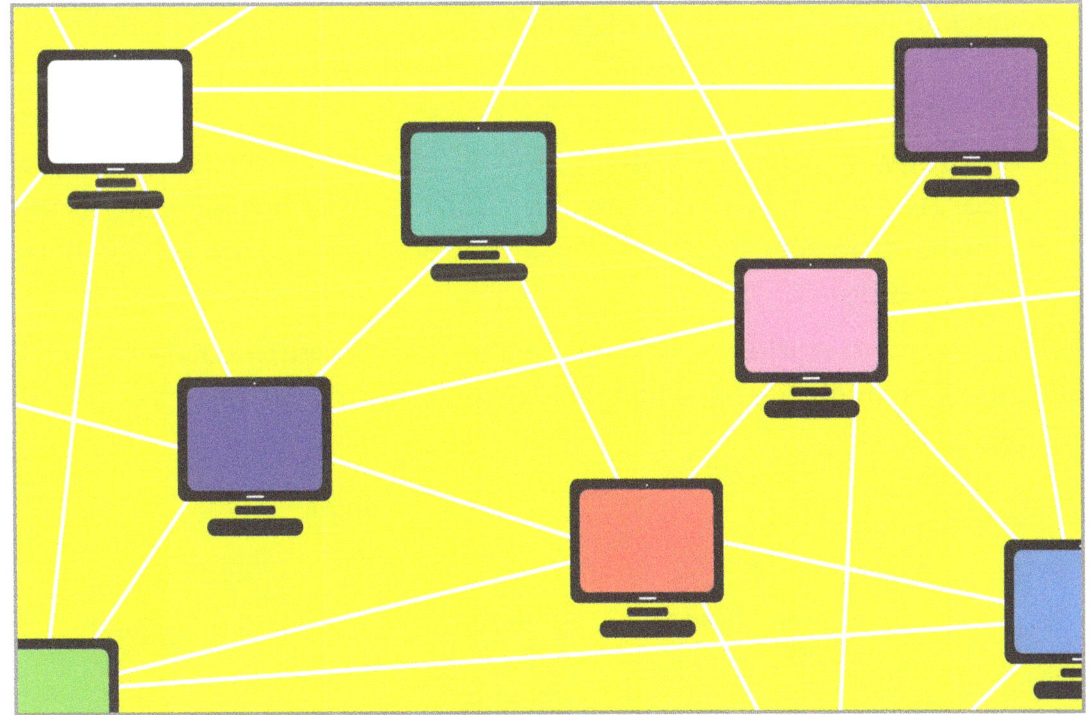

Logical

Bus, Ring, Star, and Mesh are the five main types of Network Topologies:

Bus Topology

In this kind of topology, all the computers and its devices are connected to one single cable called the Bus. This Bus network is also called linear network. The bus network transmits data, instructions and information in both directions. Only one computer can communicate at a time in bus topology. A device wanting to communicate with another device on the network, sends a broadcast message onto the wire that all other devices can see, but only the intended recipient accepts and processes the message.

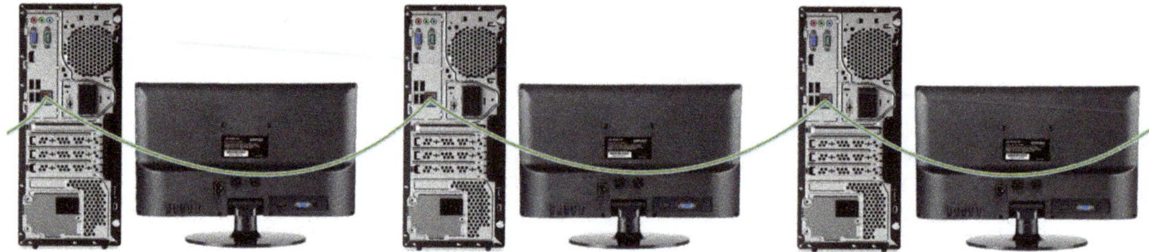

In this topology, computer system can be easily added to or removed from the network. The failure of single node does not affect the performance of the remaining network.

Star Topology

In this kind of topology, a device called a hub is placed at the centre to which all the other nodes are connected. All the information that is transferred from one computer to another on the network passes via the hub. Star networks are one of the most common computer network topologies.

It is easy to add or remove nodes. A failure in any star network cable will only take down one computer network access and not the entire network. When the hub fails then the network also fails.

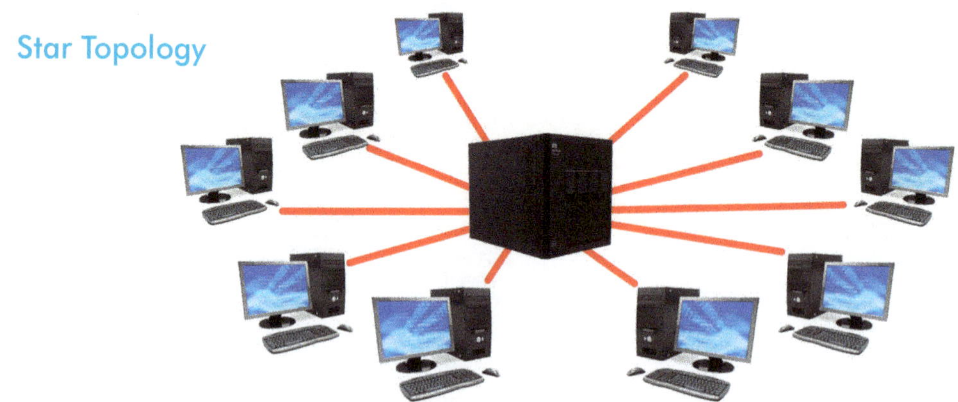

Star Topology

HUB

A hub is a device where all the cables on a network meet. Hubs are found on most modern networks. Earlier, only star network structures used hubs. It is now very common to use hubs to connect computers.

Ring Topology

In this kind of topology, as the name suggests, nodes are connected in a circular chain in which each node is connected to the next one and the last node is connected to the first one. Every device has exactly two neighbours for communication purposes. All messages travel through a ring in the same direction (either "clockwise" or "counter-clockwise").

Ring Topology

If one node fails, the whole network fails.

Computers are usually located close together. A ring network is easy to set up because computers are attached to a single ring of cable. No central connector, such as hub, is required. There is no beginning or end in a ring network.

Ring Network Model

Hybrid Topology

Hybrid topologies consist of different topologies, such as ring, star and bus. In its simplest form, only hub devices connect directly to the bus; and each hub functions as the "root" of a tree of devices. This bus/star hybrid approach supports the future expandability of the network much better than a bus (limited in the number of devices due to the broadcast traffic it generates) or a star (limited by the number of hub connection points) alone.

Wide Area Networks (WANs) are commonly hybrid networks. WANs often connect multiple network structures to create one large network. For example, a company could use the star network structure in one office and the bus network structure in another office. The individual networks could then be connected by a microwave or satellite to form a hybrid network.

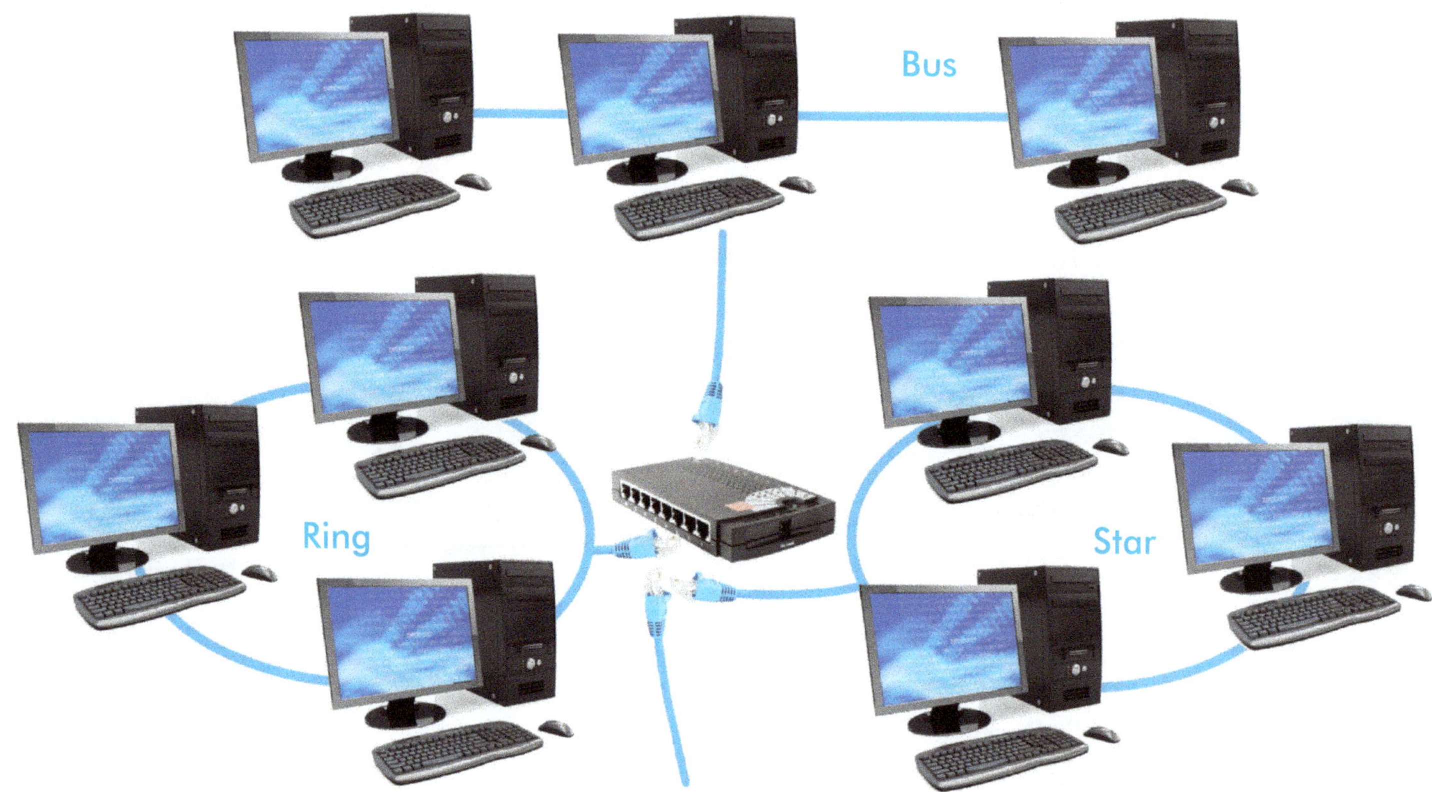

Hybrid Topology

Mesh Topology

Mesh topologies involve the concept of routes. Unlike each of the previous topologies, messages sent on a mesh network can take any of several possible paths from source to destination. Some WANs, most notably the Internet, employ mesh routing.

Mesh Topology

COMMUNICATION CHANNELS

All networks are linked to one another. Media or channels refer to cable, etc., by which data travels from the destination sources. This media is flexible, has low weight and easy to install but cannot carry data to long distances.

Most commonly used media are:

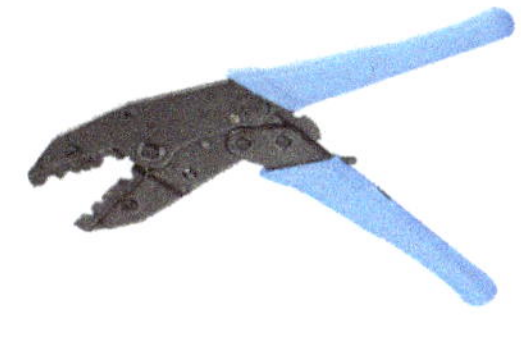

⇒ Twisted pair wire
⇒ Coaxial cable
⇒ Fibre optic cable
⇒ Wireless links

Twisted-Pair Cable

Twisted-pair wire consists of copper wire strands, which are insulated with the help of plastic sheet and twisted around each other.

Twisted-Pair Cable

A plastic coating on each wire prevents the copper in one wire from touching the copper in another. The twist helps reduce interference by preventing electrical signals on the wire radiating energy (causing interference) and by preventing signals on other wires interfering with the pair. The twists allow the signal to travel further than it could on a regular copper wire. The more twists per centimetre, the further the signal can travel.

Coaxial Cable

Coaxial cable consists of solid wire core surrounded by a wire mesh with the help of insulator in between them. This is commonly used in the cable TV networks.

Coaxial Cable

The coaxial cable provides better protection from interference by providing a metal shield. The metal shield forms a flexible cylinder around the inner wire providing a barrier to electromagnetic radiation, both incoming and outgoing.

The cable can run parallel to other cables and can be bent round corners.

A coaxial cable can carry more data than twisted pair wire. It is less susceptible to interference. It is more expensive as compared to twisted pair wire.

Fibre-Optic Cable

Fibre-optic cable is a thin strand of glass, which transmits light beams. These cables are completely noise-immune. They are fragile and need to be handled very carefully.

Light moves at different speeds in different mediums. It travels fastest through a vacuum, and slower through a medium like the Earth's atmosphere. As a result, where there is a boundary between different media, the direction of a light beam can be altered. We can measure this change, called the index of refraction.

A fibre-optic cable is made from a special medium that has two important properties: light travels easily through it, and the index of refraction is such that very little light can escape. To communicate using a fibre-optic cable, a light source produces pulses of light that travel through the cable. These pulses carry information that can be translated into a picture or voice.

Optical fibres have the following four main advantages over copper wires.

⇒ They use light, which neither causes electrical interference nor are they susceptible to electrical interference.

⇒ They are manufactured to reflect the light inwards, so a fibre can carry a pulse of light further than a copper wire can carry a signal.

⇒ Light can encode more information than electrical signals, so they carry more information than a wire.

⇒ Light can carry a signal over a single fibre, unlike electricity, which requires a pair of wires.

Fibre-Optic Cable

Wireless Link

Wireless links rely on radio signals for the transmission of data. Wireless communication is becoming popular. It is also competing with twisted pair, coaxial and fibre optic cables.

A wireless LAN links devices via a wireless distribution method (typically radio signals), and usually provides a connection through an access point to the wider Internet. This gives users the mobility to move around within a local coverage area and still be connected to the network.

Wireless LANs have become popular at home due to the ease of installation, and the increasing popularity of laptop computers. There are four common applications of wireless communication in the field of computer networking.

⇒ Office LANs can use radio signals to transmit data between nodes.

⇒ Telephone instruments can be used along with the modem to connect laptops for business communication.

⇒ LAN can be connected by using microwave transmission within the metropolitan area.

⇒ Satellites are used to connect WANs covering large distances.

LET'S HAVE A LOOK

- A network is a collection of interconnected computers.
- Three kinds of network are LAN, WAN and MAN.
- The components of a computer network are hardware and software.
- Networks can be classified into Client-Server network and Peer-to-Peer network.
- There are five basic network topologies: bus, star, ring, hybrid and mesh topology.
- The most commonly used communication channels are twisted pair wire, coaxial cable, fibre optical cable and wireless links.

BRAIN TEASER

1. Multiple Choice Questions

Tick (✓) the correct answer:

a. In this type of network, computers are connected by wires, cables, etc:

i. LAN ☐ ii. MAN ☐ iii. WAN ☐

b. It specifies rules and procedures for communication and transfer of data in the computer network:

i. Server ☐ ii. Protocol ☐ iii. Computer ☐

c. A computer that receives requests from clients and makes the resources available to them:

i. Server ☐ ii. Client ☐ iii. Computer ☐

d. This network does not have any dedicated server:

i. Client/Server ☐ ii. Protocol ☐ iii. Peer-to-peer ☐

e. The bus network is also called:

i. Linear ☐ ii. Physical ☐ iii. Server ☐

f. In Star topology, this device is placed at the centre where all other nodes are connected:

i. Hub ☐ ii. Cable ☐ iii. Node ☐

g. A topology consists of different topologies, such as ring, star and bus:

i. BUS ☐ ii. Hybrid ☐ iii. STAR ☐

h. The links rely on radio signals for the transmission of data:

i. Wired ☐ ii. Wireless ☐ iii. Cable ☐

i. Mesh topologies involve the concept of:

i. Bus ☐ ii. Routes ☐ iii. Servers ☐

j. Most commonly used media or cables in a network are:

i. Pen drive ☐ ii. Coaxial ☐ iii Tree ☐

2. Fill in the blanks:

a. ____________ area network is spread over a city or a town.

b. ____________ are also known as work groups.

c. ____________ is also called linear network.

d. A failure in any ____________ cable will take down only one computer network access and not the entire LAN.

e. ____________ is a thin strand of glass, which transmits pulsating light beams.

f. ____________ relies on radio signals for the transmission of data.

3. Write 'T' for True and 'F' for False in the boxes:

a. Networking refers to creating documents. ☐

b. Three kinds of network are LAN, WAN and MAN. ☐

c. The components of a computer network are BUS and STAR. ☐

d. Wireless relies on radio signals for the transmission of data. ☐

e. Coaxial is a thin strand of glass, which transmits light beams. ☐

4. Answer the following questions

(i) Answer each in a few lines:

a. Name the various kinds of network topologies.

b. Name the types of communication media.

(ii) Answer each comprehensively:

a. What is a computer network?

b. Explain various kinds of network.

c. Write a note on the components of network.

d. What is network topology?

e. Explain various kinds of network topologies.

f. What is communication channel?

g. Write a note on the most commonly used media in networks.

h. Write a note on the common applications of wireless communication in the field of computer networking.

5. Write a brief note on given network topologies:

a. Bus Topology ____________________

____

____

____

____

b. Ring Topology ____________________

____

____

____

____

c. Hybrid Topology ____________________

____

____

____

____

LAB ACTIVITY

1. Make a project on networking.

2. Draw the diagrams of the following and write short notes on them:

a. LAN

b. MAN

c. WAN

10 Internet Services

In this chapter, we will learn:

⇒ Introduction to Internet
⇒ Services of Internet
⇒ Various Messengers
⇒ Blogging
⇒ Shopping
⇒ E-commerce

INTERNET

The Internet is a network of networks. It is also called Net. It connects computers across the world. It is one of the major reasons why people buy computers these days. The Internet offers both information access and a fast and cheap mean of communication to the public.

Internet

The advantage of the Internet is that you can use it from a computer anywhere: at home, at work, at school or at a restaurant. Any person who gets connected to the Internet gets connected to you; you can communicate with anyone on the Internet by sending e-mail, posting messages in newsgroups (electronic bulletin boards), chatting in real time in various chats, and even telephoning and videoconferencing over the Internet.

SERVICES OF INTERNET

The Internet is a vast, worldwide network that enables people around the world to use a variety of Internet services in daily activities. Internet services allow home and business users to access the Web for activities such as conducting research, social networking, blogging, chatting, surfing and many more.

World Wide Web

World Wide Web or WWW is one of the main services of the Internet. It is a massive storehouse of information that resides on computers, called Web servers, located all over the world. Each Web server hosts one or more Web sites, and each of those

sites contains dozens, hundreds or even thousands of documents called Web pages. On the Web, you navigate from one place to another by selecting a link that appears on a Web page. You do all of this using a special software program called a Web browser.

WEB PAGE: A Web page is an electronic document on the Web that includes text, images, sound and video.

WEBSITE: A collection of Web pages created and maintained by a college, university, government agency, company, an organisation or an individual is called Web site.

WEB SERVER: A powerful computer that stores Web pages and makes the pages available on the Web for other people is called Web server.

URL: Each Web page has a unique address, called a Uniform Resource Locator (URL).

LINKS: The highlighted text or images on a Web page that are connected to other pages on the Web are called links. Links are also known as hyperlinks. You can select a link to display a Web page located on the same computer or on a computer across the city, country or world.

WEB BROWSER: A program that allows you to view and explore information on the Web is called Web browser. Safari and Google Chrome are two popular Web Browsers.

HOME PAGE: When you open a Web browser to explore information, the first page that appears is a home page.

Electronic Mail (E-mail)

Electronic mail (e-mail) was one of the original features of the Internet, enabling scientists and researchers working on government-sponsored projects to communicate with their colleagues at other locations. Now almost anyone who has an Internet account also has access to e-mail, so theoretically you can communicate with almost any Internet user in the world. This versatility has made e-mail one of the most popular Internet services.

E-mail is quite fast, easy and inexpensive. Unlike postal mail messages which can take days to be delivered and require postage, e-mail messages are usually delivered within minutes and you do not pay an extra charge to send them. Today, e-mail is rapidly climbing the popularity charts as a primary communications method for both personal and business use.

Search Engine

The Web is a worldwide resource of information. A primary reason that people use the Internet is to search for specific information, including text, pictures, music and video.

A search engine is a software program which helps find Web sites, Web pages and Internet files. Search engines are particularly helpful in locating Web pages on certain topics or in locating specific pages for which you do not know the exact URL.

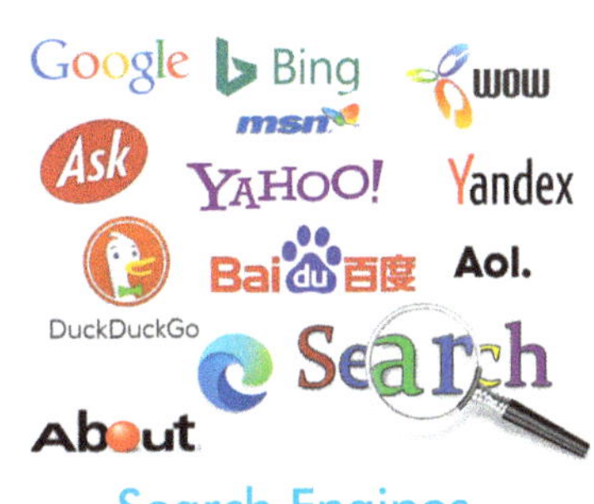

Search Engines

To find a page or pages, you enter a word or phrase, called search text or keywords, in the text box of the search engine's. Many search engines use a program called a spider to display a list of all Web pages that contain the word or phrase you entered. Also called a crawler or bot, a spider reads pages on Web sites in order to create a catalogue or an index of hits. A hit is any Web page name that lists as the result of a search.

Finding People on the Internet

The Internet provides many search sites that are primarily intended to help you locate general information, like finding people and places.

In the social networking sites like Facebook and Instagram, it's become easier to find old friends and colleagues. In these sites you can search for the people who are registered and have created their profiles.

If you're looking for a long lost friend, or maybe want to do a background check on someone, consider the following free resources to find people on the Internet. www.people.yahoo.com, PeopleFinders.com, etc. are the most reliable sources for finding people and obtaining records about them.

Another powerful search is Google's Blog Search which will find anyone who has published a blog on the Internet. Google Groups is also the most powerful tool to find someone who may have posted on the Internet a long time ago. Another best search engine for finding people through searching for all types of Internet content is 123people.

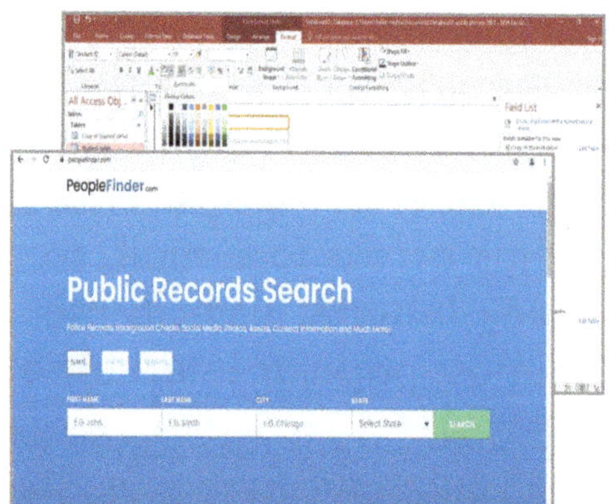

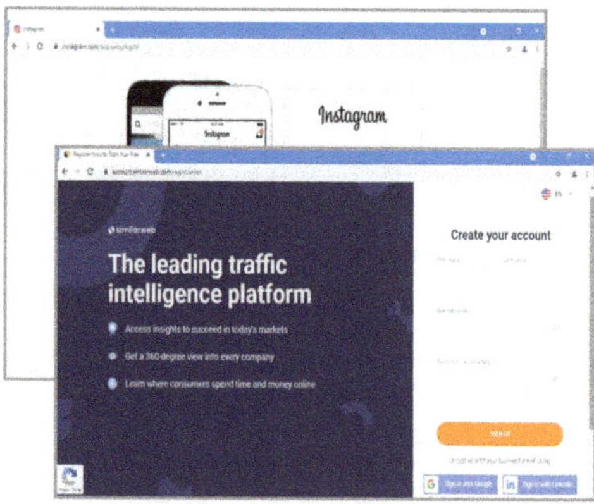

The sites shown above will help you to find details about the persons. But in most cases, you'll need a few more details about the persons, like their birthdays or the states they live in.

Online Chatting

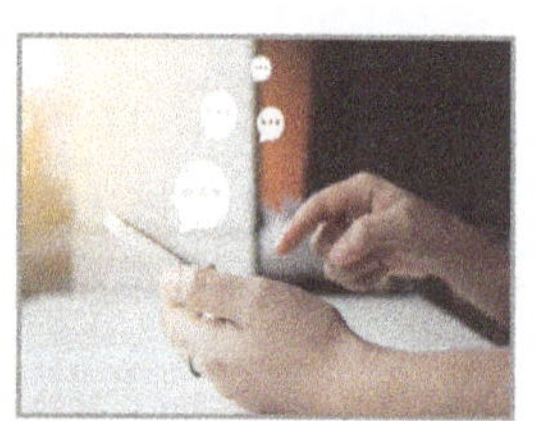

A chat is a real-time typed conversation that takes place on a computer or smartphone. It is like a text-phone. On the telephone you say something; people on the other side of phone hear it and respond; you listen to their response and reply on the spot. In the same way, in real-time chatting as you type on your keyboard, a line of characters and symbols displays on the computer screen. Others connected to the same chat room server can also see what you have typed and type the message in response to your message which you receive on the spot.

Most people use chat as a form of entertainment. You can use chat to meet new friends from all over the world. Many students use chat to discuss assignments and get help from instructors and fellow students. Chatting is a low-cost way to stay in touch with friends or relatives who have access to the Internet.

Video Conferencing

Video Conferencing

A video conference is a meeting between two or more geographically separated people who use a network or the Internet to transmit audio and video data. Essentially, it is a live connection between people in multiple locations that provides full-motion video images and high-quality audio.

The equipment required to participate or use video conferencing effectively is a multimedia computer; you need video conferencing software along with a microphone, speakers and a video camera attached to or built-in to a computer. As you speak, the members of the meeting hear your voice on their speakers. Any image in front of the video camera, such as a person's face, appears in a window on each participant's screen.

Instant Messages

You can exchange instant messages to have a private conversation with friends, colleagues and members of family on the Internet.

Instant messaging (IM) is a real-time Internet communications service that notifies you, when one or more people are online and then allows you to exchange messages or files or join a private chat room with them. Each message you send will immediately appear on the other person's screen.

You need to instal an instant messaging program on your computer to exchange instant messages with other people. You must use the same instant messaging program as the people you want to exchange messages with. Some of the popular instant messaging programs are:

WhatsApp

WhatsApp is famous as the most popular instant messaging app in the world. The app offers chat, voice call and video call services across the globe for free. It is available on iPhone and Android smartphones as well as Mac and Windows PC.

Facebook Messenger

Facebook Messenger or simply Messenger is an instant messaging app by Meta Platforms Inc. It enables users with features like voice calls, video calls, text messaging, media and files. While it is integrated with Facebook, you can also connect it with Instagram.

Snapchat

Snapchat is one of the rapidly growing instant messaging apps. It lets users chat and send instant photos to others. One of the most cool features of Snap is that you can search for people who are using the social platform within your location and be friends with them.

Telegram

Telegram is one of the most popular globally accessible instant messaging services. It is available as a mobile application as well as web. On Telegram, not only can you chat with your friends but also share large media such as photos, videos and movies. It is available on Android, iOS, Microsoft Windows, macOS, Web application, and Linux operating systems.

Social Networking Or Network Groups

Social Networking is a service on the Internet that enables you to connect with people who share similar personal or professional interests. On most social networking sites, the members are connected to one another as friends, friends of friends, and so on. The main purpose of using social networking sites is to keep track of what is going on in the life of friends, family, and colleagues, especially the people with whom you do not meet daily. It also helps us expand our friend circle and business contacts.

Facebook

Facebook is also the most popular social networking site on the Web, with over 2.5 billions users worldwide. Users can add friends and send them messages, and update their personal profiles to notify friends about themselves.

Facebook was started in 2004 as a tool for connecting students at Harvard University, but it soon expanded to other universities and then to high school students.

Entertainment on Web

The Internet provides many kinds of entertainment for you. You can download music, tune in to Internet-based radio stations, and listen to streaming audio. You can play online games with the other partner around the world. You can see the photos that people are sharing, view streaming videos, watch movies on the YouTube site.

Blogging

There are over 100 million blogs on the Internet. Blogs, also known as Weblogs, are an exciting and dynamic online medium by which you can publish your ideas, opinions and stories online. With millions of blogs available on the Net, you can read what others have published.

A blog is a Web site that consists of a frequently updated collection of entries. A typical blog combines text, images and links to other blogs, Web pages and other media related to its topic.

The entries that appear on a blog are called posts, and the act of publishing a blog entry is called posting.

A single person who maintains many blogs is known as a blogger. Some blogs allow other people to post occasional entries, and those people are known as guest bloggers. There are also many blogs that have multiple authors.

Shopping on the Web (e-shopping)

E-shopping is one of the popular services which allows shopping on the Web; you need not move out of your house. Most Web sites offer the latest information about products and prices. One can also use the Web to find reviews and ratings of the products one wants to buy. In this way, you make an informed decision before making your purchase.

On the Web, you will get the product at a less price than the price in traditional stores because companies save on overhead costs and other costs that they may incur if they have a shop, such as rent and salespeople. In fact, most products come with a discount when they are sold on the Web. One can buy almost anything on the Web from cloth and food to cars and computers.

Share Photos on the Web

You can share your digital photographs with friends, family and even complete strangers by signing up with a photo-sharing site. It enables you to upload digital photos that can be viewed, rated, tagged and commented upon by other people. You can get free accounts from many photo-sharing sites but for a less storage space. To get more storage space and more features, you can also upgrade to a paid account.

Flickr (www.flickr.com)

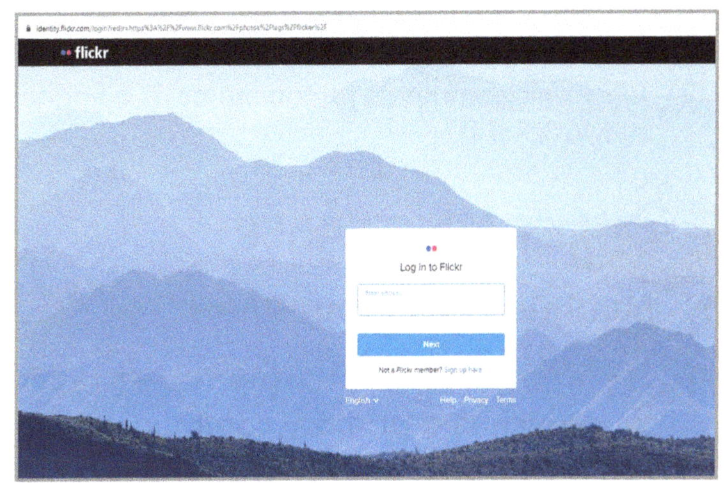

The most popular of the photo-sharing site is Flickr. It allows you to edit your photos, organize them into albums, create cards and books, and control who can view your photos. A free Flickr account enables you to upload 100MB of photos every month. You can upgrade to a Pro account, which is a paid account, that offers unlimited uploads and storage.

E-commerce

Electronic commerce (e-commerce), sometimes called e-business, is a financial business transaction that occurs over an electronic network. Anyone with a computer connected with the Internet and a means to pay (credit card, etc.) for purchased goods or services can participate in e-commerce. Two popular types of e-commerce are shopping and trading stocks.

There are thousands of Web sites devoted to online shopping. Some sites focus on one product or service, such as books or travel, whereas other sites offer a wide range of goods and services. The Web is also a great place to sell your goods and services. Now transactions can occur quickly and globally with e-commerce and a lot of time is saved by this activity.

E-Groups

E-Groups is an online group where the persons of the same interest can share their information on different topics. E-Group is also called e-clubbing where you meet the people of your taste. There are many sites that provide e-groups. Two popular e-groups are Google Groups and Yahoo Groups.

LET'S HAVE A LOOK

- The Internet is a network of networks. It is also called Net.
- The advantage of the Internet is that you can use it from a computer anywhere: at home, at work, at school, or at a restaurant.
- World Wide Web or WWW is one of the main services of the Internet.
- A Web page is an electronic document on the Web that includes text, images, sound and video.
- Each Web page has a unique address, called a Uniform Resource Locator (URL).
- E-mail is quite fast, easy and an inexpensive service used to send messages to others.
- Instant messaging (IM) is a real-time Internet communications service.
- Social Networking enables you to connect with people who share similar personal or professional interests.
- Facebook is the most popular social networking site on the Web, with over 2.5 billion users worldwide.
- A blog is a Web site that consists of a frequently updated collection of entries.
- E-shopping a service which allows shopping on the Web; you need not move out of your house.
- Electronic commerce (e-commerce) is a financial business transaction that occurs over an electronic network.

BRAIN TEASER

1. Multiple Choice Questions

Tick (✓) the correct answer:

a. Which is a primary communication method for both personal and business use?

i. Surfing ☐ ii. E-mail ☐ iii. Browsing ☐

b. A software program which helps find Web sites, Web pages, and Internet files:

i. Search Engine ☐ ii. Browser ☐ iii. MS-Word ☐

c. One of the very popular search engines:

i. Internet Explorer ☐ ii. Amazon ☐ iii. Google ☐

d. A search engine for finding people through searching for all types of Internet content:

i. Facebook ☐ ii. Jobster ☐ iii. 123 people ☐

e. A real-time typed conversation that takes place on a computer:

i. Talk ☐ ii. Speak ☐ iii. Chat ☐

f. An Internet service that enables you to connect with people who share similar interests:

i. Social Networking ☐ ii. Browsing ☐ iii. Flickr ☐

g. A Web site that consists of a frequently updated collection of entries:

i. Flickr ☐ ii. Blog ☐ iii. Orkut ☐

h. A financial business transaction that occurs over an electronic network:

i. e-commerce ☐ ii. e-banking ☐ iii. e-learning ☐

2. Fill in the blanks:

a. The Internet is also called __________.

b. A massive storehouse of information that resides on computers is called __________.

c. A __________ is an electronic document on the Web that includes text, images, sound and video.

d. A __________ is a software program which helps find Web sites, Web pages and Internet files.

e. A __________ is any Web page name that lists as the result of a search.

f. A __________ is a real-time typed conversation that takes place on a computer.

g. __________ is world's most popular instant messaging app.

3. Write 'T' for True and 'F' for False in the boxes:

a. The Internet is a small network that connects some computers. ☐

b. World Wide Web or WWW is one of the main services of the Internet. ☐

c. Each Web page has many addresses.

d. Instant messaging is a real-time Internet communications service.

e. E-mail is quite fast, easy and an inexpensive service.

4. Match the following:

a.	Internet	(i)	allows you to exchange the typed messages
b.	Chat	(ii)	very popular search engine
c.	Search Engine	(iii)	program helps find Web sites on Net
d.	Google	(iv)	also called spider
e.	Crawler	(v)	largest network

5. Answer the following questions

(i) Answer each in a few lines:

a. What is the use of social networking sites?
b. Name any one popular search engine.
c. What is blog?
d. Differentiate between Web page and Web site.

(ii) Answer each comprehensively:

a. What is e-mail?
b. Explain the use of search engine.
c What is the use of spider in search engine?
d. How will you find people on the Internet?
e. Explain social networking.
f. Discuss three instant message programs.

11 Programming in Python

In this chapter, we will learn:

- ⇒ Introduction to Python
- ⇒ Installing Python on Windows
- ⇒ Starting Python
- ⇒ Programming in Script Mode
- ⇒ Python Statements
- ⇒ Converting Values

INTRODUCTION TO PYTHON

Python is a widely used general-purpose, high-level programming language. It was created by Guido Van Rossum in 1991 and further developed by the Python Software Foundation.

It is designed with an emphasis on code readability, and its syntax allows programmers to express their concepts in fewer lines of code.

Python is a programming language that lets you work quickly and integrate systems more efficiently.

Python is used in a variety of fields, including software development, web development, scientific computing, big data, and Artificial Intelligence. It lets you work quickly and integrate system more efficiently.

Features of Python

- ⇒ **Python is easy to use :** Python is a very developer-friendly language which means that anyone and everyone can learn to code it in a couple of hours or days. As compared to other object-oriented programming languages like Java, C, C++, and C#, Python is one of the easiest to learn.
- ⇒ **Python is powerful :** Python is very powerful and it attracts developers from around the world as well as companies such as Google, IBM, Industrial Light + Magic, Microsoft, NASA, Red Hat, Verizon, Xerox, and Yahoo!. Python is also used as a tool by professional game programmers.
- ⇒ **Python is "Glue" Language :** Python can be integrated with different languages such as C, C++, and Java. This means that a programmer can take advantage of work already done in other languages while using Python.
- ⇒ **Python Runs Everywhere :** Python runs on everything from a Palm to a Cray. And, if you don't have a supercomputer in the den, you can still run Python on Windows,

Macintosh, or Linux machines. Python programs are platform-independent, which means that regardless of the operating system you use to create your program, it'll run on any other computer with Python.

⇒ **Python is Free and Open Source :** Python is free. You can install it on your computer and never pay a penny. But Python's licence lets you do much more than that. You can copy or modify Python.

Installing Python on Windows

We can easily install Python on Windows.

Download the Python Installer binaries

⇒ Open the www.python.org website in a web browser and navigate to the Downloads section.

⇒ Click on the link to download Python. A new page appears.

⇒ Scroll the window and click the Windows installer (32 bit) if you are using a 32-bit Windows. In case your Windows installation is a 64-bit system, then download Windows installer (64 bit) installer.

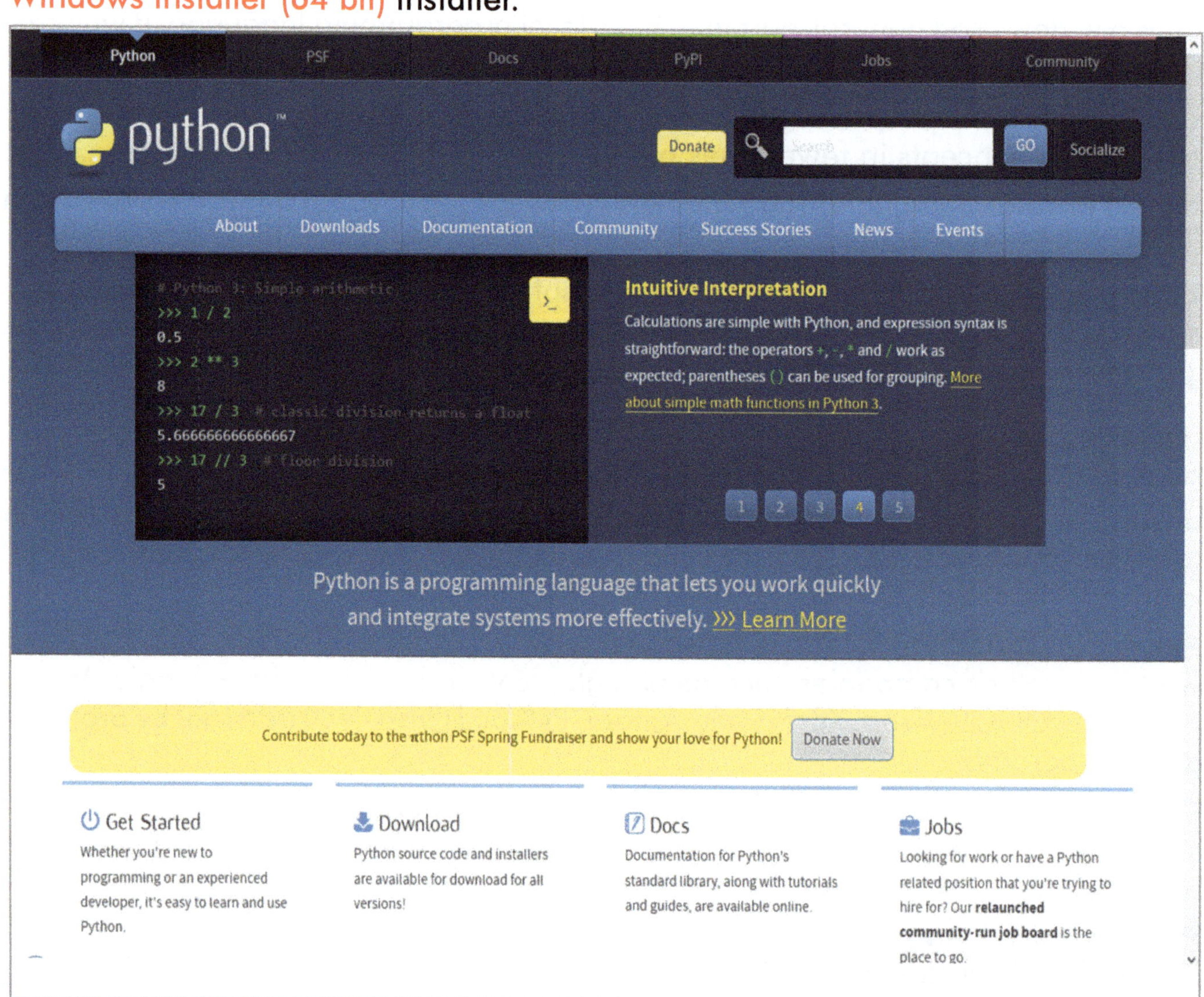

Starting Python

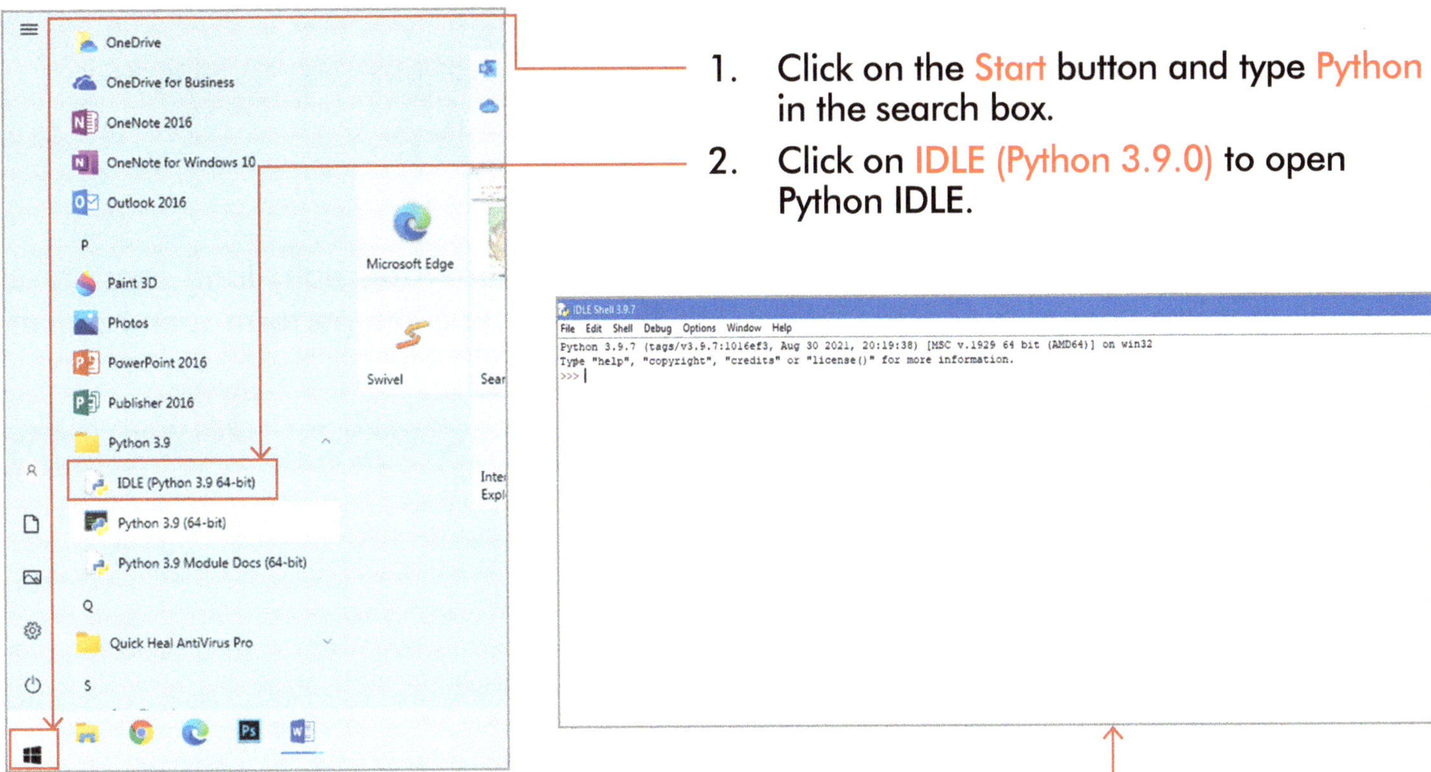

Python comes with an integrated development environment called IDLE. A development environment is a set of tools that makes writing programs easier. You can think of it as a word processor for your programs. But it's even more than a place to write, save and edit your work.

IDLE provides two modes in which to work: an interactive mode and a script mode.

Programming in interactive mode

Finally, it's time to do some actual Python programming.

The quickest way is to start Python in interactive mode.

In this mode, you can tell Python what to do and it will respond immediately.

```
IDLE Shell 3.9.7
File  Edit  Shell  Debug  Options  Window  Help
Python 3.10.7 (tags/v3.10.7:6cc6b13, Sep  5 2022, 14:08:36) [MSC v.1933 64 bit (AMD64)] on win32
Type "help", "copyright", "credits" or "license()" for more information.
print("good morning")
good morning
```

Writing Your First Program :

Let's try to display "Good morning".

Write the following command print ("Good morning") and press the Enter key.

Wow! You've written your first Python program!

Note

Python is case-sensitive and by convention, function names are in lowercase. So, print ("Hello") will work, but Print ("Hello") and PRINT ("Hello") won't.

Programming in Script Mode

Python's IDLE also offers a script mode, in which you can write, edit, load, and save programs. It is like a word processor for your code. In fact, you can perform such familiar tasks as find and replace and cut and paste.

Writing First Program (Again)

You can open a script mode window from the interactive window you've been using.

Select the File → New Window. A new window will appear, as shown along with:

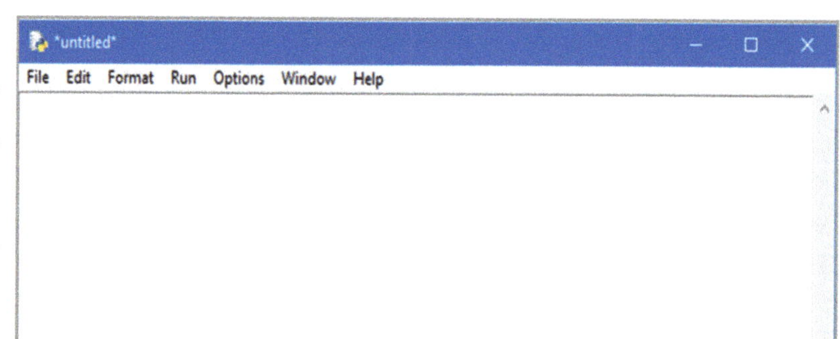

(In this new script window, type print ("Good morning") and press Enter key.

Nothing happens!

That's because you're in script mode. You are writing a list of statements for the computer to execute later. Once you save your program, you can run it.

To run your 'Good morning' program,

1. Click on Run menu.
2. Select Run Module option.

Then, the interactive window displays the results of the program.

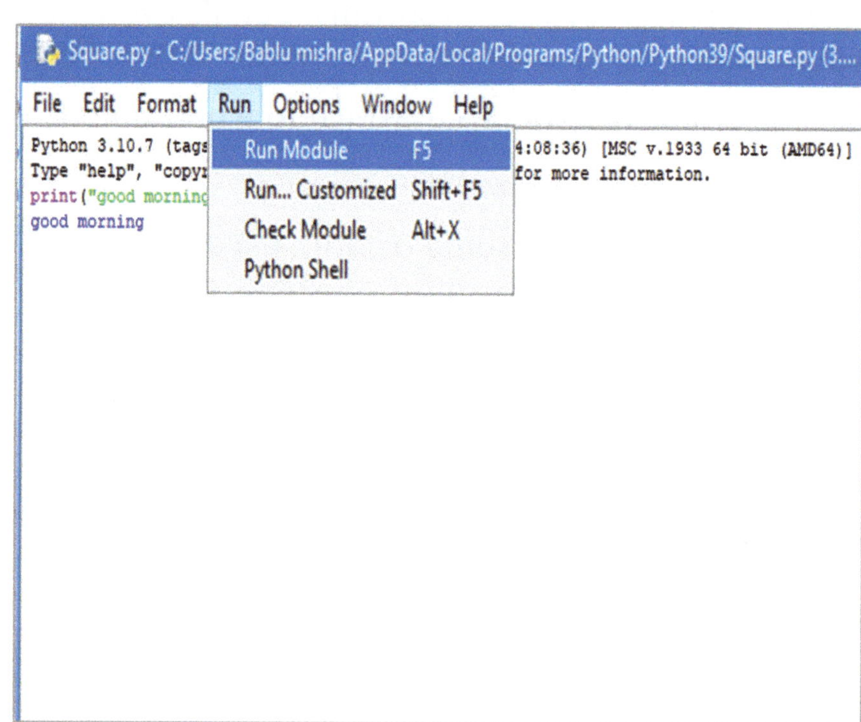

Saving and Running Your Program

To save your program, select File→Save As. Give a name to your file, e. g., 'Goodmorning.py'. By default, the file gets saved in your Python folder that was created during installation. You can also save your file at different locations.

Add this matter after you can also save your file at different locations.

To run your 'Good morning' program,

1. Click on Run menu.
2. Select Run Module option.

Then, the interactive window displays the results of the program.

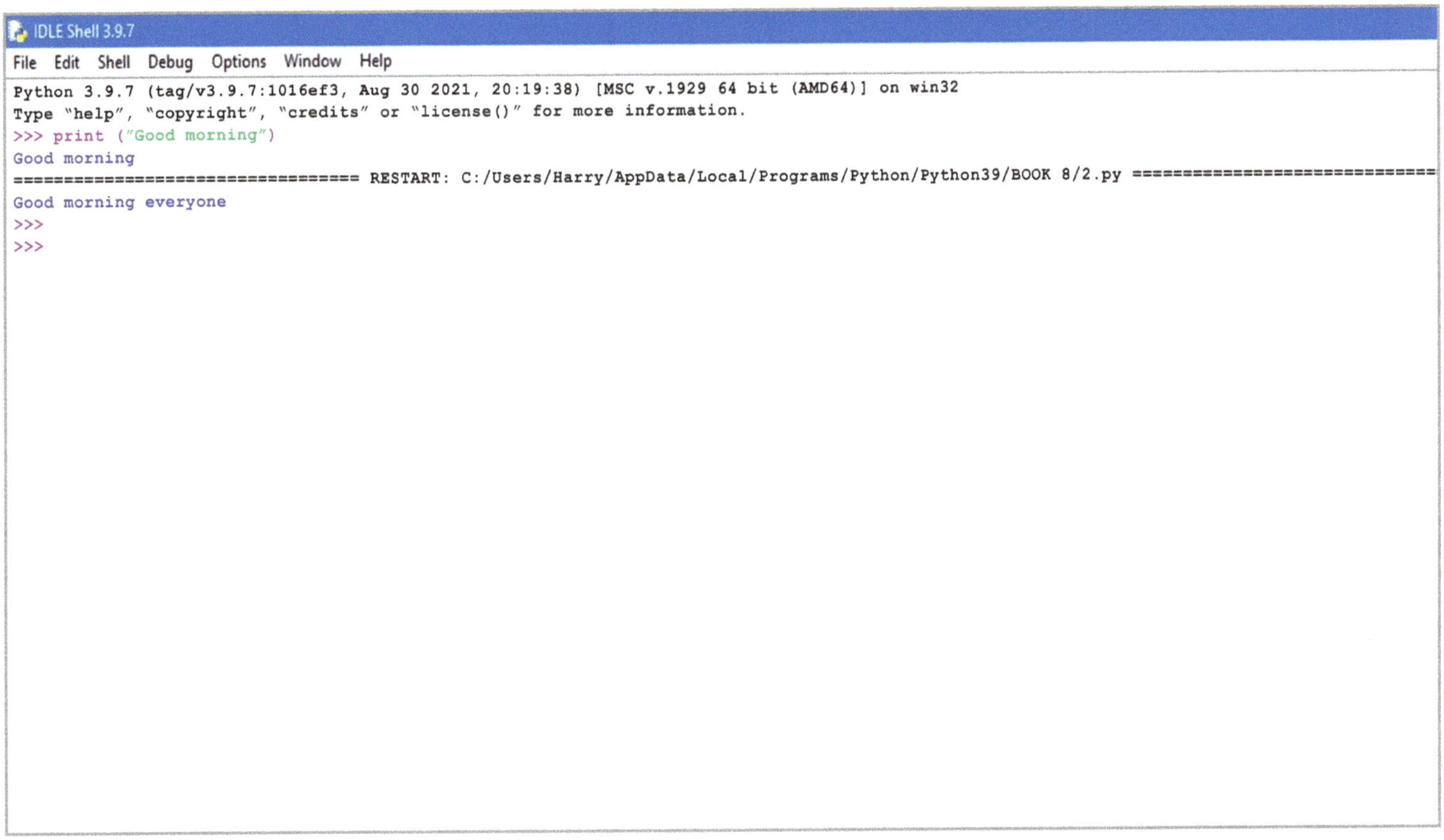

```
IDLE Shell 3.9.7
File  Edit  Shell  Debug  Options  Window  Help
Python 3.9.7 (tag/v3.9.7:1016ef3, Aug 30 2021, 20:19:38) [MSC v.1929 64 bit (AMD64)] on win32
Type "help", "copyright", "credits" or "license()" for more information.
>>> print ("Good morning")
Good morning
================================= RESTART: C:/Users/Harry/AppData/Local/Programs/Python/Python39/BOOK 8/2.py ==============================
Good morning everyone
>>>
>>>
```

You will notice that the interactive window contains the old text. It still has the statement you entered while in interactive mode, print ("Good morning"), and the results, the message Good morning. Below all of that, you will see a restart message, and below that, the results of running the program from script mode: Good morning.

Note

To run program from IDLE, the program should be saved first.

- *Interactive mode is great for trying out a small idea quickly.*
- *Script mode is perfect for writing programs you can run later.*

Using both modes together is the better way to code.

Python Comments

A comment gives extra information about your project. It is a text that doesn't affect the outcome of a code but let someone know what you have done in a program or what is being done in a block of code.

In Python, we use the hash (#) symbol to give single line comment and for multiline comment you can enclose the text in '''.....''' or """...................""".

Displaying strings in Python

print ( ) helps to display anything in python. Let us try to display "Hello", by displaying in an impressive manner, *i.e.* increasing its size.

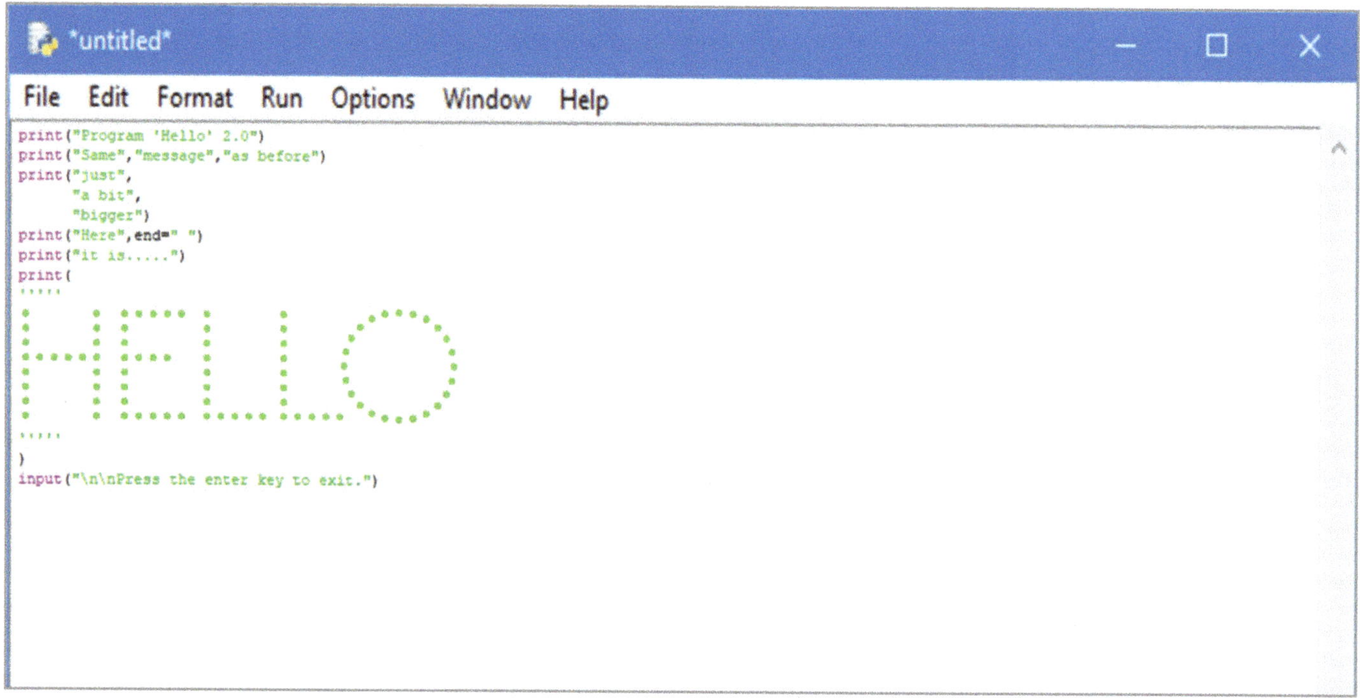

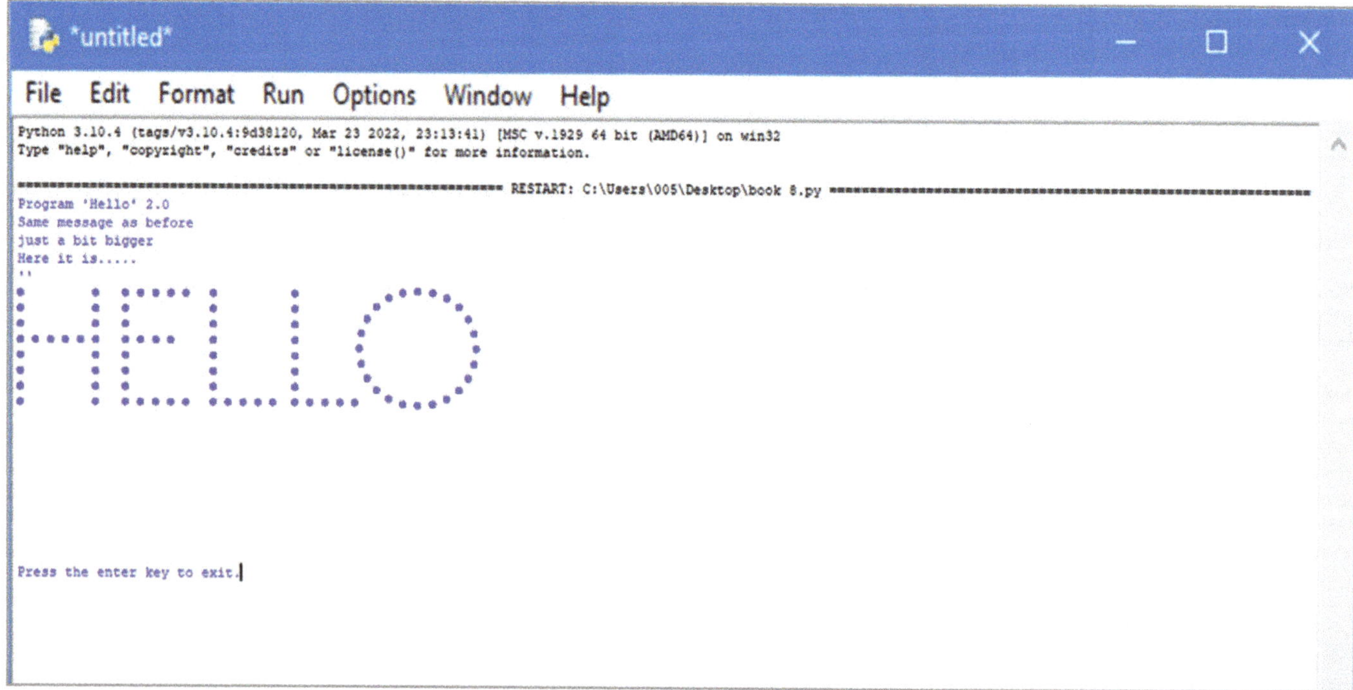

You can use either a pair of single quotes (' ') or double quotes (" ") to create string values. So, 'Hello' represents the same string as "Hello". But take a look at the first appearance of a string in the program: print ("program 'Hello' 2.0")

Here, the double quotes are like bookends, telling the computer where the string begins and ends.

So, if you use a pair of double quotes to "bookend" your string, you can use as many single quotes inside the string as you want.

And, if you surround your string with a pair of single quotes, you can use as many double quotes inside the string as you like.

⇒ You can also print multiple values with a single call to the print () function – just list multiple argument values, separated by commas.

  In the following print statement, multiple arguments are separated by commas: print *("Same", "message", "as before")*

⇒ when you have a list of arguments, you can start a new line after any of the comma separators in the list. The next three lines of the program form a single statement that prints the one line of text just a bit bigger.

```
print ("Just",
"a bit",
"bigger")
```

This method is very useful to break up an argument list over multiple lines because it can make the code easier to read.

By default, the print () function prints a newline character as a final value. This means that a subsequent call to *print ()* would display text on the following line. You can specify a space to be the final character printed (instead of the newline) while calling the print () function. This would mean a subsequent *print ()* statement would begin printing values right after that space.

This can be achieved by using end argument in the print statement as below:

```
print ("Here", end=" ")
print ("it is...")
```

PYTHON STATEMENTS

Instructions written in the source code for execution are called statements. There are different types of statements in the Python programming language like Assignment statement, Conditional statement, Looping statements, etc. These help the user to get the required output.

For example, *n = 50* is an assignment statement.

Line Continuation Character

Generally, one statement per line is written in Python. But you can stretch a single statement across multiple lines with the help of the line-continuation character- '\' (backslash).

Put it where you want to use a space (but not inside a string), to continue statement on the next line. The computer will act as if it sees one long line of code.

Variables

Variable is an object or a place in memory where an item or element can be stored. Value of a variable can be a string (e.g. 'a' 'Indian'), numeric (e.g. 674) or any combination of alphanumeric characters (XY28). In Python we can use an assignment statement to create new variables and assign specific values to them.

For example,

Case A: Assigning values to variables

Stu_name = "Jack"

Eng_marks = 22

Basic_sal = 5000.0

The following are two most important rules for naming a variable:

1. A variable name can contain only numbers, letters, and underscores.
2. A variable name can't start with a number.

Display the value of the variables

```
Stu_name="Harry"
Eng_marks=22
Basic_sal=5000.0
print(Stu_name,"secured",Eng_marks,"marks")
```

```
Python 3.9.7 (tag/v3.9.7:1016ef3, Aug 30 2021, 20:19:38) [MSC v.1929 64 bit (AMD64)] on win32
Type "help", "copyright", "credits" or "license()" for more information.
>>>
= RESTART: C:/Users/Harry/AppData/Local/Programs/Python/Python39/BOOK 8/4.py
Harry secured 22 marks
>>>
```

Declare the length and breadth of two variables and assign 60 and 30 to them, respectively. Display the area of the rectangle:

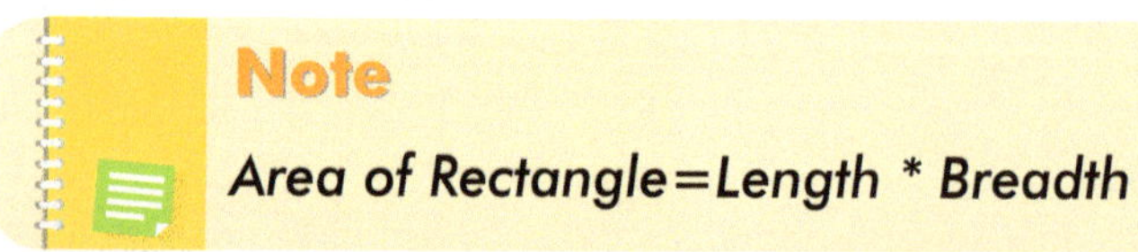

Note

*Area of Rectangle=Length * Breadth*

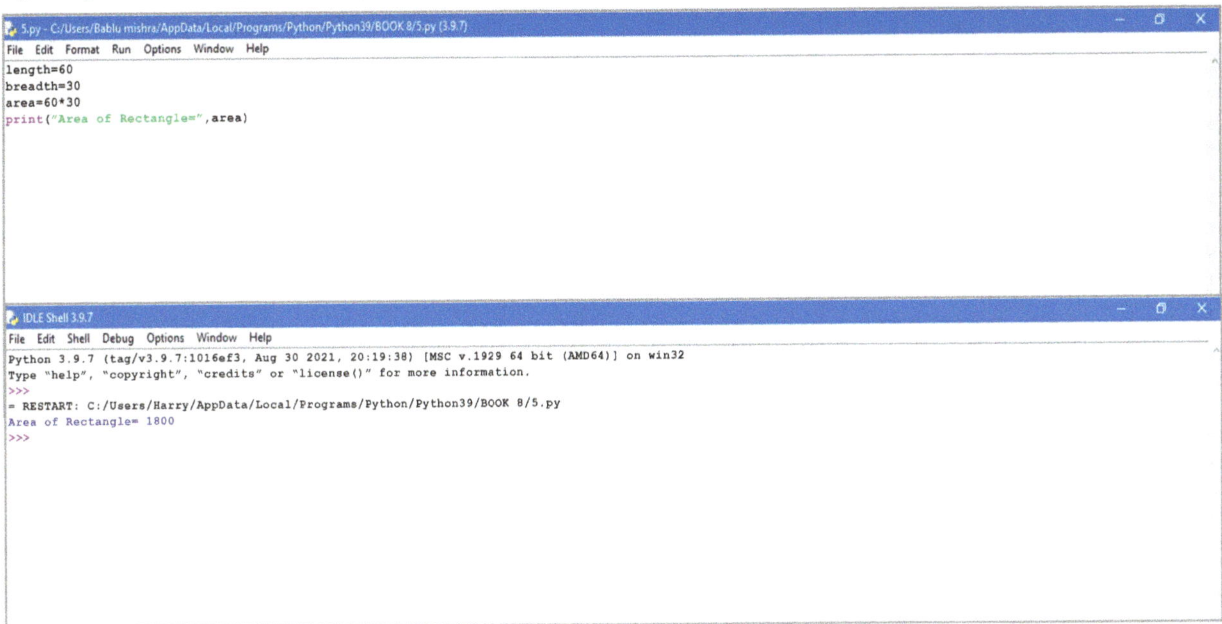

Accepting values from the user

The input () function gets some text from the user. It takes a string argument that it uses to prompt the user for this text.

For example, name=input ("What is your name")

As you can see input (), use the string to prompt the user. Input () waits for the user to enter something. Once the user presses the Enter key, input () returns whatever the user typed as a string. That string, the return value of the function call, is what name (variable) gets.

You can use print () statement to check what value was entered by the user in the variable name.

Numbers : We generally encounter two different types of data in our life, *i.e.*, either strings or numbers. Numbers are of further two types: integer numbers and decimal numbers.

Note

Python has many different types of data types to handle the different types of data. We would learn about them in higher classes.

Numerical Data Types		
Int	Integer numbers	2, -4,678, 0
Float	Real or floating point numbers	1.6, 34.67, 4.0

Display the data type of any variable with the help of type () command.

```
6.py - C:/Users/Bablu mishra/AppData/Local/Programs/Python/Python39/BOOK 8/6.py (3.9.7)
File Edit Format Run Options Window Help
age=36
name="John"
marks=28.5
print(type(age)
print(type(name))
print(type(marks))
```

```
6.py - C:/Users/Bablu mishra/AppData/Local/Programs/Python/Python39/BOOK 8/6.py (3.9.7)
File Edit Format Run Options Window Help
Python 3.9.7 (tag/v3.9.7:1016ef3, Aug 30 2021, 20:19:38) [MSC v.1929 64 bit (AMD64)] on win32
Type "help", "copyright", "credits" or "license()" for more information.
>>>
= RESTART: C:/Users/Harry/AppData/Local/Programs/Python/Python39/BOOK 8/6.py
<class 'int'>
<class 'str'>
<class 'float'>
>>>
```

Converting Values

Input () accepts only string data; therefore, we wouldn't be able to do any mathematical calculation with any values accepted with the help of input function. There are several functions that convert between types. The function to convert a value into an integer is demonstrated in the following lines:

age=int (input ("Enter your age"))

marks=float (int ("Enter your marks"))

Both the above statements would convert the string data accepted with the help of input function into integer and decimal numbers, respectively.

Function	Description	Example	Returns
float(x)	Returns a floating-point value by converting 'x'.	float("10.0')	10.0
int(x)	Returns an integer value by converting 'x'.	int("10")	10
str(x)	Returns a string value by converting 'x'.	str(10)	'10'

Python Operators

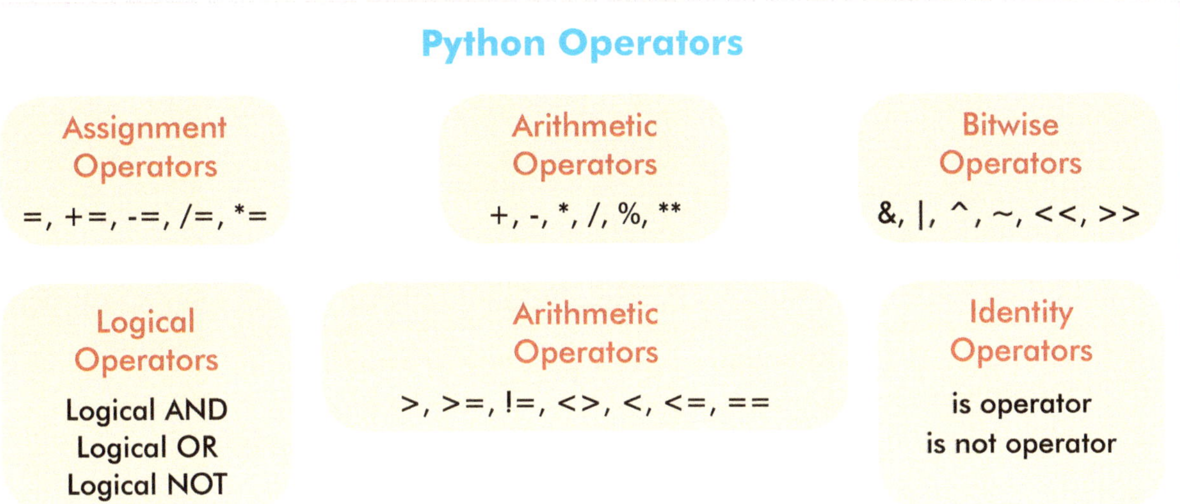

Let us understand the usage of the different types of operators:

Arithmetic Operators	**Description**	**Example**
+ Addition	Adds values on either side of the operator.	a + b = 30
– Subtraction	Subtracts the right hand operand from left the hand operand.	a – b = –10
* Multiplication	Multiplies values on either side of the operator.	a*b = 200
/ Division	Divides the left-hand operand by the right-hand operator.	b/a = 2
% Modulus	Divides the left-hand operand by the right-hand operator and returns the remainder.	b % a = 0
** Exponent	Performs exponential (power) calculation on operators.	a**b = 10 to the power 20
//	Floor Division – The division of operands where the result is the quotient in which the digits after the decimal point are removed.	9//2 = 4 and 9.0//2.0 = 4.0

Write a program to make an arithmetic calculator by displaying the output after applying any operator (+, -, *, /, %, **, //).

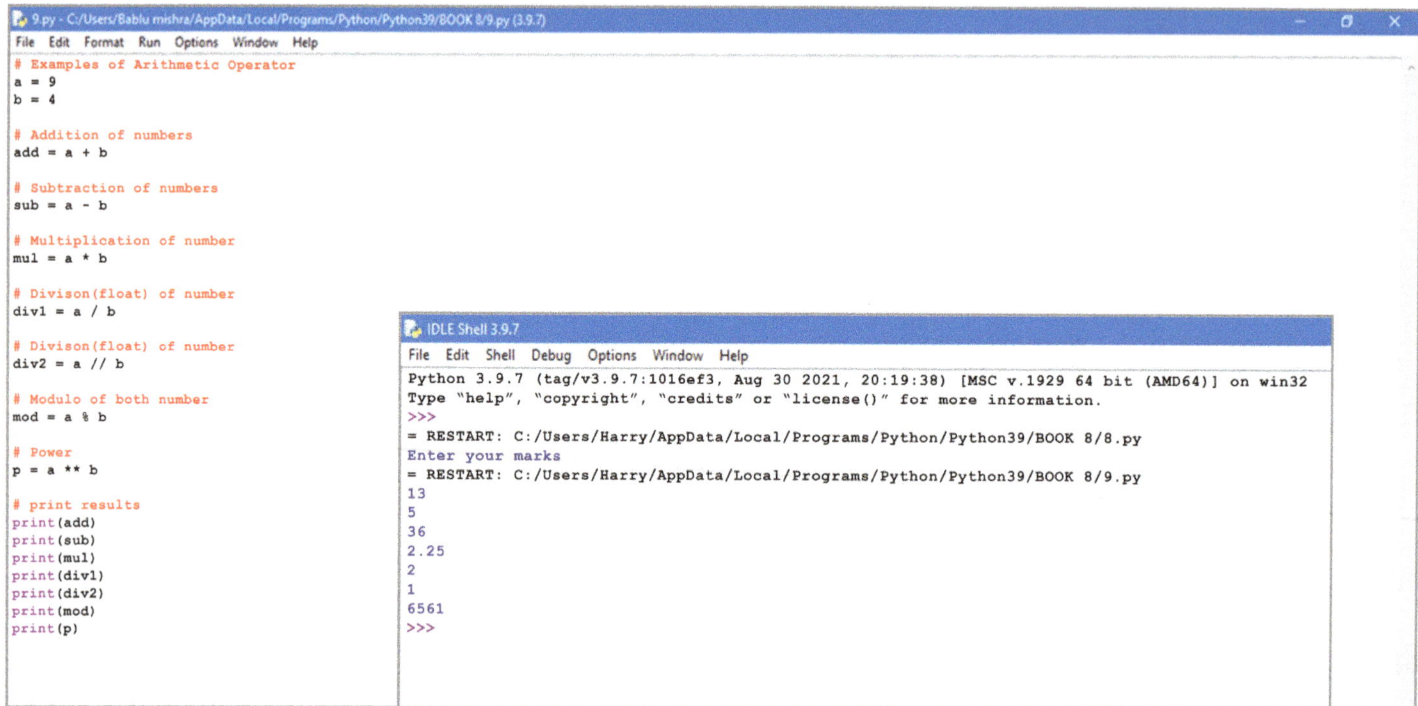

Relational Operators:

Operator	Description	Example
= =	If the values of two operands are equal, then the condition becomes true.	(a = = b) is not true.
! =	If the values of two operands are not equal, then condition becomes true.	(a \ = b) is true.
< >	If the values of two operands are not equal, then condition becomes true.	(a < > b) is true. This is similar to! = operator.
>	If the value of the left operand is greater than the value of the right operand, then condition becomes true.	(a > b) is not true.
<	If the value of the left operand is less than the value of the right operand, then condition becomes true.	(a < b) is true.
> =	If the value of the left operand is greater than or equal to the value of the right operand, then condition becomes true.	(a > = b) is not true.
< =	If the value of the left operand is less than or equal to the value of the right operand, then condition becomes true.	(a < =b) is true.

Check the relation between two variable with the help of relational operators (= =, !=, >, <, >=, <=).

```
File  Edit  Format  Run  Options  Window  Help
a=input ("Enter the first number 85")
b=input ("Enter the second number 35")

print (a==b)

print (a!=b)

print (a>b)

print (a>=b)

print (a<b)

print (a<=b)
```

```
IDLE Shell 3.9.7
File  Edit  Shell  Debug  Options  Window  Help
Python 3.9.7 (tag/v3.9.7:1016ef3, Aug 30 2021, 20:19:38) [MSC v.1929 64 bit (AMD64)] on win32
Type "help", "copyright", "credits" or "license()" for more information.
>>>
= RESTART: C:/Users/Harry/AppData/Local/Programs/Python/Python39/BOOK 8/11.py
Enter the first number 85
Enter the second number 35
True
False
False
True
False
True
>>>
```

Logical Operator:

Operator	Description	Example
And	True if both the operands are true	X and Y
Or	True if either of the operands is true	X or Y
Not	True if operand is false (complements the operand)	n ot X

Assignment Operators:

Operator	Description	Example
=	Assigns values from the right-side operands to the left-side operand.	c = a + b assigns value of a + b into c
+ = Add AND	It adds the right operand to the left operand and assigns the result to the left operand.	c + = a is equivalent to c = c + a
- = Subtract AND	It subtracts the right operand from the left operand and assigns the result to the left operand.	c - = a is equivalent to c = c - a
* = Multiply AND	It multiplies the right operand with the left operand and assigns the result to the left operand.	c * = a is equivalent to c = c * a

/ = Divide AND	It divides the left operand by the right operand and assigns the result to the left operand.	c/ = a is equivalent to c = c/ac/ = a is equivalent to c = c/a
% = Modulus AND	It takes modulus using two operands and assigns the result to the left operand.	c%= a is equivalent to c = c % a
**= Exponent AND	Performs exponential (power) calculation on operators and assigns value to the left operand.	c** = a is equivalent to c = c ** a
// = Floor Division	It performs floor division on operators and assigns value to the left operand.	c// = a is equivalent to c = c // a

LET'S HAVE A LOOK

- Python language was created by Guido van Rossum in 1991.
- It is used in a variety of fields, including software development, web development, scientific computing, big data, and Artificial Intelligence.
- Python is portable and platform-independent, *i.e.* it can run on various operating systems and hardware platforms.
- There are two modes to write programs in Python IDLE: interactive mode and scripting mode.
- In Python, we use the hash (#) symbol to give single line comment and for multiline comment you can enclose the text in ''' ......''' or """ ....""".
- As Python is case-sensitive, keywords must be written in a defined manner.
- You can use either a pair of single (' '), double quotes (" ") or triple quotes (''' ''') to create string values.
- Escape sequences allow to put special characters in the strings.
- A single statement can be stretched across multiple lines with the help of the line-continuation character, \(backslash).
- Variable in Python refers to an object or a place in memory where an item or element can be stored.
- Number data type stores numerical values only.
- String is a group of characters like alphabet, digits or special characters and spaces.
- Python has the following types of operators: Arithmetic Operators, Relational Operators, Logical Operators, Assignment Operators, etc.
- The input () function prompts the user to enter data.
- We can convert string to int by prefixing input () function with int.

BRAIN TEASER

1. Multiple Choice Questions

Tick (✓) the correct answer:

a. What is the output of the following code: print (10/14)

i. 4.5 ☐ ii. b) 4. ☐ iii. 0.71 ☐

b. Which of the following function converts a string to a int in python?

i. int ( ) ☐ ii. long (x) ☐ iii. float (x) ☐

c. What is the output of the expression: 4*1**4?

i. 64 ☐ ii. 16 ☐ iii. 4 ☐

d. What is the output of the following statement: print (3 * 2 **3)?

i. 27 ☐ ii. 24 ☐ iii. 216 ☐

e. 21% 2 in python will give ____________ in Python.

i. 17 ☐ ii. 2 ☐ iii. 1 ☐

f. What is the output of the following program: print (0.1 + 0.2 ==0.3)?

i. True ☐ ii. False ☐

iii. Machine dependent ☐

2. Find the output of each of the following program codes:

a.
```
a = 4.5
B = 2
Print a//b
```

b.
```
a = "48"
B = "52"
Print (a + b)
```

c.
```
print (2**2**3**1)
```

d.
```
a=3
b=2
print (b**a)
```

e. a=7346

```
b=10
print (a%b,end="")
a=a//b
print (a%b,end="")
a=a//b
print (a%b,end="")
a=a//b
print (a%b,end="")
```

3. Answer the following questions:

a. When would you prefer to use the scripting of interactive mode?

b. How can you give multi-line comment in Python?

c. input () helps to accept only string. How can you convert string to int?

d. What are the different ways of displaying strings in Python?

e. "Python is a case-sensitive language." Comment.

f. What are operators? Illustrate with the help of a chart the different types of operators in Python.

g. What is programming in script mode? Why would you choose this mode? Give an example of programming mode?

Write programs for the following:

1. Write a program to accept the size of all sides of a rectangle. Calculate and display the perimeter and area of the rectangle.
2. Write a program that allows a user to enter his or her two favourite foods. The program should point out the name of a new food by joining the names of original food items together.
3. Write a program to accept the basic salary from the user and calculate the net salary.

   Net Salary = Basic Salary + HRA + DA – PF

   HRA=30% of Basic

   DA=20% of Basic

   PF=12% of Basic

Formative Assessment - 4
(Chapters 9-11)

1. To create a PowerPoint presentation describing various types of computer viruses.

Description : Computer viruses affect the computer system adversely, corrupting the important data and programs, stored in your computer. These viruses can be of different types. Create a presentation explaining the behaviour and target infection of various types of computer viruses using the clue slides given on the next page.

COMPUTER VIRUS

Created by:

WHAT IS A VIRUS

Computer virus is a software written with malicious intention of causing harm to the programs and data stored in a system.

TYPES OF VIRUSES

Viruses based on their working behaviour are classified as:

TROJAN BOMB WORM

TROJAN

These are the destructive programs that hide their intentions as they appear to be useful utilities.

HOW IT WORKS?

These types of viruses remain in the system undetected and wait for a specific date to trigger.

HOW IT SPREADS?

These are sophisticated viruses with the ability to spread very fast. They do not cause any harm to the system normally.

TYPES OF VIRUSES

Viruses based on their target infection are classified as:

Boot Virus : They infect the MBR of the hard disk drive of DBR or floppy disk, e.g., very quickly.

Program Virus : These are parasite viruses infecting the program files of system. They do not affect the boot records.

Macro Virus : They infect the data files of the system. They spread through computer networks.

⇒ Apply suitable presentation design using Design Template.

⇒ Apply animation effects to the various slide objects. Also, give transition effects between the slides.

⇒ Run the slide show and record the slide timings to make an automatic presentation. Save the presentation as The Virus and close PowerPoint.

2. Name the following topologies :

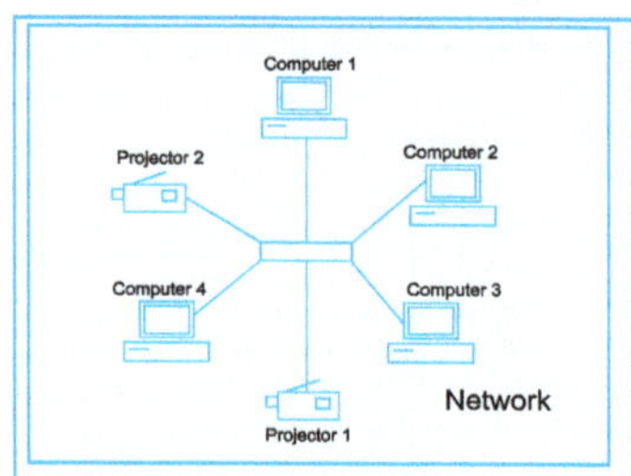

....

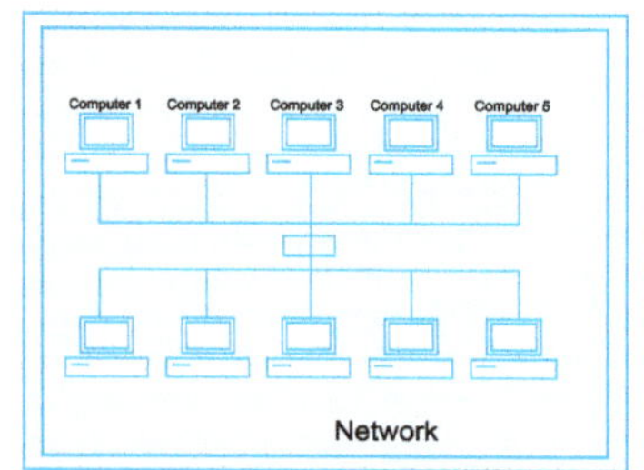

....

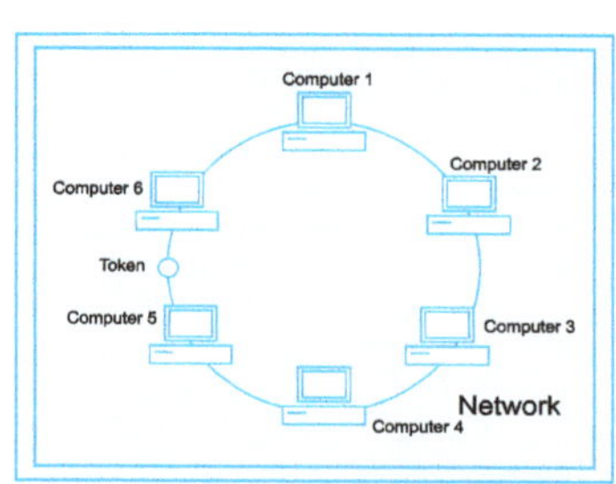

....

Summative Assessment - 2
(Chapters 6-11)

1. Fill in the blanks:

a. ______________ stands for HyperText Markup Language.

b. File extension for JPEG is ______________.

c. A ______________ is an electronic document on the Web that includes text, images, sound and video.

d. A powerful computer that stores Web pages and makes the pages available on the Web for other people is called ______________.

e. The ______________ virus is known to steal your personal and financial information.

f. E-mail viruses are spread by files ______________ to e-mail messages.

g. ______________ spread while copying the data from one system to other.

h. The first computer virus to make it to the public openly was a program called ______________.

2. Define the full forms of the following:

a. HTML ______________

b. JPEG ______________

c. GIF ______________

d. PNG ______________

3. Answer each in a few lines:

a. What do IMG and SRC stand for?

b. What is a computer program?

c. What is event in Visual Basic?

d. Name the tool used to change the size of an image.

e. Name the tool used to create oddly shaped selections.

f. Which tool is used to darken the specific area of an image?

g. Name the various kinds of network topologies.

h. Name any two anti-virus software.

4. Answer each comprehensively:

a. What is the use of alternative text?

b. What are tags?

c. What is the benefits of GUI in programs?

d. Explain Photoshop tools.

e. What is network topology?

f. Which are the most commonly used media in networks?

5. Identify the different parts of Photoshop workplace: